LOWERING HIGHER EDUCATION

The Rise of Corporate Universities and the Fall of Liberal Education

What happens to liberal arts and science education when universities attempt to sell it as a form of job training? In *Lowering Higher Education*, a follow-up to their provocative 2007 book *Ivory Tower Blues*, James E. Côté and Anton L. Allahar explore the subverted 'idea of the university' and the forces that have set adrift the mission of these institutions. The authors examine the corporatization of universities within the context of a range of contentious issues in higher education, from lowered standards and inflated grades to the overall decline of humanities, social sciences, and natural sciences instruction.

Côté and Allahar point to a fundamental disconnect between policymakers, many of whom rarely set foot in a classroom, and the teachers who must implement questionable educational policies on a daily basis. The authors also expose stakeholder misconceptions surrounding the current culture of academic disengagement and the supposed power of new technologies to motivate students. While outlining systemic shortcomings and dysfunction within our universities, *Lowering Higher Education* offers recommendations that have the potential to reinvigorate liberal education.

JAMES E. CÔTÉ is a professor in the Department of Sociology at the University of Western Ontario.

ANTON L. ALLAHAR is a professor in the Department of Sociology at the University of Western Ontario.

JAMES E. CÔTÉ and ANTON L. ALLAHAR

Lowering Higher Education

The Rise of Corporate Universities and the Fall of Liberal Education

UNIVERSITY OF TORONTO PRESS
Toronto Buffalo London

© University of Toronto Press Incorporated 2011
Toronto Buffalo London
www.utppublishing.com
Printed in Canada

ISBN 978-1-4426-4221-8 (cloth)
ISBN 978-1-4426-1121-4 (paper)

Printed on acid-free, 100% post-consumer recycled paper with
vegetable-based inks.

Library and Archives Canada Cataloguing in Publication

Côté, James E., 1953–
Lowering higher education : the rise of corporate universities and the fall
of liberal education / James Côté and Anton Allahar.

Includes bibliographical references and index.
ISBN 978-1-4426-4221-8 (bound).   ISBN 978-1-4426-1121-4 (pbk.)

1. Education, Higher.   2. Universities and colleges.   3. College students –
Rating of.   4. College students – Attitudes.   5. College teachers –
Attitudes.   I. Allahar, Anton L., 1949–   II. Title.

LB2324.C68   378   C2010-906600-6

University of Toronto Press acknowledges the financial assistance to its
publishing program of the Canada Council for the Arts and the Ontario
Arts Council.

 Canada Council   Conseil des Arts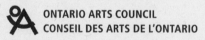
for the Arts   du Canada

University of Toronto Press acknowledges the financial support of the
Government of Canada through the Canada Book Fund for its publishing
activities.

Contents

LOWERING HIGHER EDUCATION

The Rise of Corporate Universities and the Fall of Liberal Education

Introduction

Ivory Tower Blues was written to contribute to the debate about the contemporary role of a liberal education – a broad-based, wide-ranging exposure to ideas that enhances intellectual development and civic awareness – primarily as found in university faculties of arts and humanities, social sciences, and natural sciences. Unfortunately, for a variety of reasons, that book was only partially successful in contributing to that debate.

This book adds to the debate by addressing the key issues on which this debate appears to have stalled, in part because of misunderstandings of certain issues and different understandings of other issues. A number of colleagues have encouraged us to clear up these misunderstandings and to extend the discussion of such issues as the nature of academic disengagement and the role of new technologies. Some misunderstandings appear to be due, in part, to a general confusion about the very 'idea of the university,' and whether that idea is fixed or subject to change with the times. In other cases, the spectre of ideologies comes into play.[1]

In this sequel, we use the opinions and criticisms we have encountered as reference points with which to locate key stakeholders in the 'higher educational forum.' Looking at stakeholders as part of a forum helps us to understand why otherwise cooperative people are at loggerheads about how universities should function. Our aim, nevertheless, remains the same: to stimulate debate about the type of university system Canadian society should support publicly for the current generation and the legacy that should be left for future generations. Apart from a consideration of what students should learn, a core aspect of this debate involves professors and how they teach and evaluate students as part of a liberal education. An educational system that is confused about evaluation of students is dysfunctional; a liberal educational system that is confused about *how to teach students at this advanced level* is in crisis about its mission. We firmly believe that both of these problems need to be remedied.

The title for this book, *Lowering Higher Education*,[2] was selected to signify a decline of higher learning in which the liberal arts and sciences are being appropriated to legitimize programs that are more appropriately described as *pseudo-vocational* training. These programs have been rebranded to promise that they will give students an edge in the competition for jobs. As this has happened, the pedagogical value of the liberal *education* in stimulating critical thinking abilities, and honing the skills associated with effectively communicating those abilities in writing and speech, is diminishing; thus, as universities adopt teaching practices associated with *training* people to remember formulae, systems of facts, and procedures, rather than *educating* them to develop a critical awareness of the world at large that they can defend epistemologically, we witness a fundamental alteration in the structure and function of the traditional university and its curriculum.

We carry on with the rather Sisyphean task of stimulating debate among reluctant factions heartened by the lessons learned from our first attempt. We had hoped to gain the attention of the parents of that portion of the current generation of students passing through the university system. As pointed out by some observers, this was perhaps too ambitious. As before, it is too optimistic to gain the attention of many of those actually passing through the system – university students – except for the more engaged students who want to understand the institution shaping their lives. Accordingly, the current book is directed primarily to other teachers.

In addition, administrators and policymakers should find this book useful, if not provocative. However, we are not as sanguine about having the same type of impact on administrators and policymakers as on other teachers. Sadly, there is widespread denial among university administrators about the decline of the liberal arts and sciences, and their reactionary stance remains a major impediment to bringing together all of the important stakeholders in the debate, as we discuss in chapter 2.

The strongest moral support for the positions we advocate comes from other teachers at all levels of the educational system, and it appears that any changes to the system have to come from the grassroots of that system. This grassroots support will hopefully be bolstered by teacher unions and faculty associations, but these organizations can be reluctant to openly discuss certain issues if they perceive doing so risks placing their members in a negative light. These representative bodies must be convinced that there is an urgent need to address deteriorating working conditions. It will take the collective opinion of their member-ships to change this skittishness among unions and faculty associations about admitting that some dysfunctions in the system are tied to cur-rent teaching and evaluation practices, and are not simply tied to fund-ing levels.

One other important goal of the current book is to offer suggestions about how some dysfunctions in the system might be rectified, or at least how a beginning can be made toward rectifying them. It appears that an array of potential solutions needs to be specified and laid out for the public to become involved. Public opinion is currently too grid-locked for change to occur otherwise.

The Canadian scene is the focus of this book. The American pub-lic and its educators have been much more open in their discussion of these issues, and do not need us to point out their problems any further. Fortunately, because of that openness, there is a wealth of literature from the United States of comparative value that can be drawn upon when it is illustrative of what Canadian universities are experiencing.

The Plan of This Book

This book is divided into three parts. The first part is a two-chapter examination of the wider issues underpinning the higher education de-bate, putting it in the context of a historical examination of the forces producing the mission drift that has left liberal education at the mercy of vocationalism (chapter 1) and the competing interests of various stake-holders in the general 'educational forum,' where a certain amount of chaos now prevails as a result of mission drift and misguided leader-ship (chapter 2).

The second part comprises four chapters mapping the specific issues associated with the mission drift evident in the ongoing transformation of liberal educational programs into pseudo-vocational ones. It begins with an 'on the ground' view of the university system in chapter 3, ex-amining 'entitled disengagement' and the declining standards reflected in historically high levels of grade inflation, academic disengagement, and the unreadiness of many students for the rigorous intellectual journey that a liberal education can provide. This view is focused on students, faculty, and the system itself, in which the 'BA-lite' is becoming the norm, and is an extension of our previous book. This chapter will refresh the memory of those who read our previous book and will provide new readers with a primer on that book, but it goes beyond it in many ways.[3]

The other chapters in Part II 'drill down' into several hot-button questions regarding the state and health of the university system: Are the problems severe enough to warrant being called a crisis (chapter 4)? What is academic disengagement and is it inevitable in our universities (chapter 5)? Is the answer to disengagement the embracing of the new technologies that might be used in teaching and learning (chapter 6)?

Part III then presents in a single chapter a summary of the recommendations for the direction that university missions should, and should not, take into the new millennium – the second millennium of 'the university.' Hopefully, framing the view of the university in these expansive historical terms will help readers appreciate the gravity of what is at stake.

Taken as a whole, this book should provide a useful guide for those who want to understand our universities, what is wrong with them, and what needs to be fixed. Contrary to what some defenders of the status quo might claim about critics of the university system, we do not believe the sky is falling; are not advocating an élitist approach to student access to universities; do not want to return to some imagined Golden Age of education; and are not lamenting that 'kids these days' will ruin Western Civilization.

To the contrary, universities are here to stay (in some form, but we should strive to direct their future in a democratic manner that involves all stakeholders); students from disadvantaged backgrounds should be adequately prepared for, and welcomed to attend, liberal universities; we need to look to the needs of future generations of students and not be guided by either the imputed sins or the imagined glories of the past; and there are many good students who deserve to be better served by our universities. If readers can bear these points in mind, they will understand the arguments to follow much more clearly.

PART ONE

The Rise of Pseudo-Vocationalism

1 A History of a Mission Adrift: The Idea of the University Subverted

The University in Historical Perspective: The First Millennium

The word *university* is derived from the Latin *universitas magistrorum et scholarium*, which is roughly translated as referring to a 'community of teachers and scholars.'[1] In the present context, however, the term 'university' will be understood more specifically to refer to the degree-granting institutions that came into existence in Europe as early as the tenth century and that have since evolved to today's modern entities.[2] The idea of the modern university really emerged out of the Enlightenment, the ferment of the French Revolution, and the Romantic Conservative reaction to that revolution. In these developments, the principal debates revolved around the differences between theological knowledge and scientific knowledge, and whether the universe could be subjected to the will of *man*.

Those debates occurred in the context of Europe's passage out of the Dark Ages, the retreat of religion, the rise of science, and an emboldened and irreverent questioning of the traditional comforts and privileges of the monarchy, the nobility, and the clergy by the nascent bourgeois and proletarian classes.[3] The beginnings of modernity can be identified here, along with the scholarly quest to develop a more objective and detached view of the world that is free from prejudgments, superstitions, and personal interest. Those who have followed the standards associated with this quest are commonly referred to as 'modernist scholars.'

Looking through their ethnocentric eyes, the élites of the day saw their European literature, philosophy, art, and poetry as defining *the* classics, and in their Eurocentrism defined them as setting the global standard for culture and civilization. Theirs was a clear embrace of the 'liberal arts,' and for a long time their vision was largely unrivalled. Recently, though, another group with revolutionary ambitions appeared. They shared the view that a university education was best conceived of as a liberal education, but disagreed on what should constitute the curriculum and who should comprise the teachers and the taught. This latter group, commonly called postmodernists, wanted to de-Europeanize the classics – to understand history as also having been made by non-Europeans, non-Christians, non-Whites, and even non-males. Building momentum in the 1980s and 1990s, those who can be referred to as 'postmodernist academics' – to distinguish them from modernist scholars[4] – challenged the so-called European canon and called for a democratic ethos to be extended to the university. But they also embraced a decided element of cultural relativism and tied it to a politics of advocacy, supposedly tailored to defending the alleged victims of the excesses of certain élites. In turn, these postmodernist positions have been used to trump the traditional standards of academic scholarship developed during the modernist period following the Enlightenment. Within the academy, this postmodernist group is identified by its rejection of modernist ideals of objectivity as well as standards that can be universally shared.

In the estimation of one educational philosopher, John Brubacher, those who advocated this postmodernist ideal of the university were counter-cultural radicals bent on revolutionizing from within the élites' vision of the university as a place where the children of the leisured classes went to be schooled in the ways of their parents. In its stead, these postmodernists favoured a more inclusive and permissive learning environment that was treated somewhat derisively by the defenders of the old order. As Brubacher states,

> ... the activists of the counter-culture paradoxically proposed a 'nonuniversity' within the existing university. There students would be freed from the conventional lock steps of academic requirements and would be allowed to paint, record, write, improvise and study non-Western, nonrationalist cultures like those of the Orient.[5]

These 'radical' postmodernists embraced the 'political correctness' that emerged at this time and raised the cry of 'democracy' when they charged that as a public institution the university ought to reflect the composition and broad interests of the public at large. At the same time, others increasingly saw a university education as a ticket to a better life,[6] and when the call for more democratic access gained traction, the public also began to demand that their tax dollars be spent on more practical and results-oriented pursuits.

This was to have an unintended, contradictory consequence for those driven by a postmodernist agenda. Paradoxically, the calls for democratization and transparency fed into the views of those who opposed the liberal arts and favoured vocationalism, a position that resonated well with governments, which are financially accountable to the public. As a result, more university funding began to be directed toward the STEM disciplines (i.e., science, technology, engineering, and mathematics), while fewer grants were channelled into the liberal arts disciplines that the politically correct radicals tended to favour. And within the social sciences, where political correctness took firm footing, the contradiction was evident when those branches of specialization that are driven by the more positivist and modernist assumptions regarding the nature of truth and knowledge, and that focused more on the production of quantitative knowledge, came to be privileged over those that had more humanistic, qualitative pursuits. So even in today's grants-driven social science faculties, a two-tiered system has emerged: the 'upper tier' emphasizes specialization, utilitarianism, and a more immediate, results-oriented curriculum, while the 'lower tier' embraces generalization, reflexivity, and a more humanistic stock of knowledge for its own sake.[7]

Meanwhile, public support for the mission of the university shifted away from that envisaged by either postmodernist academics or modernist scholars, both of whom have attempted to preserve the liberal arts, albeit from different points on the political spectrum. In difficult financial times, one might expect calls for rationalization and accountability from members of the public, who are understandably suspicious of the traditional beneficiaries of university education – the wealthy élites. Because the majority of the public do not attend university and are not attuned to what goes on there, they are also understandably more likely to be interested in practical outcomes of expensive educational investments and in curricula that promise tangible returns on governments' spending of their tax dollars.

To generalize from these trends: in the current public mind, the classics are out and instruction manuals are in; for many postmodernist academics, the classics are out and victim-based narratives are in. In the meantime, modernist scholars find themselves increasingly squeezed between these incompatible pressures of vocationalism and relativism.

The Drift Associated with Massification

The idea of the university is not as straightforward as some would think. Clearly, it is a place where certain types of knowledge are pursued, produced, and shared. But unlike other places where knowledge might also be pursued and produced, universities do so at a high level of abstraction and in a pointedly systematic and rigorous fashion. Often described as places of 'higher' (as opposed to 'lower') learning, universities are thus seen to be engaged in the production of knowledge that is somehow more sophisticated or refined than one might get from so-called 'lower' education.

Although it is often taken as an élite institution with élitist concerns, the university can be viewed differently. While the pursuit of higher education at the university is meant ultimately to serve the public good, the public *per se* is not necessarily equipped with the specialized skills and knowledge to dictate the terms of that pursuit. For even after the massification of the system that took place over the last few decades, only a minority attend university. Consequently, only a restricted segment of the population in question will have direct familiarity with what goes on at university. This produces a challenge for the university today when the public is demanding more transparency in its governance, more say in its offerings, and more democratic access to its hallowed halls.

These demands are understandable, for whether or not one agrees with what universities do, it is clear that over their careers, university graduates generally do better than non-graduates occupationally, economically, materially, health-wise, and so forth.[8] But at a more general level, as long as such successes and failures are understood individualistically and not structurally in class and economic terms, it is easy for those who do not attend university, and who do not boast the trappings of material success, to blame themselves for lower occupational and economic achievements. Sociologically, such self-blame is an effective way of guaranteeing social order, so that it is in the interest of the élites to have the non-élites construe public issues (low rate of university attendance by the non-affluent) as personal troubles (unemployment and poverty) and in so doing deflect attention away from the structure of privilege in the society, especially in terms of public education at the primary and secondary levels.[9] And, as noted, the latter level of public education is increasingly being exposed as inadequate in many regions of the country and as not being up to the task of preparing its students for the rigours of a higher education.

In view of these issues, while democratization of access is a good thing, it presents a serious challenge: how can access be made more broad and inclusive of the public at large while maintaining high standards? This is a challenge not because the more affluent are more naturally gifted, which they are not, but because the wider class inequalities that characterize the system guarantee the affluent a better chance at preparation for higher learning or a university education through private forms of education and tutoring.

This said, as soon as one mentions the idea of the university and links it with the question of knowledge production, the first question it provokes is: 'Knowledge for what?' This question suggests that one could either have 'knowledge for knowledge's sake' (i.e., knowledge as an end in itself),[10] or knowledge for its material or exchange value – what can one gain from knowing? Writing in the mid-nineteenth century, John Henry Newman, one of the earliest thinkers to reflect on the idea of a university and to philosophize about the nature of knowledge in that context, remarked that 'knowledge is capable of being its own end. Such is the constitution of the human mind, that any kind of knowledge, if it really be such, is its own reward.'[11]

Newman's observations are premised on the reflections of an even earlier philosopher, Antoine Nicolas de Condorcet (1743–94), who was convinced that the invention of the printing press made possible the spread of 'every degree of knowledge' such that 'the boundary between the cultivated and the uncultivated had been almost entirely effaced, leaving an insensible gradation between the two extremes of genius and stupidity.'[12] In agreement with Condorcet, Kern Alexander, Professor of Excellence at the University of Illinois, recently went to the heart of the matter by arguing that since the invention of the printing press in 1440 'a brisk and universal trade in knowledge has emerged; that universal trade is what universities are all about – their reason for existence.'[13]

For Newman, the idea of a university was synonymous with the teaching of liberal arts and the preparation of 'proper citizens' who would contribute to a rich civic experience for everyone. His conservatism and élitism were unmistakable in statements such as the following:

'A cultivated intellect, a delicate taste, a candid, equitable, dispassionate mind, a noble and courteous bearing in the conduct of life; these are the objects of a university.'[14] Newman saw the university as a place of higher education where ideas could be pursued as ends in themselves, where intellectual culture rooted in literature was unquestionably superior to both mechanical culture based in science and practical knowledge with all its utilitarian concerns.[15]

We hasten to add that the notion of 'higher' in relation to education is not meant to concur with the misplaced sense of hubris or arrogance that is commonly exhibited by some more affluent members of society. The élitist orientations of the latter, who have traditionally been the recipients of university education, have led them to feel that they are somehow better than the 'masses,' who historically have not attended university. Rather, we understand 'higher education' to refer to the order of abstraction required for grasping certain types of knowledge. In their approach to the world, some people are more philosophical and reflective, while others are more practical and hands-on. The former, for example, will want to know *why* things work, while the latter will want to know *how* things work; *why* speaks to analysis and explanation, *how* speaks to description. This has nothing to do with 'natural ability' but can be conditioned by one's social and economic location, not to mention personal preferences and the (structured) choices one might make.

The Drift toward Vocationalism

When considering higher education in terms of the personal/intellectual transformative potentials of the liberal arts and sciences and the competency-enhancing potentials of vocational-type programs, it is thus pedagogically crucial to distinguish *education* from *training*.

On the one hand, education is more general and envisages as an end product a more cultured, open-minded, and civic-minded citizenry. On the other hand, training is more given to specialization and the acquisition of a narrow range of skills and information associated with a discrete or specific task, challenge, or problem. Disciplines that train students also tend to undertake research typically associated with, but not restricted to, the hard or physical sciences and the positivist concentration on precision and quantification as a superior approach to knowing.

Training, therefore, is equally important, but speaks to acquisition of technical knowledge and the details that are specific to a given field. As such, training is more narrow, particular, and instrumentally geared to meeting definable goals and honing personal careers. It is what the would-be engineer learns about structural stress in simulation experiments, what the medical student learns in a laboratory, or what the aspiring lawyer learns about precedent.

Such examples illustrate clearly that education and training are discrete learning activities. Yet, as the educational philosopher J.M. Cameron asserts, many people 'have difficulty with the idea that education at its finest consists of a set of speculative activities that are not to be justified by their being directly useful to society or by their tendency to further the betterment of mankind.'[16]

For these reasons, we argue that while one may be *trained* in engineering, one can only be *educated* in the liberal arts and sciences: education and training are not inimical to one another; they merely speak to different moments in the complex process of teaching, learning, and sharing information. We are reminded here of the observation by the political philosopher Leo Strauss, who lamented over a half century ago the ascendance of the scientific mind when he wrote that 'science is the only authority in our age of which one can say that it enjoys universal recognition.'[17] Hence, to be labelled a 'rocket scientist' is a positive evaluation of one's talents and abilities, but there is no equivalent elevation of a student who is an outstanding literary scholar or a highly accomplished musician or painter.

Arguing against those who feel that humanity's future could only be safeguarded by scientific research and the advance of scientific knowledge, we are of one mind with Max Weber, who spoke of the emerging materialist sensibility and the embrace of science in the service of 'the modern economic order with all the related technical requirements of machine production.' For Weber, this social and economic order can be akin to an iron cage controlled by 'specialists without spirit, sensualists without heart; this nullity imagines that it has attained a level of civilization never before attained.'[18]

Then there is Kern Alexander, who echoes Weber and argues that having morality-based value systems is a necessary means for tempering what can be a blind and unbridled faith in science. For him, it is up to the university to bridge the two cultures by promoting both the arts and the sciences: 'The university should be a bulwark against a rudderless progress that would have unforeseen and perhaps dire consequences.'[19]

Believing that scientific knowledge alone is insufficient for addressing or solving all the problems of humanity, and acknowledging the dangers inherent in embracing science as a panacea, Strauss cautioned that 'this science has no longer any essential connection with wisdom. It is a mere accident if a scientist, even a great scientist, happens to be a wise man politically or privately.'[20] What Strauss is getting at is the essential difference between education and training and the fact that wisdom – as a reflexive and ethical awareness of the world schooled in different forms of knowledge – must not necessarily be equated with the latter. This relates to the above reference to 'rocket science' whereby popular understanding elevates hard or physical science to an intellectual level far superior to literature, the arts, or the social sciences.

For us, a university education speaks to the elevation of our *democratic* and *egalitarian* concerns and embraces the central philosophical issues at the heart of the human community: the promotion of social justice, the inculcation of a sense of morality and social responsibility, a commitment to the pursuit of social equality, and the recognition of the dignity of all people irrespective of class, race, gender, sexual orientation, culture, or country (and, for us, postmodernism can paradoxically make the attainment of these ideals more difficult because of its indefensible relativism). Science alone cannot guarantee the pursuit of these goals, but in the educational process they can be addressed by putting the stock of human knowledge in the service of humanity, especially the least fortunate and least able, and not using it to diminish some and elevate others. Thus construed, a university education ought to be conceptually separate from job training. Again, the former is more general and ideally produces well-informed, cultured citizens, while the latter is more specific and instrumentally geared to 'getting the job done.'

The Drift toward Corporatization

Unlike the United States, where there are both public and private universities, in Canada universities are for the most part public, which means they are supported in large measure by government funds that are derived from the taxes levied on citizens. One might then assume that the government and the taxpayer should have a say in how universities are run, what universities do or produce, and how answerable universities ought to be to those who fund them. However, as the public university in Canada becomes increasingly corporatized, it begins to respond to the same demands of the private university, and this is bringing about serious difficulties for the professors and students who are caught between the corporate interests and the university administration that increasingly thinks in terms of the bottom line (profits). As Simon Marginson, professor of higher education at the University of Melbourne tells us, '… private universities produce private goods.' And as a result of this, they 'have a lesser compass of responsibility, a greater freedom to engage in commercial markets and otherwise pursue their own ends free of state intervention, but they must finance their own operations themselves. This is a simple and transparent symmetry.'[21]

This corporatization goes counter to the idea of the public university as a place where ideas are pursued as ends in themselves; a place where, even if unpopular, such ideas are to be exempt from censorship, partisan politics, and the demands of corporate sponsors or donors. As such, the utilitarian approach to ideas is out of place in the traditionally conceived university that stresses education over training, and community health over personal enrichment. The driving ethos in today's modern, corporatized university, conversely, emphasizes the vocational thrust that is premised on utilitarian considerations and is coming to eclipse the traditional 'idea of the university.' The modernist scholar puzzling over abstract philosophical problems that address the nature of truth, the (non-)existence of God or the origins of the universe, the commonsense understandings of race and gender inequality, or the contradictions of democracy, is now on the defensive.

Increasingly, the public is calling for 'relevance' and 'accountability,' and the modernist scholar is being asked to provide compelling material justifications for his or her scholarship, especially in times of severe economic downturn. And as funding is tied to programs that produce tangible and immediate results, the traditional idea of the university is giving way to the results-oriented mandate which sees the modern university being run by CEOs or those trained in their methods, and which hears the language of business in discussions of departmental budgets while witnessing the replacement of non-instrumental decision-making practices with rational business models. Thus, talk of 'total quality management,' or TQM, 'is not just something imported into the university from business in an attempt to run the university as if it were a business'[22] – it is to acknowledge that the university has become fully commercialized. Appropriately, Bill Readings, University of Montreal professor of comparative literature avers: '… we can ask a number of questions about what constitutes "quality" in education. Are grades the only measure of student achievement? Why is efficiency privileged, so that it is automatically assumed that graduating "on time" is a good thing? How long does it take to become "educated"?'[23] If we continue the current trend toward corporatization of the university, the public would soon come to 'the recognition that the university is not just like a corporation, it is a corporation.'[24]

In reference to the idea of 'quality,' the factory or customer service industry comes to mind and suggests such things as quality control, client satisfaction, and product inspectors. University campuses, on the other hand, do not lend themselves quite so easily to quality considerations and their measurements, for scholarship and learning do not always have clear quantifiable ends in mind. As Cameron writes:

> Liberal education goes with a certain largess in the style of life of teacher and taught; material cares are assumed to be, if not altogether banished, at least not to be too consuming; the life of liberal study is free of perpetual occupation with small tasks, with concern about means to unconsidered ends, that is, it is a life of leisure, though by no means a life of idleness.[25]

The Drift Associated with Social Engineering

To return to the earlier question of democratization, when we insist that the university be publicly accountable, we mean that knowledge of what the university does has to be made accessible to a wider audience who, though literate, is not specialized in a given branch of knowledge. Add to this a society-wide embrace of a democratic ethos, which means that not only is greater transparency being demanded of the public university, but also the latter has been pushed to make access to higher education more readily available to the population at large. In principle there is nothing wrong with this just so long as those gaining access have the necessary preparation and motivation for the pursuit of truly *higher* education as we have described it above, and just so long as academic standards do not have to be lowered in order to accommodate political decisions or desires.

This, then, is the challenge. How does one broaden access but keep standards high when the affluent are traditionally the ones with access to better schools and learning opportunities? Indeed, as the distinguished sociologist Randall Collins has warned us, while credential inflation is a serious problem facing both the university and its students, it also has consequences for the wider economy and society.[26]

The well-known social theorist Craig Calhoun elaborates on this when he notes that although sharing does not diminish knowledge, the easy availability of credentials is another matter. Recognizing that for a long time a central function of universities has been the credentialing of the children of the wealthy, he writes that 'expanded access may imply more open and meritocratic distribution of the existing credentials, but of course … it actually produces an inflation of credentials and a new emphasis on prestige differentiations among apparently identical credentials.'[27]

One consequence is that hitherto élite credentials are no longer as scarce and as prized, and another is much duplication of effort and costs as universities compete over empty spoils (prestige rankings). And finally, while students are caught up in escalating tuition debt and the mindless pursuit of ever more paper, in the end the economy is not noticeably more productive. We thus witness a classic 'arms race' in which expensive efforts to gain individual advantage through the status associated with higher degrees cancel each other out and the collective is impoverished in what becomes a 'race to the bottom.'

These types of problems have led Calhoun to suggest that a kind of confusion has set in:

> … the opening of universities to students from working class backgrounds, women and ethnic minorities have all brought important advances in knowledge and in the capacity of universities to fulfil their public missions. Yet they have also brought ambiguity about just what those public missions are.[28]

With their missions adrift, challenges of broadening access while maintaining standards remain, and the goal of reducing the structured inequalities in the wider society and economy goes unaddressed.

The Spoils of the Culture Wars

On many university campuses, stand-offs between hard science and the humanities, between quantifiable knowledge and qualitative understanding, and between vocationalism and the liberal education have been part of what have been called the 'culture wars' in which modernist, Enlightenment conceptions of knowledge and truth are challenged by postmodernists. Postmodernists challenge the scientific method and posit in its place the idea of a 'socially constructed' truth. The culture wars therefore fundamentally involve the conflict between postmodernists and modernists noted above.

Much to the chagrin of modernist scholars, postmodern social constructionists, who initially rode the bandwagon of political correctness and identity politics, called into question the taken-for-granted idea of White, male, heterosexual, Western, middle-class, Christian (etc.) privilege. As is well known, the birth of the university was essentially the work of men of status and property (the élites at the time). Therefore, whether dealing with the founding religious authorities or their class, race, and gender allies in government, the traditional gatekeepers of university education, knowledge production, and power-brokering were essentially conservative in that they supported the status quo. By the last third of the twentieth century, however, this status quo was seen as always being subject to contestation and re-examination.

In assessing the changes, the conservative education commentator Roger Kimball argued that 'these developments have helped to transform liberal studies into an ideological battleground that is also, all too often, an intellectual wasteland.'[29] Many modernist scholars were angry at 'the new breed' of academics 'who cut their teeth on the identity debates' and turned their world upside down.[30] Dubbing liberal education 'illiberal,' a leading American conservative would charge that 'instead of liberal education, what American students are getting is its diametrical opposite, an education in closed-mindedness, and intolerance, which is to say, an illiberal education.'[31]

Unfortunately, the culture wars have obscured the differences between the 'vocational' and 'liberal arts' functions of the university, and allowed vocationalism to creep into more and more programs as liberal arts professors became preoccupied with symbolic issues.

Those on the Right within the liberal arts and sciences found themselves critiquing both postmodernists and the old Left, who were also housed in liberal programs. In the process, the Right often confused the two and painted the 'Left' with the same brush. (Postmodernism morphed out of the New Left of the 1960s as its centre broke down, while the old Left has maintained its Marxism-based objectivist/materialist assumptions that are incompatible with postmodernism's subjectivist/constructivist assumptions, yet those on the Right could not tell the difference in their positions.)[32]

Meanwhile, on the Left, postmodernists critiqued both the old Left and the Right, also often confusing the two to the extent that both make their case on the basis of objectivist assumptions. In fact, many of those in the Marxism-based old Left believe that the Right poses less of a threat than postmodernism to the political cause of addressing economically based inequalities, and establishing a common ground upon which equality can be based.[33] Yet, all three groups share in common an endorsement of liberal education principles.[34]

At the height of the culture wars in the mid-1990s, Todd Gitlin, an ex-president of the 1960s New Left organization Students for a Democratic Society, published *The Twilight of Common Dreams: Why America Is Wracked by Culture Wars*, expressing his disappointment in the New Left and noting how the political correctness of postmodernists was undermining the efforts of the old Left to find a common ground, thereby making it possible for the Right to dominate American politics. Linking wider political concerns with the politics of the academy, the dust cover of this book sums up his argument as follows:

> The Left, which once stood for universal values, has come to be identified with the special needs of distinct 'cultures' and select 'identities.' The Right, long associated with privileged interests, now claims to defend the needs of all. The consequences are clear: since the late 1960s, while the Right has been busy taking the White House, the Left has been marching on the English department.

Regrettably, the distraction of this infighting has allowed a corporatization of universities to go uncontested for decades, whereby vocationalism has crept unnoticed into certain hitherto liberal programs, eclipsing the citizenship function and converting the contemporary university into an extension of the corporate world: where research and development are geared to the market; where generous, targeted private-sector grants drive the creation of research centres; where corporations endow professorial chairs;[35] and where sustained critiques from the Left of the neo-liberal influences on this transformation have only recently emerged.[36]

Re-engaging the University

When a university education is conceived as an open forum for the discussion and dissemination of ideas, both democracy and freedom are strengthened. Defining education as 'intellectual engagement,' Gregory Prince, former president of Hampshire College in Massachusetts, brings student and professor disengagement into the open. But Prince extends the concern with disengagement when he affirms that student and professor disengagement does not exhaust the matter, for many universities, and their administrators too, need to become more engaged with their students and the communities that house them. At the same time, it must also be acknowledged that intellectual engagement can involve by necessity politically contentious ideas.

Still, many modernist scholars disagree on this point. For example, Max Weber did not think that political activism should be part of the university's mandate. A century ago, in 'Science as a Vocation,' Weber argued that the university should be neutral, just as students and professors must ensure that 'politics is out of place in the lecture room.'[37] More recently, the well-known conservative John Ellis added: 'Twenty years ago no one would have believed it possible that professors, of all people, would one day argue that the universities should have an overtly political function.'[38] To this list can be added Stanley Fish, Distinguished Professor of English, the title of whose 2008 book, *Save the World on Your Own Time*, captures the essence of his thinking. Too many professors and students, he feels, have become too activist and are distracted from the main tasks of higher education. He writes:

> Pick up the mission statement of almost any college or university, and you will find claims and ambitions that will lead you to think that it is the job of an institution of higher learning to cure every ill the world has ever known: not only illiteracy and cultural ignorance, which are at least in the ball-park, but poverty, war, racism, gender bias, bad character, discrimination, intolerance, environmental pollution, rampant capitalism, American imperialism and the hegemony of Wal-Mart; and of course the list could be much longer.[39]

In contrast, Prince insists that 'you cannot educate without engaging'[40] and that it is sheer denial for the university to pretend it can be neutral. But far from advocating a call to armed struggle, what is being demanded is that students be taught how to challenge authority in a civil manner, for in so doing when they, in turn, are challenged by life's situations, they will know how to respond appropriately. The posture of neutrality, which plays into the hands of the more conservative modernists, is ideological and should be eschewed. While universities cannot be expected to take a stand on every social issue, still those same universities cannot always refuse, in principle and under the guise of neutrality, to do so.

Students learn better when they are intellectually engaged and challenged. They do not look for or expect neutrality in their professors, any more than engaging professors relish passive compliance from students. Neutrality, therefore, is not to be confused with objectivity, truth, or a propitious learning environment. As Bruce Smith et al. remind us, 'Although students may encounter what they see as bias from time to time, they are neither helpless victims nor pawns in the grip of forces beyond their control.'[41] For today's students, even the disengaged, are very empowered; they are not passive learners, but rather 'are encouraged to question their professors, and they rarely have problems expressing their own views to their teachers in or out of the classroom.'[42] This leads Prince to insist that 'democratic cultures need an education that stimulates questioning and active engagement of the student,'[43] and the most able companion of a democratic order thus conceived is a liberal education.

'How can we not seek to conserve our liberties,' Smith et al. ask, 'even while we argue over what it means to be free?'[44] A proper liberal education will excite student voters over the issues, make them aware of the importance of their voice, and alert them to the potential pitfalls and benefits of any given choice. Readers should note that the origin of the term 'liberal' is the Latin *liber*, meaning 'free,' and the liberal education is associated with the idea that education (broad knowledge) can set one free from the confines of one's ignorance.

As pointed out above, this liberal point of view is at definite odds with those conservatives who feel that the university should be 'neutral' and should stay away from advocacy and activism, even if these liberals and conservatives share other educational values. Nonetheless, it should be acknowledged that in many instances activism has tended to give way to political opportunism and reformism. So in an age of identity politics, specific groups usually issue calls for democracy and transparency with specific ethnic, racial, national, religious, gender, or sexual-orientation claims of disadvantage. In this case, we are dealing with what the conservative commentator Shelby Steele calls

a politics of difference, a troubling, volatile politics in which each group justifies itself, its sense of worth and its pursuit of power, through difference alone. In this context racial, ethnic and gender differences become forms of sovereignty, campuses become balkanized, and each group fights with whatever means are available.[45]

It is very rare that leaders of these opportunistic groups will seek to characterize their groups' problems in more sociological terms by raising the question of social class inequality and its organic links to the capitalist structure of the wider economy and society. In the process, their politics become quite conservative as they eschew questions of class struggle and comprehensive system change in favour of a politics of accommodation that sees individual groups striving to carve out a separate space for themselves *within* the existing system of oppression and exploitation. Without recognizing the ideological slant of their own position, members of such groups are quick to reject traditional truths (the canon) as one-sided, sexist, and racist. Given their political posturing, Kimball asserts, the very idea that students should have to become familiar with

> great ideas which have influenced the actions of man in the past, and continue to do so in the present would instantly elicit a whole range of objections from the feminist complaint about the use of 'man' or 'men' to the more general complaint that there is no agreed-upon set of 'great ideas' that speaks equally to every ethnic and racial constituency.[46]

Equally ideological are those who favour the vocational university, and for whom pedagogy is a straightforward matter involving the objective imparting of 'objective' knowledge and skill, the building of a disciplined mind, and the development of character. These views are heavily laden ideologically, but as in most politics of this sort, those who articulate them are blind to their ideological content and prescription;[47] they see themselves as objective and reasonable and maintain that advocacy and activism are not tailored to opening up closed minds and encouraging independent thought, but rather to persuading and converting the student. And because of the power imbalance between professor and student, such advocacy and activism amount to intimidation and abuse of the professor's privilege.

On the matter of engagement, then, we are not dealing with an either/or phenomenon, for it is clear that dis/engagement is a matter of degree. The key concern is whether the university in question is engaged *enough*. We are persuaded that engagement speaks to the university's reaching out, not only to the students and professors within, but also to those in the wider community. To the extent that the university is a microcosm of the wider society that surrounds it, the protection of women's rights, abortion rights, civil rights, gay rights, workers' rights, animal rights, and even the human rights of illegal immigrants, is vital to a flourishing democracy. As a servant of the community, the university thus has a responsibility to advocate on behalf of those both within and without. And this is where some critics, both conservative and liberal, have sought to draw the line. Once more, the question of the idea and role of the university is recast.

Conclusion: Into the Second Millennium of the University

Those who embrace the vocational function of the university, and who see it primarily as serving the needs of the economy, are supported by some conservative modernists who feel that the university should stick to the traditional Eurocentric curriculum with the traditional definitions of what constitutes appropriate history, literature, music, and related subjects for instruction. Whether in Canada or the United States, these very conservatives feel that the Left has hijacked the university system and that a 'liberal bias' has enveloped the nations' campuses.[48]

In a study that contradicts such claims, Smith et al. conducted a comprehensive survey of administrators, professors, and students that enables them convincingly to expose the 'liberal bias' as a myth that is propagated by the Right. For while they found that professors are generally more liberal than their students, and their students are more liberal than the citizens at large, they also found that universities clearly do not discriminate against hiring conservative professors, and students with conservative points of view are not disadvantaged with regard to grades.[49]

To repeat an earlier claim, education is political. Therefore, to oppose the vocational function of the university often leads to the charge of 'élitism' being levelled against those who feel that the university is a special place where ideas, sometimes even unpopular ones, are pursued as ends in themselves, where knowledge is produced, and where the practical and utilitarian demands of everyday life should not drive the agenda. It is a 'space' where complex ideas are unpacked, dealt with in abstraction, and then recombined in the form of concepts, theories, hypotheses, and ultimately policies applied back to the outside world. For these reasons, the university is a 'space' that is quite different from the pub, the football stadium, or the cocktail party, and should not be governed by the norms or rules that apply in the latter venues. At the same time, there are those – usually, though not always, conservatives – who feel that political activism has no place on the campus or in the classroom, and who would like to reserve for themselves the right to determine what is and is not fair game in a neutral university.

The challenge is both practical and political: in pursuing a balanced and inclusive curriculum, should the professor be required to teach the ideas surrounding Holocaust denial, creationism, scientific racism, and the supposed inferiority of woman to man? Should s/he be permitted to teach that belief in God is really a supreme manifestation of irrational behaviour? Should a physics professor be permitted in class to criticize the prime minister's decision to go to war as morally reprehensible?

In answering these questions, we must guard against the tendency to homogenize students, especially to infantilize them as incapable of engaging in such discussions, and thereby miss the fact that there are as many divisions and differences among students as there are among faculty members. Indeed, while some professors are opposed to the corporatization of the university, others are not, and there are still others who 'wanted patronage,' but 'found it difficult to live with the patrons.'[50] More important is the understanding of the university as one among several social institutions, each of which bears a separate responsibility to the wider society and culture that surrounds and nurtures them. A key responsibility of universities has been to provide a liberal education that contributes to the creation of an informed citizenry that is capable of engaging in value-based discussions. This responsibility is being eschewed as universities drift toward a vocational – or, worse, a pseudo-vocational – mission. Is this to be the legacy of the beginning of the second millennium of the university – our legacy? And, what will historians at the turn of the next millennium say about our stewardship of this system?

2 Stakeholder Relations: The Educational Forum

People from different walks of life have been willing to share with us their experiences with various aspects of the educational system – experiences that are unique to their particular position in society vis-à-vis the educational system. Combined with the comments from critics discussed in Part II of this book, this feedback helps us locate the various higher-educational stakeholders in relation to each other when we use the metaphor of the 'educational forum,' where conflicts are played out in the arena. In this chapter, we share this construction of the educational forum with readers as a way of illustrating how difficult it is to change a system toward which so many opposing views are held.

In addition to bringing the abstractions from the last chapter to the concrete realities of today's society, two goals can be accomplished by identifying the conflicting views of the various system stakeholders.

The first goal is to make readers aware of how complex the politics of education systems are in modern democracies like Canada where there is little central planning. The sad fact is that because no one is 'in charge' of Canada's university system, no one can be called upon to fix it. In place of central planning, myriad compromises are made among stakeholders. In some of these compromises, a certain amount of complicity can be found to not challenge the status quo of prevailing assumptions, even when evidence to the contrary is available.

The second goal is to show that the politics of education are essentially conflictual, rather than harmonious, given the centrality of education to economic and cultural systems, political ideologies, and personal worldviews. This realization can help us to understand better what would be entailed for reform efforts to restore the 'idea of the university' by providing an environment supportive of a liberal education.

We conclude from this exercise that reform efforts need to begin with those stakeholders who are closest to what takes place in classrooms, especially teachers/professors. This is the case because those who exercise the most control over the system – administrators and policy-makers – are most remote from what is currently taking place in the nation's classrooms and are therefore more likely to be out of touch with the nitty-gritty of daily teaching/learning and understandably may even deny that these things are taking place.

Accordingly, in this chapter, we introduce the metaphor of the 'forum' with a central arena where the action takes place. In this sense, readers are asked to visualize what it would look like if all of the stakeholders were brought together in a forum in which their relation to the arena is represented by the row of seats in which they are placed. This is a useful visualization to the extent that it helps us imagine just how remote various stakeholders are from what actually takes place in the classroom. In addition, if we imagine asking each stakeholder to speak up, we see that those closest to the classroom, and therefore those whose voice should be most influential, are actually the least influential in policies that govern what happens there.

Figure 2.1 provides an illustration of how we would seat the various stakeholders in a 'higher educational forum.' In the first row are the on-the-ground participants, most directly students and professors, but also, less directly, counsellors and various campus staff.

The second row represents those who have a direct stake in the system but less direct knowledge of what takes place in the classroom: parents and administrators who have day-to-day stakes in the educational system, and faculty associations and parent-teacher associations that have more symbolic involvements in the system.

Being seated in the next row affords these stakeholders an even more distanced view of the classroom, but their views and actions affect what happens there inasmuch as they provide information input and feedback for the system. The importance of these third-row stakeholders varies to the extent that they produce information used in directing the actions taking place in the classroom. For professors, this is the academic research community; for parents, it is the mass media, especially those producing rankings of universities; for administrators, it is the shadow research community, which is often funded by governments in search of confirmation that their policies are working; and for counsellors and other campus staff, it is various specialized associations that attempt to provide information and support for their interests.

Figure 2.1 The higher education forum

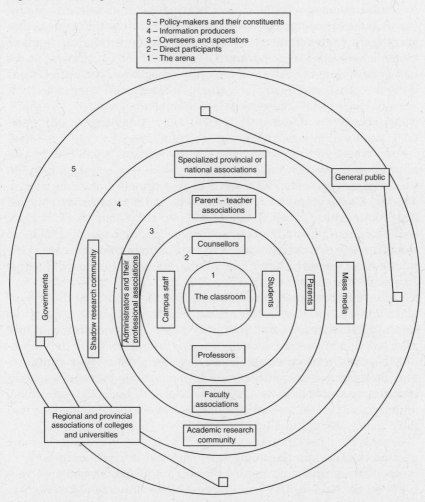

5 – Policy-makers and their constituents
4 – Information producers
3 – Overseers and spectators
2 – Direct participants
1 – The arena

And, finally, most remote from the classroom, but in many ways most important, are governments that set policies, various associations representing provincial/state and national governance, and, of course, the general public. Governments make major funding decisions, and their decisions are often made pragmatically to appease the voting public on a short-term basis (i.e., the number of years until the next election) rather than in response to paying attention to the evidence provided by researchers, to the pleas from administrators, or to the needs of professors and students.

Of course, in reality, the interests of these groups are not as neatly and clearly aligned as the figure suggests, but the figure and the forum metaphor serve heuristic purposes. As noted, the conflictual nature of higher education is implied in the figure (imagine all parties yelling at the same time, cheering for their favourite team, or, in some cases, calling for blood). In addition, given the potential cacophony from so many competing voices, in conjunction with the inevitable power differentials, many issues go unacknowledged (and can, like grade inflation, become 'the elephant in the room'). Indeed, many people would like not to hear about, or would prefer to suppress, issues we raise on behalf of professors. This disinterest and animosity can be found among administrators, government policymakers, and elected politicians. Students have similar issues that go unacknowledged, except among their representatives in local student councils and provincial and national students associations, but even then only a limited number of issues, such as tuition levels, are the focus of reform efforts.

Conflict and Complicity: Case Studies

Some of the sources of, and solutions to, the system crisis are widely acknowledged, yet little is being done to reform the system in Canada. This is especially the case with the nature and quality of education offered at the secondary level, and how universities are increasingly called upon to compensate for deficiencies at that level. Some of the more pressing problems undermining the liberal mission in Canadian universities include the following:

- The lack of preparation at the secondary level for a rigorous post-secondary liberal education, or the absence of an intermediate level of preparation like the CEGEP system in the Province of Quebec;
- The increased funnelling of students into academic programs at the secondary level, and the decline of vocational programs at the secondary level;
  .(Vocational programs have been dumped at the secondary level because they are more expensive and workplace co-ops require personnel to coordinate these programs with the labour market. However, the result is simply a delay of vocational training for increasing numbers of students who, because of mismatches of

interest and ability, dilute academic programs in secondary schools and overburden liberal programs in universities. This is evidenced in the significant numbers of students who, after completing the BA-lite, go back to 'community colleges' – in jurisdictions like Ontario where these vocational institutions exist at the post-secondary level – and seek to acquire 'practical skills' that might enhance their chances of employment.)

- The use of universities as a part of social engineering attempts to reduce wider economic inequalities.
  (It is wasteful to matriculate unprepared students into university settings because they will experience a sense of marginality there from the start, and have a very high risk of dropping out;[1] but apart from an unfairness to prepared students and engaged professors, it is especially unfair to do so to unprepared students from 'under-represented groups' because they have less chance of converting credentials into better paying jobs, while incurring large student-loan debts. Consequently, this type of social engineering does not necessarily produce more social justice.)

To alleviate these problems, the following measures need to be undertaken immediately:

- Students from under-represented groups (i.e., lower social-economic and certain ethnic backgrounds) need to be targeted at the primary and secondary levels if they are to aspire to, and benefit from, a higher education;
  (The reluctance of students from these groups is more cultural and psychological than economic; that is, offering grants and student loans at the eleventh hour will not sufficiently entice them to participate at the tertiary level, and is too late if they are not academically and psychologically prepared. As it stands, the primary and secondary systems effectively eliminate many of those from under-represented groups from the educational system, even many of those with academic interests and abilities. This must be addressed before universities can perform their transformative function.)[2]
- A systemic culture of learning – one that is not anti-intellectual – needs to be established at the lower levels of education, so that students respect knowledge acquisition;
  (This will not only engender respect for rigorous higher learning, but it will also enhance people's contributions to society [citizenship

and leadership roles], the economy [international competitiveness], and the common culture [continuing to advance the frontiers of knowledge and understanding], regardless of their level of education.)

- It needs to be acknowledged by policymakers that the ultimate goal of a liberal education should be to educate the best and brightest from all backgrounds to their highest potential, so that they can make their maximum contribution to society.
  (Other students, with lower levels of academic abilities, but who demonstrate some university-level promise, should be welcomed into the system, but not pandered to with inflated grades and an acceptance of academic disengagement. The point of reference for standards needs to be [true] excellence, not mediocrity.)

We will now turn to some examples of how these solutions to the system crisis are stymied by the conflict and complicity among key stakeholders.[3] In the final chapter, we revisit and extend this discussion of problems and solutions.

Conflicts in the Arena

Students' Frustrations: Where Is My Education?

Many students find contemporary universities to be highly alienating. This is likely a chief motivational factor behind some student-induced disengagement. Nonetheless, as explored below in chapter 4 (in the section 'The Crisis Experienced by Students'), universities must bear responsibility for not providing sufficient challenge and structure to students who have the ability and motivation, yet find there is little there to stimulate them.

Two cases of university students who have recently spoken up in the print media about this sense of alienation and waste are reviewed here. The first case is of an English major, who, along with her classmates, received high marks for mediocre work but was frustrated that she did not benefit more from her education in terms of learning how to write at an advanced level. Similarly, the second case is of a psychology student who did all that was required of him but felt cheated because he was not sufficiently challenged; instead, he was required to engage in little more than textbook memorization.[4]

The first case was written for the *Globe and Mail* as a poignant article titled 'My Best Marks Were in Partying 101.'[5] This student was fed up with the congratulations she was getting for earning an A average in her university courses when she did very little to earn it. She knew the little work she did was mediocre, yet she consistently received marks purporting that her assignments and exams were excellent, despite the fact that she skimmed required readings for only a few minutes before classes and studied for exams the day before. Instead of active engagement in her courses, she and her friends spent most of their time socializing in a local Starbucks.

Her lowest mark was a B+ and she writes that many of her friends received equivalent marks in spite of their lack of interest in book reading beyond Harry Potter novels. She not only knew that she did not deserve the praise that should go with feats of excellence, but she actually felt somewhat guilty about her hollow accomplishment. The sophistication of her prose suggests she has much untapped potential for creative narrative. In one passage, she writes: 'Taking only one step up a mountain, when there are thousands more to go, and then being told that one step is more than enough, seems to cheat one out of reaching the summit and seeing the valley below.'

She goes on to take some of the blame, but also places some blame on the system that condones the disengagement she and her classmates experienced: 'It is my own fault for not taking more steps and getting closer to the mountaintop, but it is not my fault for receiving a higher mark than I deserved. I was not given a chance to work hard for something, because slight efforts were enough.' Still, she cannot feel proud of herself or the school she attended, thinking that

> when the mediocre is accepted as excellent ... discouragement is the only appropriate response. There is almost no incentive for excellence. Nothing more was expected of me than the pittance I gave, and there is something almost insulting in that.

One has to wonder what untapped potential lies within this student, who appears to have a flair for writing and mistakenly looked to a university to help her develop it. Clearly, bright students such as she are being cheated by a system that inflates grades and in so doing removes the types of challenges that would nurture their potentials and push them to strive for true excellence.

The other case involves a fourth-year psychology student from York University in Toronto who spoke up in the magazine *Psynopsis*.[6] He also complains about not being given assignments and assessments that were challenging, and instead being subjected to continual testing in large lecture courses. His tally of the total assessments he received in his nine second- and third-year psychology courses was one essay, one report, three literature reviews, two group projects, two research proposals, and *twenty-six multiple-choice tests*. He feels his BA in psychology qualifies him only for 'Jeopardy or hitting the North American Trivial Pursuit circuit,' and he resents owing $20,000 for what he 'could have acquired by reading an encyclopaedia.' His greatest regret was that the 'critical thinking skills that should have been fostered … from the beginning become ancillary. Without discussion, without critique, without thinking, why is this education?'

These examples emphasize that students are not a homogeneous body and not all of them are keen to take the easy way out. What the examples also do is touch on a common form of alienation from the *process* of acquiring a university education. In addition, a substantial proportion of graduates are also frustrated by the *product* of that education, with up to one-half of graduates discovering that it is very difficult to find a job that they feel is commensurate with their qualifications, while at the same time carrying a heavy debt. To begin one's adulthood with a debt load that is equivalent to a small mortgage, with little hope on the horizon of achieving financial independence, is certainly not a situation to be envied.

No doubt a lot of student dropout and underachievement is a result of this alienation, and a sense of futility about wasting time and money. Students who have affluent parents to pay their bills for them likely experience this alienation as well, but because of the parental and societal pressure to get the degree, they can simply 'cooperate and graduate.' With little recognition of these problems, students often do not know where to direct their frustrations to the extent that the source of the conflicting stakes between students and the system is not immediately obvious.

What are the sources of this alienation that students are experiencing? Let's follow the trail.

Professors' Frustrations: 'I'm Leaving!'

Meanwhile, professors experience frustrations in trying to reach – and thus teach – alienated students in a corporatized environment where the goals of education are not shared with students or administrators. Although many professors may not be able to locate the source of their malaise, the conflicts they experience in this environment on a daily basis can wear them down. Instead of identifying the systemic sources of their frustrations, they are likely to take their frustrations out on students, or on themselves. Hence, the high levels of stress and stress-reducing medications reported below in chapter 4 (in the section 'The Crisis Experienced by Faculty').

In spite of high stress levels, professors generally keep their malaise to themselves. Those who openly voice dissatisfaction with their jobs to the public do not receive much sympathy, partly as a result of misconceptions about how much work is involved in the job. A recent exchange in the on-line news source *Inside Higher Ed* illustrates this lack of sympathy for professors' complaints.

The article 'I'm Leaving,' written by a professor using the pseudonym John Smith, stimulated this exchange. He was tenured at a liberal arts college in the United States and had even served as the Chair in his department. His primary reason for wanting to leave was expressed as follows:

> After too many years at this job (I am in my mid-40s), I have grown to question higher education in ways that cannot be rectified by a new syllabus, or a sabbatical, or, heaven forbid, a conference roundtable. No, my troubles with this treasured profession are both broad and deep, and they begin with a fervent belief that most of today's college students, especially those that come to college straight from high school, are unnecessarily coddled. Professors and administrators seek to 'nurture' and 'engage' and they are doing so at the expense of teaching. The result: a discernable and precipitous decline in the quality of college students. More of them come to campus with dreadful study habits. Too few of them read for pleasure ... They are terribly ill-prepared for four years of hard work, and most dangerously, they do not think that college should be arduous. Instead they perceive college as an overnight recreation center in which they exercise, eat, and in between playing extracurricular sports, they carry books around. If a professor is lucky, the books are being skimmed hours before class.[7]

He was also critical of the disengagement of some of his colleagues:

> Far too many of my colleagues are dialing in – showing up late, popping in videos during class, assigning group projects, or sitting in a circle and asking students how they feel. Why they have abandoned classroom rig-

or is something that only they can answer. But one answer is simple – students flock to these popular classes, probably because they cater to the students' worst sensibilities. Homework is minimal, or sometimes optional. Surprise quizzes are considered unfair. Late assignments are not failed. Some grades are even negotiable.

Professor 'Smith' continues by stating his refusal to get on the latest bandwagon of coddling students and looking to new technologies for magic solutions:

Such a pedagogy runs counter to the school, undergraduate and graduate training that I received, but it is openly embraced by nervous administrators who encourage faculty members to be innovative, experimental and experiential. They speak openly about pandering to student demands, but opt not to use the word 'pander,' employing instead the curious and the trendy phrase 'student empowerment.' I prefer to empower them with reading skills. But such a mission is considered old-fashioned. Maybe I should attend a seminar (don't worry, the college will pay for it) titled 'Technology in the classroom' or 'Innovative pedagogies in the 21st century.' I pass.

As telling as the confessions of this frustrated professor are, even more telling are the large number of comments (sixty-six comments over a several week period) in response to his article. Many are hostile and demeaning to the disillusioned professor, using various forms of name-calling, with titles like 'poor baby' (written by a chronically unemployed holder of a PhD), 'good riddance,' 'grow up,' and 'Good! Leave!' (the last comment with the opening sentence 'I really, really need a job, and a gig "coddling" your liberal arts college students sounds like an absolute dream').

These comments reveal a widespread lack of insight among stakeholders into the system-level problems cited by 'Smith.' Instead of grasping the problem as systemic, these commentators in this 'cacophonic forum' adopt individualistic explanations that 'blame the victim.' Indeed, we invite readers to visualize the education forum in this case as a Roman circus with spectators shouting for blood and their thumbs down.

One commentary reveals a source of this systemic problem in the mission drift of the liberal arts, recommending an unabashed embracing of a corporate-based vocational mission by universities:

It is time for education to be run as a business and less as a [*sic*] elite society of scholars. Education is preparing an individual for their [*sic*] future. Education is not creating scholars – we are *training* individuals for their future employment. (Emphasis added)

There were a number of sympathetic voices, showing that not everyone is out for blood, but these were mainly from those also working in this 'row' of the arena. One graduate student did not want to see professors like 'Smith,' who 'get it,' to give up and leave her to the mercy of professors who do not 'get it':

From the perspective of a current grad student, I sadly couldn't agree more. I've seen many faculty dumbing down lectures and handing out undeserved passing grades. Most of my peers during undergrad were going through the motions or working under the stupid assumption that they were going to be doctors when they couldn't understand why they had to take Microbiology. For the good students, and the bad who need to be weeded out, don't abandon the school and speed the decline. I've only been a lowly TA at this point, but I understand the pain of entitled students. Please don't leave students like me wondering why I demand more of undergrads than professors.

If the hostile reactions to a professor being honest about how he feels about this dysfunctional system are typical of what happens when someone goes public, it is little wonder that more professors are not speaking up.

Secondary-School Teachers' Frustrations (1): 'Let Me Do My Job!'

In a small Ontario town, a group of high-school teachers has organized to raise the consciousness of the public about the decline in the secondary system there. Prompted by a lack of responsiveness from the local school board and the Ontario Ministry of Education, they are also attempting to get more say in the administration of public schools. For the past few years, they have organized events and maintained a blog[8] that informs interested parties about local and provincial developments. According to their blog, their mission is to initiate discussions about changes that would counteract the 'top down system [of the current secondary school system, where] ... the information flows only one way.' Their 'Mend Education' mandate is to work together to create the kinds of students we all value – students with character. But we believe the education system is not doing this as well as it should. This is manifested in:

- students ill-prepared to meet the expectations of the next level (junior to intermediate, intermediate to senior, senior to workplace/college/university)
- no meaningful input garnered or accepted from students, parents, teachers, trustees.

They feel that local administrators are insensitive to their concerns, and therefore are taking their own measures 'to improve our educational system for all students.' This group is helping frustrated teachers and parents voice their concerns, and the support the group is garnering can be seen on their website. This type of grassroots organization can be expected to grow as the frustration levels increase among those most closely seated in the educational forum to 'the arena.'

At the provincial level, a grassroots organization formed in Ontario in the late 1980s has since become more formalized as the Society for Quality Education. Its mandate is as follows:

[We are] parents, educators, and citizens who believe the poor quality of our education system can no longer be ignored. Many of us learned the hard way that public schools are failing our children. We discovered that today's school boards are unimaginably bureaucratic and unaccountable. For many of us, this discovery (and the implications for our children's futures) was one of the most painful experiences in our lives. Some of us were forced to find expensive private alternatives for our children. As we watched real learning taking place, while at the same time making huge financial sacrifices, we simply could no longer accept that quality schools should be out of reach for most families. Now we're determined to do something about it! In Ontario, the status quo is unacceptable and unsustainable. School systems around the world have implemented better and more equitable ways to teach children. We want to be an agent for change; a force for better-quality schools. We're up against a powerful inter-locking monopoly – the teachers' unions, the school boards, the faculties of education, ministry officials, and other vested interests.[9]

The Society for Quality Education is playing an information-dissemination function that helps interested parties to educate themselves about alternatives to the heavily bureaucratized public school system, and its heavy-handed, top-down ways enabled by its monopoly.

Also relevant here in terms of how parents are seeking alternatives to an unresponsive educational system is the Canadian Centre for Home Education. According to its website, the Canadian Centre for Home Education (CCHE) 'is a non-profit, sister organization to Home School Legal Defence Association (HSLDA) that was formed in order to fill the void of quality research in the area of home education, and to train volunteer home education leaders from across the country.'[10] This organization recently released the results of a study reporting that those who are home-educated have above-average outcomes as adults on a number of indicators. The study began in 1994 and followed a sample for fifteen years, finding that compared to Canadian averages obtained from Statistics Canada, as adults, those who were home-educated

> were more socially engaged and almost twice as likely to have voted in a federal election. Average income was higher with more sources of investment income and self employment, and no cases of government support as the primary source of income. They were happier in their work and their lives in general. When reflecting on the value of being home educated, most felt that it was an advantage in their adult life.[11]

Although it can be argued that there is a selection bias in terms of who receives home schooling, especially in terms of parents who are more involved with their children's education and knowledgeable enough to oversee it themselves, it is clear that there is widespread and growing discontent among parents as well among the secondary-school teachers who teach their children. Ontario seems to have more problems at this level than some other provinces (such as Quebec and Alberta)[12] and jurisdictions in other countries, but this seems to be a matter of degree, not kind. Will a full-fledged grassroots movement form among these stakeholders to gain more control of high-school governance? Are administrators and bureaucrats getting it? It appears not, at least in Ontario, as the next case study illustrates.

Secondary-School Teachers' Frustrations (2): 'The Ministry of Truth'

In the spring of 2009, things came to a head involving what have been dubbed the Ontario Ministry of Education's 'no-fail' policies. At the heart of these policies are recent initiatives by the ministry to increase high-school completion rates to 85 per cent of secondary students by 2010-11 (from a rate of 77 per cent in 2009, constituting an increase of only 8 per cent). Like some other provinces, Ontario has had a relatively high 'dropout' rate, and the attempts that have been made to reduce it are based on concerns about the poorer economic prospects of those who do not complete high school.[13]

According to a 'memo' posted on the ministry website in May 2009,[14] the ministry's policies aim to separate students' 'behaviour' with respect to attending class, completing assignments, and sitting for exams, from their academic 'performance,' or how well they actually do on assignments and exams. In other words, and in a clear case of the tail wagging the dog, grades cannot be deducted for lateness on assignments, and students must be allowed to write make-up exams whenever they are ready to do so. Further, a 'Credit Recovery' program is in effect to allow students to quickly make up for missed classes, assignments, and exams near the end of each year.[15] As phrased in the memo, '... the decision to separate reporting of performance from behaviour was made a decade ago and is reflected in current Ministry policy.'

As benignly as the Ministry of Education has attempted to spin this policy, the ripple effect is being felt far and wide. As these students have gone on to university, their professors have been scrambling to teach them that they must abide by the self-management standards expected of responsible adults. Professors thus find their workload and frustrations increased in terms of more frequently having to 'herd' students to complete assignments on time and to show up for tests on their scheduled dates.

The only people who seem to be happy about these Ministry of Education initiatives are ministry officials, and perhaps some high-school administrators who can more easily appease students and parents by raising grades by fiat. High-school teachers are hopping mad about it and in the spring of 2009 released the results of a study on the negative consequences of these policies. A petition protesting aspects of the 'no-fail' practices was also circulated.[16] In the meantime, as discussed below in chapter 4, a recent study of university professors in Ontario found that most professors feel that incoming students are not as well prepared in terms of both skills and motivations to benefit from the university experience, and have greater 'expectation of success without the requisite effort.'[17] The national media even picked up on both of these expressions of dissatisfaction,[18] but the Ontario Ministry of Education did not indicate any willingness to consider seriously these concerns.

This is a prime example of stakeholder gridlock. There appeared to be little understanding in the Ontario Ministry of Education regarding why teachers might be concerned about the issue of failure among their students. When large numbers of students put out little or no effort in a course, any self-respecting teacher would be upset, especially when there is also pressure to pass such students. In this case, there are numerous reports from teachers who feel obliged to fail students on substantive grounds but face various obstacles in doing so, primarily because of the unpleasantries they face from their administrative personnel. The Ministry of Education seems to think, as its memo implies, that teachers unhappy with these policies are calling for a quota of F's. To the contrary, the students·whom these teachers feel should be failing in the current system are not meeting the barest of standards, such as attending classes and sitting for exams.

To be fair, these problems are not limited to Ontario. A recent study found that in Canadian schools, 'social, academic and intellectual engagement show a marked decrease with grade level ... participation falls steadily as grade level increases and [regular] attendance decreases from a high of 90% in Grade 6 to a low of about 40% by Grade 12.'[19] Undoubtedly, many adults who have not kept up with changes in Canadian high schools will be astonished with the finding that just over half of fifteen-year-old Canadian students have regular attendance, compared to about three-quarters for comparable students in other OECD countries (regular attendance is defined as not skipping classes or missing days without a reason in the month prior to the survey). The authors of this study note that these findings are consistent with previous Canada-OECD comparisons 'on sense of belonging and student attendance, which found that Canadian students have very low levels of engagement ... [with] less than one-half of Canadian students ... deeply engaged in their study of school subjects.'[20] The public should rightly ask why Canadian ministries of education enable this widespread disengagement.

Findings like these raise a host of questions about how it is that Canada is touted as a world leader in·education. For example, some ardent defenders of the Canadian educational system (through all levels) point to Canada's performance on the Programme for International Student Assessment (PISA) tests, as does this Ministry of Education memo.

Their logic is that if Canadian students are scoring high on these standardized tests, which are administered in dozens of countries, then critics of the Canadian system must be wrong.

Then again, there are several serious problems with using the PISA as a defence of the Canadian system, and other educational systems for that matter, especially when it is implied that if the PISA is an assessment of academic excellence, then those countries scoring 'high' on it must also have excellent educational systems.

First, the PISA is specifically designed to assess the ability of fifteen-year-olds to use simple skills to solve everyday problems. Moreover, the questions, exam conditions, and grading are not rigorous; the questions use simple wording and only short answers are required; grading does not take into account spelling and grammar errors; students can use calculators during the test; and part-marks are given for wrong answers.[21]

Consequently, these tests do not assess an advanced academic aptitude that would be associated with a readiness for the university curriculum. In fact, if we look at the results for reading literacy, only a small minority of Canadian fifteen-year-olds scores at the highest level of literacy (Level 5), the level that would be most compatible with university-level reading comprehension. The majority of students of this age are capable, at best, of only a moderate literacy – Level 3 or lower. In conjunction with the evidence of low engagement levels, looking at the results in this way helps explain why so many high-school students have such difficulty with other literacy tests (e.g., the EQAO tests in Ontario), and why so many high-school graduates currently have difficulty making the transition to the university level.

Second, other international tests assessing more advanced abilities tell a different story about the 'success' of the Canadian system, placing Canadian students in the middle on international comparisons (e.g., the Progress in International Reading Literacy Study (PIRLS) and the Trends in International Mathematics and Science Study (TIMSS).[22] Furthermore, there are recent indications that Canada is slipping even from its mediocre position. As a result, Canadian students are not well represented among the front-runners of these more difficult tests, and it is with the more advanced abilities that we should be concerned in preparing students who would go on to our universities.

But, to return to the issue of incentives and structure for students, common sense tells us that if students know there are no penalties for non-compliance with course requirements, some will play the system.

The emphasis here is on 'some' students. A system can certainly ensure that virtually all students complete high school by ignoring non-compliance with basic academic standards and behavioural requirements, but what kind of education are these students receiving? It is naïve to assume that the entire system should bend for the sake of a minority of students who do not have the behavioural maturity to meet basic course requirements. And, given what those on the ground – teachers and students – are reporting about the deleterious effects of these practices, the majority are being made to suffer for the sake of this minority. Given that the Ministry of Education is trying to graduate only marginally more students (as above), the extreme disruption to two levels of the educational system is a high price to pay.

Why won't the Ontario Ministry of Education listen to those who have the most experience with the consequences of its policies? The answer seems to lie in the patronage among stakeholders in the more remote levels of the 'educational forum.' That is, the ministry is apparently willing to pay more heed to the abstract expertise of a few individuals in the shadow research community (level four) than to the multitude of voices who directly experience what is taking place in the arena.

The ministry memo takes recourse to this, referring to (unreferenced) research on assessment, making a claim to authority by stating that 'some of the top international experts on student assessment are from Ontario,' as if consultations with these experts has made the Ontario secondary system some sort of world leader. The memo further claims that this research goes against 'conventional wisdom' about tying grades to both behaviour and academic performance, implying that this research proves that giving students low grades, or failing them, discourages them from trying harder.

We strenuously disagree with this characterization of both the research and people's beliefs. Obviously, if people believe they are good at something, they are more likely to persist in that activity until compelling evidence to the contrary is presented. That point is so obvious as to not require extensive academic research (and we hope that the ten years of research mentioned in the memo have investigated more than this). What is not mentioned is that people's *beliefs* about their abilities need to match the *reality* of the situation and that false feedback is extremely harmful, merely setting them up for future failure. Telling people they are good at something when they are not does not increase their ability level, and is not what research about the 'self-fulfilling prophecy' is about.[23] Grades need to be used as accurate feedback, not as a false reward to pump up self-esteem or feed narcissism.

As elsewhere, before the introduction of these ministry policies, Ontario teachers routinely gave students who encountered difficulties in meeting deadlines second chances, and they took these circumstances into account when assigning grades. Besides, grades are only seen as punitive when someone thinks they are unfair. If this memo is representative, the ministry's view of teachers seems to be that they are insensitive to students' needs and psychological states, and that they use grades punitively, a view that further infuriates teachers.

The memo makes other statements that fly in the face of both common sense and established research. For example, it claims:

Some critics appear to believe that only so many students are capable of completing high school or being successful in postsecondary education. Yet everything we know denies this supposition.

Are we to assume that those at low levels of intellectual functioning are as capable as those at high levels of completing a rigorous high-school and university education? Can we really take people at random and turn them into doctors, physicists, or philosophers simply 'by providing lots of encouragement,' as the memo would have it? Again, common sense tells us otherwise, as does decades of psychological and educational research. There are clear differences in abilities among people and there are different types of abilities, of which academic ability is only one.[24] As discussed below in chapter 3, effort can make a difference in people's ability levels, but the evidence shows that it is *tremendous effort* that makes a difference, not the modicum of effort required to hand in assignments late or attend a few make-up classes, as the ministry's Credit Recovery program allows.

When the ministry asserts that many people can improve themselves by trying harder, we wholeheartedly agree. But not everyone is good at everything, and part of growing up is learning what one is good – and not good – at. Finding this out, even if it means failing occasionally, or finding out that one is just 'average,' or even below average, in terms of certain skills, is part of 'life's package,' with which we must all learn to live. Those who discover what they are truly good at, and then expend tremendous effort in developing those abilities, are the ones who go on to reach their full potentials.[25]

This ministry memo concludes by urging teachers to challenge criticisms of government policies by talking about 'Ontario's high standards.' In doing so, it is advocating a public-relations approach that massages issues rather than rectifies problems. It calls for 'public confidence,' when it means public compliance and the submission of teachers to seriously misguided policies established in remote offices based on some unspecified research.

We now turn to a consideration of why those who have the most say in educational policies can be so misguided in the policies they champion.

Complicity in the Grandstands: The Scourge of Human Capital Theory

This section traces the links among governments (in row five of the forum), through the shadow research community that advises them (row four), to university administrators (row three). Administrators are the lynchpins of how university missions are defined and 'lived' on the basis of the beliefs held by the upper-level stakeholders. The focus here is with how those in these three rows share a common thread of thinking about the university mission, as well as a common 'language' to share their beliefs. Exposing their common beliefs helps us see why those at these three levels are so resistant to listening to those in rows one and two, who have direct experience in today's classrooms and who operate under a different set of beliefs. This exposé also reveals why appeals for reforms are likely to be ignored or dismissed – to the detriment of the system – by those with the most power over the educational system.

Stakeholders 'seated' at these three most remote levels of the educational forum tend to think in terms of the rational-choice logic that is central to the discipline of economics. Most influential in *education economics* is human capital theory, which hypothesizes that individual and societal investments in education yield economic returns for those individuals and societies. In the case of university-level education, these stakeholders invariably point to studies that show that university graduates have lower unemployment rates and higher salaries than those with other types of education.

The appeal of human capital theory for these stakeholders is that if all educational credentials represent human capital, then the more credentials a person has the better. And, if no consideration is given to what these credentials really represent, then logics of efficiency can prevail: because academic streams in high schools and liberal programs in universities are the cheapest to offer, it is more efficient to pile students into them than to offer the more expensive vocational and professional programs.

Although some evidence does provide some support for human capital theory, there are competing explanations for why graduates of liberal programs do better than those with 'lower' levels of education. In particular, these credentials can have a 'positional' quality implicated in status competitions for jobs that employers use in selecting among prospective employees, especially for jobs that do not require advanced, specialized skills.

In fact, when all of the evidence from a variety of disciplines is examined, the theory works much better in explaining outcomes for applied and professional degrees, which are designed to increase the concrete skills sought by employers. Because those in these three upper rows of the forum do not recognize this distinction between concrete and abstract skills, they keep advocating the general university education as if it had the same marketability as the applied education. Hence, it is not that human capital theory is not still useful, but rather that its acclaim far exceeds its utility to the point that the policies based on it are actually creating a multitude of problems, sometimes making it *more* difficult for many people to integrate into the workplace.

For example, university graduates experience a bottleneck on their way to the job market that cannot be explained by the notion that 'more education is better' regardless of the type or content of that education. This bottleneck involves the high probability of *under*employment, especially for graduates of general programs.[26]

One way of understanding this underemployment or 'overqualification' is as follows:

If the proficiencies ostensibly represented by *any* post-secondary credential constituted marketable skills to the extent claimed by human capital theorists, even liberal-arts graduates would not face a bottleneck in matching their 'skills' to jobs. Even if existing jobs that needed their skills were saturated, their 'human capital' would convert into more lucrative employment outcomes, including the creation of their own productive enterprises. However, only a small number of liberal-arts graduates create their own employment outside of such existing institutional contexts as government, schools, and businesses.

What is more, if job marketability closely adhered to *any* type of education, then years of schooling would correlate with earnings and outcomes independently of whether a credential is attained, but this appears not to be the case. Instead, empirical studies find a 'sheepskin' or 'signalling' effect of credential attainment.[27] Hence, to the extent that a university education has become a prerequisite for just about any type of white-collar job, even where the skill levels are obviously mismatched, the impact of these credentials needs to be understood sociologically rather than just economically.

This confusion was identified in the earliest peer-reviewed academic publications that developed the claim that human capital investments were analogues to other types of capital investments. Those publications made more circumscribed designations of human capital than those that currently inform researchers and policymakers. For example, in a 1935 article in the *Quarterly Journal of Economics*, J.R. Walsh argued that *only investments in training for a profession* would constitute 'a capital investment made in a profit-seeking, equalizing market, in response to the same motives which lead to the creation of factories, machinery, and the like.'[28] Walsh did not recognize general forms of education as involving this type of profit-producing investment motivation:

> At the outset is to be noted the obvious fact that some education is clearly not the result of 'rational' profit-seeking calculations. The training children receive up to and including that in secondary school is not primarily intended to develop vocational skills. Rather it is the intent of the parents and the state to promote the education of citizens. The purpose is to provide political and cultural education in the widest sense. And although abilities which have their economic significance are developed as a part of the process of training an intelligent electorate, these abilities are by no means the preconceived object of the training. Their appearance is incidental to the major purpose.[29]

In spite of these caveats, it was economists like Gary Becker[30] who, in the 1960s, popularized the concept of human capital, claiming its equivalence to other types of capital investment (like buying more machinery) and thereby making it attractive to policymakers. Although Becker cited Walsh as supporting his popularization, Becker's influential work constituted a departure from these earlier assumptions that applied the concept of human capital only to vocational and professional forms of education intentionally pursued for their concrete economic returns. According to earlier economists like Walsh, this would exclude most secondary education in academic streams, as well as liberal arts programs at universities, both of which are now uncritically assumed to constitute forms of capital investments on par with applied streams.

More contemporary research is confirming that earlier formulations of human capital theory were more precise than current ones in limiting their predictions to the outcomes of specific forms of vocational and professional education. As David Walters recently concluded in his analysis of the skill use of post-secondary graduates in Canada, human capital theory is 'more applicable to applied and technical programs.'[31] In an analysis that specifically tests this theory against credentialism theory, Walters found that

> there are a large number of graduates, particularly those of liberal arts programs, who are in jobs that are not related to their schooling. This finding lends support for the credentialist perspective, that there is widespread mismatching of credentials in the labour market.[32]

At the same time, the extent of the earnings advantage of university graduates is being increasingly questioned, especially for those graduates who did not do well in their studies because of motivational and ability shortfalls.[33] It also appears that the bases for some past calculations are faulty, as in cases where the average earnings of *all* university graduates is used (which are generally in the 60–70K range), instead of the earnings of just those with bachelor's degrees, who constitute the majority of university graduates (and their salaries are generally in the 40–50K range).[34] An estimate of the lifetime earnings of those with just an undergraduate degree would be about one-third to one-half of that estimated on the basis of the earning power of all university graduates.[35] Other sources report low returns for undergraduate degrees relative to other investments, taking into consideration what would have been gained from the investment of income lost while attending university (opportunity costs).[36] These questions about economic returns are being asked of graduate degrees as well. For example, according to Statistics Canada, the economic return of a PhD is now not much greater than an MA, so that there is little financial incentive to spend those three to five (or more) years pursuing a doctorate:

> The median annual earnings among those who were working full time in 2007 was lowest for college graduates at $35,000. This increased to $45,000 for bachelor's graduates, $60,000 for master's graduates and $65,000 for doctorate graduates. Therefore, the earnings gap was 33% between the

bachelor's and master's degree, and 29% between a bachelor's and a college degree. But it was only 8% between the master's and doctorate levels.[37]

Policymakers and Their Advisors

One reason for the massive expansions of universities is that recent cohorts of students have been taking refuge there from a labour market that is not kind to young workers in terms of opportunity, remuneration, or respect. The youth labour market collapsed in the 1980s in developed countries around the world,[38] and many governments have done a poor job of re-establishing it. Rather than addressing the *demand side* of youth labour – jobs themselves – many governments have elected to address the *supply side* through policies directed at producing more educated workers.[39] These policies appear to have been misinformed by human capital theorists. As the underemployment research shows, the supply-side strategy has not worked out as it should have. Ironically, instead of altering course as it became increasingly obvious that these policies were not working for a large segment of the youth population, governments have resorted to increasing the rhetoric about the need for highly educated labour. This has produced an unacknowledged triple-whammy hindering the integration of young people into the labour force: (1) good jobs are scarce for them; (2) those who can afford it have to pay for more education in hopes of getting even entry-level jobs; and (3) many find that even university credentials are not easily converted into job opportunities.

Readers may ask how it is that the research upon which these policies have been based would not have revealed these problems, redirecting policy efforts to more effective solutions for helping young people integrate into the labour force. After all, aren't current policies in advanced democracies evidence-based? Well, it turns out that the research exposing the problems with these policies has been largely ignored in favour of evidence that verifies the initial conceptions formed by a human capital theory – the 'confirmation bias' discussed below in chapter 4. Some of this non-confirmatory research has come from peer-reviewed academic journals. However, the various governments across Canada have apparently ignored this research and relied on research produced by their own researchers and 'shadow research communities.' The problem with this source of research is that it is often constrained by the parameters set out by governments' belief in economic theories such as the human capital model. As a result, this research has merely confirmed the preconceptions of policymakers, leading them further and further off course, perseverating rather than adapting.

Some insight into this hiatus between research and policy comes from William Rees,[40] who argues that while academics believe in accurate data and precise analyses, policymakers make decisions largely based on political expediency and what will appease public sentiments, which may be at odds with academic understandings of policy issues. He summarizes this as follows:

> Unfortunately, politics is among those domains of human activity least beholden to sound academic research. First, politics – indeed, social relations of all kinds – is about power, ambition, social status, and personal prestige. Thus, while politicians will readily adopt research that supports their beliefs, many show little affinity for results that challenge their political survival. Indeed, they will readily abandon science that speaks to the long-term public interest, giving way to powerful special interests if to do so helps ensure re-election …
>
> Second, politics is ideological and, like other mythic constructs, a political ideology can be a rather ungainly concoction of fact and values, assumptions and illusions. It often gains credence only after frequent repetition and ritualistic affirmation. But while people may come to believe profoundly in a particular political position, ardent belief alone cannot true that position with reality. In these circumstances, we would do well to recall Henry Kissinger's dictum that 'It is not a matter of what is true that counts, but a matter of what is perceived to be true.' In other words, policy action is often propelled more by myth than science.[41]

We next provide several Canadian examples of the misdirection of research associated with the political use of human capital theory.

STUDIED IGNORANCE OF KEY FACTORS

The Canadian government's own internal research into university graduate underemployment, and thus knowledge of this problem, date back at least to the 1980s,[42] and periodic reports have been released since.[43] Yet aspects of these reports that do not confirm human capital theory have apparently been ignored. As recently as 2006, statements such as the following can be found in reports published by Human Resources and Skills Development Canada (HRSDC), a major branch of the federal government:

The proportion of university-educated individuals in lower-skilled occupations has risen from 12% in 1990 to about 17% in 2005, providing some evidence that there *may be signs* of oversupply of university graduates. Although admittedly, this is an area that *requires further research*. (Emphases added)[44]

'May be signs … requires further research'! Incredibly, none of the many previous government studies dating back to the 1980s is even mentioned in this report. Instead, the report takes a Pollyannaish view of the future labour market that is possible only through the selective use of evidence. To the extent that politicians read and believe these types of reports, the scourge of human capital theory continues.

It is difficult to say just what the federal government's position is on youth *under*employment, given such buried, ignored, and contradictory reports. It certainly must be an 'elephant in the room' among those who advise politicians. What is apparent is no action has been taken to alleviate underemployment, so that the policy of sending more and more young people to universities simply exacerbates the problem.

The trail of how these misguided beliefs have become entrenched in government policy can be followed by examining Canada's primary research department charged with studying education-to-workplace transition issues, HRSDC.

HRSDC published a report in 2005, *HRSDC Policy Research and Survey Plan: Directions for the Next Three Years*, after it was realigned and renamed (from Human Resources Development Canada, in 2003). This rebranded department defined itself as

> now primarily a research, policy and program design department, [whose] knowledge base is one of our most important assets for achieving our mandate. Therefore, it is important to have a Knowledge Management Strategy (KMS) in place; there must be a systematic approach to research planning across the department; there must be effective mechanisms for connecting with departmental expertise; and research products need to be disseminated to all interested groups so that they are used effectively.[45]

This report laid out some forty-five studies that were underway or to be undertaken to ensure that the 'quality of human capital … [be sustained to maintain] Canada's comparatively high levels of effort as measured by expenditures and certificates and degrees granted, and outcomes, in terms of directly measured skills and abilities.'[46] This report is infused with the logic and language of human capital theory, with the term used thirty-two times in the discussion leading up to the specifications of the studies to be undertaken, and fifty-one more times in delineating these studies. The public will be interested to know that each of these studies involves tens of thousands of dollars, with the overall research initiative costing taxpayers into the millions of dollars.

One of these proposed studies was titled 'Can a Supply of Highly-Qualified Labour Create Its Own Demand?'[47] It is described as follows:

Canada has tended to take a 'production function' view of potential growth, based on the premise that by increasing the supply of human capital, either via quantity or via quality (as in educational attainment and skills) the economy will be able to grow faster and macroeconomic policy (largely via the setting of monetary conditions) will engineer the demand growth consistent with that faster potential growth.

This project is to consider whether a 'supply will lead to its own demand' approach is appropriate, either in the short run or the longer run. In particular, the project should identify the transmission mechanisms by which increasing the supply of more highly qualified human resources helps stimulate demand for those resources, and whether the supply can be stimulated to a point of oversupply and consequent labour market imbalances, possibly reducing the return on that higher investment in human capital.

These forty-five studies were tendered to sources outside HRSDC through 'requests for proposals' (RFPs). The RFP for 'Can a Supply of Highly-Qualified Labour Create Its Own Demand?'[48] was issued in July 2006, with part of the justification for requesting papers on this topic specified as follows:

Between 1976 and 2000 ... the post secondary education (PSE) participation rate in Canada jumped from 15% to 30%. More Canadians are developing higher levels of formal human capital. Given the importance of identifying the role that human capital accumulation plays in economic development, it is also imperative to understand the microeconomic relationship between the demand for labour and the supply of human capital. This research should establish whether it is possible for human capital accumulation to exceed demand, therefore resulting in a waste of valuable resources. If human capital accumulation can exceed demand, then it is possible that job-education skill mismatches may occur. The microeconomic theory of supply and demand suggests that if human capital accumulation can exceed demand then individuals may be overqualified for their jobs, implying an underutilization of their existing skills and talents. A high proportion of qualified graduates raises questions at a broad level regarding the education system, the availability of jobs and the structure of the labour market. If widespread underemployment does exist, it may decrease the attractiveness of careers in a given discipline, causing current graduates to seek other employment opportunities, and deterring future generations from entering particular fields of study.

That's right: in spite of human capital theory driving Canadian education policy for decades, in addition to the forty-four other papers, this government department was only recently seeking opinion about whether the policy might be creating underemployment! From the above discussion and references, readers now know that an extensive literature has already been produced by the Canadian government on this issue, along with an extensive sociological literature, with both sources of evidence indicating that the policy does create underemployment. So why is the question still being asked as if it is a new concern?

One answer comes from the statement in the RFP, following this quoted material, that 'HRSD is aware that the research proposed above may be addressed from either a microeconomic or a macroeconomic perspective.' In other words, anyone applying to write a paper for them had to adopt a framework from the discipline of economics, presumably accepting the logic and language of human capital theory. Apparently, sociological perspectives on the topic were not welcome, so that the whole literature on credentialism was out of bounds, and in consequence presumably will not make it to policymakers' desks when these reports are written. We have been unable to find the papers on the HRSDC website that were commissioned by this RFP. Indeed, little is available there connected with this huge research initiative sponsoring multiple papers on forty-five topics. Apparently, these papers are not for public consumption.

So goes the world of 'evidence-based' policy in Canada, as least as it applies to higher education and its relation to the labour market. The major stakeholders here are fixated on a theory with limited validity; they think and speak in terms of its logic, and contradicting evidence that would lead to revisions of the theory and introduce new, more applicable ideas is not made available to them. And, in addition to the damage done to the careers of Canadian citizens, the Canadian higher education system is driven further and further off course as hitherto liberal programs have scrambled to 'retool' to resemble vocational training programs.[49]

THE SHADOW RESEARCH COMMUNITY AND THE PROMOTION OF PSEUDO-VOCATIONALISM

In addition to government departments conducting their own in-house and tendered research, many countries have 'shadow research communities' that conduct policy research, often bidding on these tendered papers and studies. Unfortunately, this 'community' shows signs of biases in producing research that supports the policies of those hiring them. For example, one observer argues that this type of research supports such American educational initiatives as 'school choice,' even though there is mixed empirical support for policy claims. He argues that as a result of widespread public support for such policy initiatives, biased research goes unchallenged and instead is 'spun' by

the media and political savvy of influential advocacy coalitions that have coalesced around the choice issue. Concerted groups of think tanks, issue organizations, and policy advocates in academia have demonstrated a notable ability to shape policy discourse and action around this issue primarily by shaping public and policymaker perceptions through engagement with the media regarding research on the issue ... [Certain] advocacy coalitions [are] creating a new political economy of research production and dissemination around US policymaking. A key component of this effort is the strategy of by-passing and thus marginalizing traditional scholarly processes that were designed to instill an element of quality control on knowledge production. In this new 'marketplace' of ideas, research rigor is often less important than talking points, rapid response, and institutional branding, all driven by a well-resourced coalition of advocacy groups. In the new 'marketplace' of ideas, ideas calling for free markets are heavily subsidized.[50]

In Canada the emergence of this shadow research community has not been as well documented, but as the above discussion of the HRSDC and the discussion of the Educational Policy Institute to follow suggest, a shadow research community has emerged here with respect to such initiatives as higher educational 'access.' In both countries, these various 'consulting' groups and 'think tanks' essentially have become tools of governments. They influence the wider research community by bypassing peer review processes with academic experts in the fields of interest, sometimes doing their own internal 'reviews,' making them vulnerable to 'groupthink' processes and denying policy-makers alternative perspectives on problems of interest. In turn, these organizations are positioned to use their government sponsors to gain legitimacy with the mass media, which will pay attention to their press releases and mass distribution of their non–peer-reviewed publications via the Internet. In this way, they play a public relations role of instilling public confidence in the government initiatives that they have been paid to 'research.'

An alternative model to a shadow research community would be to make this research money spent by governments available to independent academics as peer-reviewed grant money to allow them to research these problems from a variety of theoretical perspectives (rather than exclusively from the hegemonic human capital theory) and disseminate their results through peer-reviewed journals. Because it is also problematic that Canada has so few academic journals, new journals could be launched that are devoted to public policy issues in such fields as education, to be financed with this money as well. In this model, the editorship would be entirely independent of the government of the day and the influence of the bureaucrats connected with the shadow research community. If these reforms were made, the 'evidence-based' policy that governments used would be of higher calibre and not prone to the groupthink that characterizes the current policy research that is done under the auspices, and by the grace, of the governments of the day and according to how their departmental and ministerial mandarins deem to disperse millions of research dollars.

In contrast to a balanced source of information, we have seen that in Canada much government research is framed in a way that privileges the discipline of economics and its pet approach, human capital theory, so that those in the shadow research community must write their bids in the logic of this theory if they hope to be awarded contracts. Some researchers have formed companies or 'Institutes' whose livelihood depends on this source of government funding. One such institute is the Educational Policy Institute (EPI), whose mission is

to expand educational opportunity for low-income and other historically-underrepresented students through high-level research and analysis. By providing educational leaders and policymakers with the information re-

quired to make prudent programmatic and policy decisions, we believe
that the doors of opportunity can be further opened for all students, resulting in an increase in the number of students prepared for, enrolled in,
and completing postsecondary education.[51]

The EPI began in 2002 as a non-profit organization based in Virginia,
but had 'for-profit' branches in Canada and Australia, and a 'for-profit'
consulting firm in the United States.[52] The EPI is characterized as 'a
non-partisan think tank,' but the above mission statement belies this
claim. The EPI targets funding and carries out research on post-secondary 'access' and 'retention,' and is thus an advocacy organization.

Alex Usher, a self-styled educational consultant and 'higher-edu-
cation advisor,'[53] headed the Canadian branch, which recently closed
shop. Usher reviewed our previous book,[54] bringing his views to our
attention. His review is critiqued here because it illustrates views that
are entrenched in human capital theory's logic and language, and how
the theory can lead people to simultaneously acknowledge problems
and dismiss their gravity. That is, human capital theory has now been
stretched in so many ways as to appear to its advocates to cover all circumstances, leading them to make contradictory claims. For example,
Usher argues that we should just get used to credentialism; that there
are no problems with the youth labour market; and it is no big concern
that universities are devolving into high schools. In other words, he
not only accepts the lowering of higher education, but he also seems to
celebrate it. Rather than addressing this decline in higher education, he
advocates keeping everyone in school for a prolonged period, regardless of how poor the quality of education is and how disengaged the
students are. And, these views are apparently held alongside a blind
faith that graduates' 'skills' will find a place in the economy.

This sort of argument is classic human-capital orthodoxy, shored up
by a dogmatic claim that 'there is very little good information' supporting alternative positions. For example, Usher argues that the youth labour market is healthy because youth unemployment has not increased
in the past few decades relative to adults, staying at twice the rate.
While this rate comparison is factual, the interpretation is ill informed
because it fails to consider that the unemployment rate has stayed as
such as a result of large numbers of young people seeking refuge in
post-secondary institutions. Consequently, a good number of students
are not rationally seeking to invest in applied skills, but attend universities because the alternatives are unpalatable, and a good proportion of

these reluctant students are disengaged from their studies and merely seeking credentials, bloating our universities to the point where about half of those now attending put out minimal effort, and are therefore not acquiring so-called human capital skills. Therefore, one problem with this argument is that if all of these disengaged university students were to drop out immediately, the youth unemployment rate would double to some 25–30 per cent of those aged fifteen to twenty-four.[55]

Usher also claims that salaries for university graduates should have declined if there was a glut of them, but he fails to acknowledge that youth salaries in general have declined by 20–30 per cent over the past few decades, while those of university graduates have been stagnant, such that the better earning power of graduates is relative to non-graduates of the same age-range, and not to older workers.[56] He also does not mention the fact that a significant proportion of graduates take lower paying jobs as part of a downward cascading effect,[57] displacing workers with less education, including those in low-skilled jobs, as identified above in an HRSDC report.

Finally, Usher claims (1) that 'recent graduates often take time to find ways to use their skills properly'; and (2) 'that one of the ways that skills spread throughout an economy is by people with higher levels of education taking on jobs that previously did not require such levels.' For a human-capital theory advocate, these points may be obvious, but they are not to others. On the first point, he fails to consider that students who are disengaged while attending university would pick up few skills to eventually use 'properly,' exposing his blind faith in schooling (i.e., that mere attendance will inculcate skills, independent of student effort). On the second point, he ignores the obvious point that those graduates who drifted through university putting out a minimal effort would not have many skills value-added by their university experience to 'spread throughout an economy.' He also apparently ignores the fact that even engaged students who eventually find themselves underemployed after graduation, in say menial clerical jobs, could not reasonably apply many of their skills to these jobs. How many writing skills could be applied to the job of barista or store clerk, for example?

At the heart of views such as this is a failure to distinguish liberal and applied degrees, and an assumption that both will provide the same potential for integration into the labour force. The consequence is to promote a form of pseudo-vocationalism, as if all that is done at university is job training.

Usher concludes his review by saying that professors just have to get used to universities being big, with an emphasis on efficiency and 'productivity,' and that it is the fault of universities themselves for allowing 'the undergraduate experience to massify to the point of becoming the new high school.' At the same time, he claims that universities did not figure out how to accommodate unprepared students, and 'as a result we have a lot of unhappy professors out there, teaching unengaged students.'[58] These are strange statements to make for someone who is ostensibly devoted to the causes of 'access and retention' of low-income and historically under-represented students – in effect, advocating sending them into dumbed-down holding pens where they will be unhappy, graduating with credentials no better than the high-school diploma of recent generations.

It is counter-productive to blame universities entirely for their own decline. Universities are being pushed into this lowering of higher education to become the 'new high school,' especially in jurisdictions that have suffered serious declines in funding, such as Ontario, but where government policies promote 'university for all' on the basis of research produced by Usher and others in the shadow research community. He simply adds insult to injury by blaming those inside the system for problems to which he contributes from the outside!

Administrators in Denial

Confronted by governments (and their minion researchers) who believe that all investments in educational systems constitute 'capital investments,' a belief ostensibly supported by empirical research, university administrators find themselves having to speak this same language as they captain universities that have themselves evolved into corporations where the logic of capital investments prevails.

Meanwhile, those closest to the arena in liberal programs have been complaining for years about the inappropriateness of this language and logic for what needs to take place in the classroom. There are thus two sets of stakeholders speaking in different languages and utilizing different logics, ostensibly in pursuit of the same goals. And, given that administrators feel they are more accountable to those in the upper rows of the forum than to those in the lower rows, it is more expedient for them to deny that any problems exist in the classroom or in the mission ostensibly governing what takes place there.

Even if they do take the time to listen, it is easy for administrators to miss the point that front-line teachers are trying to make to them:

namely, that in many universities the mission has drifted away from providing a rigorous liberal education to a watered-down system that attempts, but fails, to emulate a vocational training for the labour force where economic gains are directly tied to investments in specific skills.

We are not trying to offer up administrators as scapegoats for the ills of the university system, but rather to explain how those who rose through the ranks of the professoriate to administrative positions could then become so detached from the realities of the contemporary classroom. On the one hand, as noted, they find themselves in a corporate environment where they are accountable to those who think in terms of (misguided) economic theory. On the other hand, they are now removed from the classroom, and the longer they stay in administration the more remote they become from how it has changed.[59] This is now happening in many secondary schools, as principals – a designation formerly meaning the 'principal teachers' – have been assigned by governments to purely administrative positions for which no classroom teaching is required, and they are no longer members of the teachers' unions.[60]

With livelihoods and loyalties shifted to the rows above them in the educational forum, it is far easier for administrators simply to deny what their teachers try to tell them needs to be done to get the system back on course, and as time goes on the system drifts further and further off course. In the meantime, the administrations' public-relations mantra has been 'excellence, excellence, excellence,' in complete denial of the realities on the ground.

Complaints about this mission drift may not be new, but the problems have become increasingly severe, exposing the system and its main actors to a series of crises that are explored in chapter 4.

Conclusion: Whither Free Enquiry?

The current education system and the politics governing it have become increasingly complex as it has expanded to include more and more stakeholders. While the positions taken by the various stakeholders can be understood in terms of how their livelihoods and futures are implicated in what takes place in the classroom, assumptions underlying the policies directing this system at the highest levels are misguided and are producing a mission drift that threatens to obliterate the centuries-old liberal education. Can the 'idea of the university' survive in such an educational forum of competing interests, attempts to silence critics, and blanket denials of obvious problems? It is ironic that institutions that are held as bastions of freedom of enquiry are being undermined by these very undemocratic influences in countries that claim to be beacons of liberal democracy.

The next part of this book keeps this question in the background while it examines the landscape of specific issues that often obscure this question and divert attention away from articulating a clear mission for universities that would take us into the new millennium.

PART TWO

Issues Associated with the Drift to Pseudo-Vocationalism

This part of this book tackles the more concrete issues that can interfere with a full consideration of more general issues discussed in Part I. While it is understandable why the various stakeholders of the educational forum might make the arguments they do, given their positions in the forum, many of the squabbles that take place among these stakeholders can generate much more heat than light. In turn, this heat produces a smokescreen, if you will, obscuring the larger issues associated with the mission drift of universities away from a liberal education toward forms of pseudo-vocationalism undergirded by a corporate mandate.

In dealing with these more concrete issues, hopefully the way can be cleared for stakeholders to see the wisdom of allowing universities to deliver liberal educations of the highest quality in the twenty-first century and beyond, into the third millennium.

3 Standards: Schools without Scholarship?

With the exception of a small group of well-known critics who commonly express their views in the opinion pages of leading newspapers, criticizing the university system is not a popular thing to do, partly because the public receives a steady diet of good-news stories about the economic necessity of having large numbers of university graduates. Moreover, few in the public have had the opportunity to delve deeply into the literature on the role of the university in modern societies. Instead, most people are exposed only to the conventional wisdom that universities do great things for students, financially and personally.

Most certainly, there is research evidence from the decades since the 1970s of many personal/intellectual gains and financial benefits associated with earning a university degree, or more commonly now, degrees:[1]

- Personally, students can expand their understanding and awareness of the world, and develop specialized knowledge sets. University graduates take more active citizenship roles, including political engagement, whether locally, provincially, regionally, or nationally. Intellectually, students can enhance their skill sets in numerous areas: critical thinking, quantitative reasoning, writing, and public speaking.
- Financially, the research shows that *on average* the benefits outweigh the costs for most people,[2] either soon after graduating for those in applied programs, or eventually for those in general liberal arts and sciences programs. The lifetime earnings differential in comparison with a high-school diploma can be large, and women in certain

ethnic groups have more to gain relative to (white) men because they make much less without a degree.[3]

Our concern is that much of this in jeopardy, and the empirical evidence to support this concern is accumulating. When Canadian universities are examined in terms of what it is like currently 'on the ground,' two sides to this risk to future benefits can be identified, as epitomized by the 'disengagement compact' between students and teachers. In this compact, students and teachers have a tacit agreement not to challenge each other to work harder.

To reiterate the thrust of Part I of this book, the mission drift that has taken place is partly due to a decrease in government funding and the response by universities to market their (job) credentialing services. Conversely, general undergraduate programs largely emerged out of the liberal tradition in which learning is an end in itself, even if that learning may have eventual practical benefits. In other words, in its ideal form, the process of learning in a liberal environment is valued irrespective of the product (a grade or a credential). Regrettably, this mission has slowly changed such that many undergraduate degree-granting institutions implicitly or explicitly promise that a credential is both the ultimate goal of the experience and a ticket into white-collar jobs. Given the obvious irrelevance to any future jobs of the curriculum that is subsequently delivered, university students can become alienated from the process of learning, a problem that has plagued high schools since they became mass institutions whose credentials are now perfunctory requisites for most jobs.

As a result of these changes and the resulting pressures, a culture of disengagement can be found in many 'mass schools,' even among smaller upper-year classes. In this respect, mass schools should be compared with 'élite schools,' which historically service the children of the wealthy for whom cost is no object. Élite schools, as in the so-called Ivy League, have low student-teacher ratios, often less than 10:1, while mass schools have ratios that are frequently two to three times higher, and individual professors often teach hundreds of students each term, rendering their individual 'student-teacher ratio' much higher. Given that mass schools service the vast majority of students, and are promised by governments to be the solution to all sorts of problems plaguing disadvantaged groups in terms of access to the labour market, we hope to bring these problems to the public's attention and generate a public debate about remedies. For as laudable as it may be to believe that every citizen should experience a rigorous post-secondary education, it is just not realistic, in part because a university education is not appropriate for all people. This view does not mean that the latter are second-class citizens, but rather it reserves a university education for those who are academically prepared and at the same time recognizes that there are hundreds of thousands of bright, hard-working Canadians who do not have a university degree. It is only the élitist who thinks that a university degree makes one 'better' than someone who does not hold one. Thus, those who feel that any criticisms of mass education threaten the progress made by the Left in addressing social-class and other economic inequalities need to be reminded that sending young people from disadvantaged backgrounds through faulty systems based on false promises does not represent social justice.

If the risks to the liberal arts and sciences are to be faced, the numerous and complex issues associated with those risks need to be understood clearly. The remainder of this chapter provides a close-up view of what is happening 'on the ground.'

The Student Side of the Disengagement Compact

As noted, there are strong indications that students are benefiting less from an undergraduate education, especially in undertaking liberal arts and sciences degrees. Personal benefits are threatened as fewer students put an honest and sustained effort into their education. Students benefit personally and intellectually from university in direct relation to the effort they put into their studies, so that low-effort graduates are not likely transformed in any of the ways that the research suggests can be part of the benefit of a liberal education.[4] Financial benefits are at risk as a result of the glut of undergraduate credentials, a situation compounded by (a) an excess of credentials now routinely awarded to (b) students who put little effort into their studies.

With this glut of bachelor's degrees of dubious merit, competition among degree holders for entry-level jobs and placement in post-graduate programs has gone to a new level: multiple and combined degrees and diplomas. Consequently, more and more graduates are seeking multiple degrees and diplomas to get even a foothold in the labour force or on the short-list of professional programs like medicine, law, and education.[5]

This problem is serious enough to attract the attention of the Maritime Provinces Higher Education Council (MPHEC),[6] which recently reported that the average debt-to-earnings ratio of graduates of Maritimes universities from 1999 was 12 per cent overall, but 14 per cent for arts and sciences graduates (versus 10 per cent for those from applied and professional programs). A debt-to-earnings ratio greater than 8 per cent produces a situation where 'difficulties with payments become significant.'[7] In addition to the lower salaries paid to liberal education graduates, this debt load is traceable to the fact that 82 per cent of these graduates pursued further post-secondary credentials after earning their bachelor's degree (while only about a half of those from applied/professional programs did so).

Lamentably, indications are that when universities based on the liberal educational model take on these mass-educational qualities, the benefits found among past graduates diminish. The 'canary in the coal mine' in these settings is the extent to which a culture of disengagement has gripped the program or school, for many students funnelled through academic programs in the secondary system have insufficient motivation or ability to benefit from what the liberal arts and sciences have to offer, especially if those programs are strained financially and as a consequence have high student-teacher ratios.

It seems the culture of disengagement first appears in high schools when higher grades are given to students for lower-quality work as a way of discouraging dropout or attempting to increase academic interest. As more students motivated by these false grades and misleading feedback about their accomplishments and scholastic aptitude enter universities, this culture of disengagement spreads, forcing universities to either fail large numbers of students – and lose significant amounts of funding – or to redefine standards and water down course requirements to handle them. For combined with disengagement there is also a very strong sense of entitlement and empowerment that is characteristic of recent cohorts. To keep students happy and in the system, higher grades are awarded for lower performances from first through final year, and just as in high schools, very few are ever allowed to fail.

It is in these ways that universities with mass access – particularly those that have not attended to standards in a climate of underfunding – have found themselves mired in the twin problems of grade inflation and academic disengagement, which feed each other. University students in these mass systems are enabled by these systems to treat their studies much like a part-time job, yet they can still earn a B average with relative ease. The traditional standard for an average performance was a C, but that is now outdated in many mass universities. Students in these institutions can expect Bs for putting out a modicum of effort that produces mediocre work, and As if they do any more than this. Grade inflation is in this way institutionally induced as universities have attempted to adapt to massification in the context of underfunding.

Given that grades are at the heart of this problem, and are its most visible manifestation, grade inflation will be examined first.

Grade Inflation

Based upon numerous reports, university-level grade inflation is being reported as a serious problem in many countries, with websites set up to call attention to it in the United States[8] and the United Kingdom,[9] as well as Ireland, Europe, and Australia.[10] Apparently, little progress is being made to bring it under control wherever it is happening, perhaps because it is the proverbial 'elephant in the room': at some level, most people know it is there, but few want to talk about it.

Even when it is discussed, a common reaction among administrators is that although grades may be inflated, it makes no difference, because universities are dealing with the best and brightest students, especially those transitioning from high schools to universities.[11] Unfortunately, it appears that this reaction is widespread among administrators who have little or no recent experience in the classroom, and so do not see the types of repercussions of the problem.[12] For example, many students who shone in high schools do not necessarily fail at today's university, but have performance levels that would have resulted in failure in the past. The question for these administrators to answer is, what would happen if professors were to start failing these students? Would these administrators stand behind their professors' authority, or would they cling to their belief that the grades of students they are sending to professors are not inflated? Or, do such administrators view students more as 'customers,' who in a business transaction would always 'be right'?

The fact that grade inflation is not being counteracted suggests that many educators have lost sight of some basic pedagogical principles concerning why it needs to be combated: grade inflation lowers standards and expectations, so that all students are challenged less. It needs to be rectified for the following reasons:

- Grade inflation is bad for bright students because they can achieve high grades with little effort, and so are not challenged by a curriculum that should be higher-order. They are therefore less likely to

develop their intellectual potentials in ways that would enrich their lives and contribute to society and the economy.
• Inflated grades are also bad for those who have academic abilities that are average or below because they are given higher marks for their mediocre work – false feedback – and are not told how to improve. Abilities can be improved with effort, but if little effort is required of a student, little change in ability level will occur.

When little is asked of students, and no feedback is given regarding how to become more proficient in areas where improvements could be made, many will simply drift through the educational system and into the workforce without knowing what they are – and are not – good at. Being rewarded for what one is good at, and not rewarded (or failed if warranted) for what one is not good at, provides crucial information for young people in terms of what life and career goals they should set, where they can find their purpose in life, and how to develop a stable sense of identity.

One problem faced by those who try to bring grade inflation to public attention is that many people appear to be unaware of the meaning of the standards that grades represent.[13] The Canadian and American university systems emerged out of the British system, in which no more than 5 per cent of students were awarded the equivalents of As ('firsts,' to acknowledge their outstanding written and/or oral performance in a subject area), and another 30 per cent given Bs ('seconds,' to acknowledge their 'very good' performance). Combined, then, only one-third in a given large group would be judged to be above average (with the 'average' subgroup constituting about 40 per cent of the group).

We urge readers to think about this for a moment. By definition, 'outstanding' may be treated as a synonym for 'exceptional.' Forty per cent of people drawn from the general population cannot be exceptional at something when they are their own reference point, but this is what current grading practices would suggest when 40 per cent of students are awarded As in a given class.

If students from across the country who were deemed to be exceptional in comparison to their classmates in terms of, say, their math, chess, or video game abilities, were put into one class, it would still be possible to distinguish those who are outstanding within this highly select sample. The majority of students who were exceptional in relation to their local classmates ('big fish in small ponds,' if you will) would now only be mediocre when compared to all of those students across the country who are outstanding at math, chess, or video games (they become 'small fish in big ponds'). Most certainly, people are willing to recognize differences among, say, top (exceptional) hockey players when they are compared with one another. In other words, outstanding hockey players plucked from each community across Canada and placed into an NHL draft will not perform identically. The same principle applies to students.

At that level of population comparison, then, only a few people will be outstanding, and this fact can be obvious even to the casual fan of hockey. There are only a few players of the calibre of Hull, Howe, Gretsky, Crosby, and so forth. The rest can be ranked or graded as 'very good' or 'good' NHL players, while the remainder might be cut from the team because they do not have sufficient talent (yet) to play in the 'big league.' Those who are dropped from the 'big league' may still play in the lower leagues, and they might be outstanding at that level. There is no shame in this sorting of hockey talent, just as there should be no shame in the sorting of academic talent.

To turn to a consideration of *normal distributions* of grades, statistically the largest category of students (about 40 per cent) should be judged as average (producing 'satisfactory' work for that level of education), assuming that commensurate standards are employed (note that low standards in relation to the group in question would produce non-normal, inflated grade distributions). This 'normal distribution' of ability/performance – where most cases cluster around the mean or average – is a statistical fact of life when large numbers of people are compared. Currently, in many schools twice the percentage of students is receiving 'above-average' grades – As and Bs – than a normal curve would indicate. Not coincidentally perhaps, a recent survey of first-year American students found that 70 per cent rate themselves as above average,[14] a phenomenon understandable in terms of a 'cult of self-esteem,' but not in terms of statistical probability.

Readers will be interested to know that the grading logic is used in differentiating the work done by professors as well, when they apply for grants or submit articles to journals (which often use 4-point rating scales). Likewise, this logic can be found in the merit scores that many universities assign professors in annual performance reviews. The rubric used in our own department is as follows in assigning our annual performance scores in the areas of teaching, research, and service: 0 = below the acceptable; 1 = acceptable; 2 = good; 3 = very good; 4 = outstanding. It is understood the departmental average each year

will equal 2.2 points (in essence a C average). If the departmental average is higher than 2.2, the dean adjusts all members' scores down by a
constant number.

We are among the many voices that call for high schools and universities to get a grip on the standards they use in evaluating students
and assigning grades, and recommend the European Credit Transfer
System as a point of reference. This system was originally set up to
coordinate student exchange programs among institutions in some
thirty countries. Now in use by hundreds of universities, it allows participating universities in each country to convert grades to a common,
non-inflated standard. In this sensible system, As are awarded for outstanding performances (about 10 per cent of cases), Bs are given for
performances that are very good with few errors (about 25 per cent), Cs
go to good work that is generally sound with notable errors, and Ds or
less are awarded to work with significant shortcomings.[15]

Those who dismiss this logic as an arbitrary imposition of 'grading
on the curve' do not understand the nature of the population distribution of abilities and performances, and the usefulness of feedback
regarding these things. So long as assessment procedures are set up
to accurately reflect proficiency of performances, grades are a powerful pedagogical tool. In the liberal education, the objects of assessment
are chiefly written and oral communication of learned knowledge, the
critical analysis of material, and an application of principles. When
these types of grading standards are used to provide feedback for –
and thus nurture – those skills, students have more for which to strive,
excellence is rewarded, and those who need to improve are given appropriate feedback.

There appears to be an especially strong resistance among Canadian
educators to admit that grade inflation is a problem in Canadian universities, even though they may point to it in other countries like the
United States. However, an examination of National Survey of Student
Engagement (NSSE) data indicates Canadian university students report receiving grades that are only slightly lower to those in the United
States. Some educators also believe that it is more of a problem in large
research-intensive universities, but again the NSSE studies suggest
there are no substantial differences among types of universities.[16] In
view of these findings, these educators would do well to learn about
how Canadian university students' subjective definition of the meaning of grades has shifted away from the traditional standards mentioned above, in no small part as a result of the inflated grades they
received through primary and secondary school. Robert Runté from the

Table 3.1
Changes in subjective definitions of grades among
university students

1985	2005
A = excellent	A+ = excellent
B = respectable	A = respectable
C = satisfactory	A−
D = scraping through	B+ = satisfactory
F = failure	B
	B− = scraping through
	C+ = failure

University of Lethbridge argues that these subjective definitions have shifted between 1985 and 2005 as indicated in table 3.1.[17]

A variety of arguments among educators and the public can be found concerning why grade inflation should *not* be addressed. These arguments generally follow a vague notion that an innocuous evolution of grades is taking place. We could not disagree more. The 'evolution' that has taken place is outside of sound pedagogical principles. In some cases, grades have become status symbols, detached from any substantive meaning, that interfere with the learning process; in other cases, credentialism drives grade inflation.[18] And, given the current aversion to being 'average' at anything, the B, which is the current average grade assigned at most universities, will come to be defined as beneath certain students' dignity. What is to be done, then, to deal with the obvious problem of grade compression into the B/A range: develop double- and triple-As (AA and AAA), and when these become stigmatized, develop double- and triple-A pluses (A+A+ and A+A+A+)? Then what?[19]

This 'just get used to it' logic, and the ancillary recommendation that teachers recalibrate their assessment of 'satisfactory' or 'average' to a B, is flawed on a number of grounds.

Unlike monetary inflation, which has no ceiling, grade inflation does. We are hitting the ceiling and are literally running out of letters.[20] Unless measures are taken to de-stigmatize the designation of 'average,' this problem will continue to plague educators. Abilities can be differentiated in terms of at least four categories, and this differentiation is essential for effective assessment and feedback. To lose sight of this is to lose sight of the promise of education, and reduce high schools to holding pens (for young people not needed in the economy) and universities to recreation centres (for the children of well-to-do parents or those willing to amass a major debt). Increasingly, there are calls to reverse the wider societal trend in which individualism has morphed into 'specialism,' where children are raised to believe they are not only individuals, but are also special in ways that unfold for them without any particular effort on their part. In her book *The Self-Esteem Trap*, Polly Young-Eisendrath argues that we need to teach our children the value of 'being ordinary':

> Ordinariness is rooted in a wisdom about our human condition and a knowledge of how we are all connected, always making use of one another. Basing our lives on the importance of being ordinary – a member as well as a leader, dependent as well as dependable, and compassionate about the demand that life makes on all of us – is a whole new approach to self confidence. [21]

We understand that grades can be used to motivate students in certain ways, and may temporarily increase a student's self-esteem, optimism, and persistence. But, this is a short-term solution that creates long-term problems.[22] The student given false feedback is in many cases being set up for future failure, pointing to a fraudulent practice that does not bode well for the ethics and integrity of the educational systems involved; and what is perhaps worse, it does not prepare the student in question to deal constructively with such failure.

A 2007 report from the Atlantic Institute for Market Studies underscores this point about accurate feedback.[23] The report, aptly titled 'Setting Them Up to Fail? Excellent Marks Don't Necessarily Lead to Excellent Exam Marks,' surveyed high schools in two Maritime provinces, finding that teacher-assigned grade 11 mathematics marks were on average about 14 per cent above those of standardized provincial tests, producing a B average in courses (73.7 per cent versus 60.1 per cent). From his analysis, Robert Laurie, the report author, concluded: 'It is clear that grade inflation is alive and well in many New Brunswick and Newfoundland and Labrador high schools. It is also clear that grade inflation is much more prevalent in some high schools than others.'[24]

Laurie notes that excuses can be made for this difference in test scores, including the claim that teachers know their students better than do examiners of standardized tests. However, the relationship between the variation among schools in teacher-assigned marks and provincial test (PT) scores belies this excuse. In these provinces, schools varied dramatically in teacher-assigned versus PT scores, with some schools showing no difference in these scores all the way to a 25 per cent difference.

It turns out that there is a negative correlation between variation in teacher-assigned marks in a school and average performance of that school on PTs: low-inflation schools have highest PT results (e.g., where teacher-assigned grades are 70 per cent and PT results are also 70 per cent), whereas high-inflation schools have lowest PT results (e.g., where teacher-assigned grades are 78 per cent and PT results are only 53 per cent).[25]

Speaking directly to parents to tell them why this an issue, Laurie states:

> So what you ask? Let's assume the following hypothetical situation to see the impact and seriousness of this situation. Suppose your child attends Canterbury High School and your nephew Southern Victoria High School, two high schools in the New Brunswick Anglophone school system. Your child brings home a report card with a math mark of 75% and your nephew a mark of 77%. You would naturally assume that your child and your nephew are performing at about the same level in math. How would you explain that your child will probably score about 30% less on the provincial exam while your nephew's mark will probably remain the same? Welcome to the world of grade inflation.[26]

Laurie's report concludes that unrealistically high teacher-assigned grades reflect lower standards, and therefore produce lower performances. He recommends that some schools need to challenge their students more, especially struggling students, because doing so can increase their performance; not challenging them sets them up for later failure. Additionally, he contends that

> inflating grades is a set-up for massive disappointment later on. Sooner or later reality will catch up to the students and 'success' won't come so easy. The cost of failure may be as high as being forced to withdraw from post secondary institutions, loss of job opportunities, and even jobs themselves. These individual failures reflect an education system which fails students and society. Without a serious and concerted effort to change the practice of grade inflation everyone loses.[27]

We also understand that low grades can demoralize students and alienate them from schools. Nevertheless, this point misses the indispensable utility of proper grading systems for providing useful feedback and assessment for students, helping students to discover their strengths and nurture their abilities. As such, this feedback is crucial to identity formation. Accurate feedback is important because it helps students discover what they are good at and what they are not good at; where they have potential and where they do not. This feedback thus helps students to set goals and develop a realistic sense of purpose, both of which are chief components of identity formation.[28] It can also prevent later misdirected efforts and personal disappointment that can ultimately have consequences for both society and the economy, whether covertly in terms of the social mal-integration of the person, or overtly in terms of economic marginalization and exclusion. Attempting to use inflated grades as a 'great leveller' will fail on these grounds. Schools need to do other things, such as attend to informal learning needs and provide extensive individualized counselling, to help those who encounter difficulties with the formal educational system.[29]

Finally, several types of grade inflation need to be identified. The first is likely what most people think of, where higher grades are given for work of the same standard. This is sustainable only if the students coming into classes each year are as prepared as were students of previous years. As we see below in the section 'Unreadiness,' this cannot always be assumed. Consequently, what many teachers do to maintain a normal distribution – but are really doing so to avoid failing large numbers of students – is to give the same grades, but for lower standards (e.g., giving Cs for what may have earned an F in the past). This second type is 'hidden' grade inflation and clearly leads to lower standards. The third type of grade inflation occurs when professors allow a 'double whammy' and give higher grades (e.g., a B average) for work of a lower standard (e.g., work that would be failed if higher standards were imposed). This contributes most to a disintegration of standards, and is tied to the disengagement of professors.

To rephrase Winston Churchill's famous quip about democracy, grading is the worst system, except for all the others. Those who want to ignore grade inflation or do away with grades entirely need to realize that in the case of the liberal education, it is not the grading system that is at fault – it is often the method of assessment that is at fault. As we argue, when the liberal education is mistaken for vocational training, and only test-taking skills are the basis of grades, the unique benefits of the liberal education – written and oral skills, and the critical thinking underpinning them – go unassessed and unacknowledged. As a result, students are not given feedback on these skills or helped to develop them. These students are not being educated to develop the skills of critical reflection and argumentation: they are being trained to memorize course content, and many resent it. Paradoxically, since memorization is easier than understanding/learning, we have found that the majority of students in our classes are now happier with the former and prefer to be tested using methods that cater to memorization and regurgitation, as opposed to tests that require conceptual thinking and effective writing.[30]

Academic Disengagement

The annual NSSE studies, along with other sources, consistently show that on average Canadian and American students treat their full-time studies like a part-time job. A full-time course load (five courses) requires that fifteen hours per week be spent attending classes. NSSE results indicate that students spend on average only about thirteen to fourteen hours per week preparing for their classes. As a result, typical university students spend fewer than thirty hours per week on all aspects of their studies – the equivalent of a part-time job – and this does not take into account the fact that daily attendance is typically between only 50 and 70 per cent.[31] Given this modicum level of effort, it appears that Canadian and American universities now routinely award a 'BA-lite' to the bulk of graduates, not necessarily because students want it but because this is what universities require for graduation.

Nonetheless, our chief concern is specifically with the 40 to 50 per cent of students – disengaged students – who spend fewer than ten hours per week in all aspects of class preparation and assignments. Those who put in fewer than five hours, some 15 to 20 per cent, can be defined as *hard-core disengaged students* for whom a 'faux-BA' will be awarded if they pass all of their courses. And, it should be stressed that if students can graduate university with this paltry level of effort, it is the system that needs to take the bulk of the blame, not the students involved. As one of our colleagues puts it, 'Administrators let them in but professors let them out.'

While the necessity of dealing with grade inflation may be difficult to grasp for some people, the problem of dealing with the disengaged student can be even more elusive for them, especially those who have never taught in an undergraduate classroom, as is the case for those in the upper rows of the educational forum. A common reaction is to ask why teachers do not simply require their students to 'engage.' What is missing here is a firm grasp of what it means to engage. Some people seem to think engagement involves just attending class or speaking up periodically. Others appear to think it is to be interested in a subject, especially to be engrossed by it.

The image that seems to drive these uninformed conceptions of engagement in the university classroom is that of the cool 'super prof,' as portrayed in movies and in television shows. This cool prof casually walks into a classroom and puts on a performance by standing on a desk and uttering a few profundities, dazzling the class with her or his brilliance and wit for a few minutes until a bell rings and the class is dismissed. The reality of the day-to-day teaching that takes place in a university classroom is far different from this, and not the least significant difference is that classes can run as long as three straight hours (and there are no bells to end them). Standing on a desk and spouting profundities would get stale very quickly, and a prof trying this in every class for three hours would become a laughingstock of his students, and likely be seen as a candidate for psychiatric institutionalization by his colleagues.

As George Kuh has stressed, the traditional assumption regarding the time commitment that university students need to give to their courses to become proficient in the topic area is two hours – the 'two-hour rule' – for every hour spent in class. This is part of an *implicit bilateral contract* between students and teachers stipulating that if students prepare for classes, teachers will give them something 'value added' to that preparation. The value-added component comes from the teacher's expertise in the subject matter, which allows him or her to draw on a wealth of knowledge derived from years of study. Students who do the necessary preparation in advance of the lecture will also derive greater benefits than those who simply sit passively in the class with little advance preparation for it. The grade they receive would be another matter, though, and should be as much a reflection of the student's ability as demonstrated in class assignments and exams as the time and effort devoted to class preparation and attendance.

This expertise at universities is traditionally the hallmark of 'the professor,' as opposed to an 'instructor' whose knowledge of a subject is derived mainly from reading the textbooks written by experts in the field. A professor who has done decades of research in an area can extemporaneously expound upon material and answer questions that students have of the readings and clarify issues arising from the readings. A professor with a research program is also more likely to be on the cutting edge of the field, bringing back fresh insights from conferences and contacts with other experts, and provide students with state-of-the-art knowledge of the field. With this expertise, the professor can put the details into context and help students make sense of the big picture. In this way, students who are prepared for the class can move up the learning curve of the subject area more readily.[32]

Those who think that all learning should take place during class time in universities are confusing the 'tip of the iceberg' with the 'iceberg': *what takes place in the university classroom should be the tip of the iceberg of learning, not the iceberg*. And, effective teachers can use the 'tip' as an indication of how much deep learning is taking place for individual students and the class as a whole.

As suggested above, effective university-level learning requires that students read the assigned material in advance of a lecture or tutorial. At the university level, the quantity and quality of knowledge on any given topic has traditionally been too extensive and nuanced to be presented in full in a lecture, regardless of the teacher's skill. Accordingly, students need to actively engage themselves in their learning by thoroughly reading in advance the material upon which a lecture is based. The lecturer can then dispense with the rudiments and draw the material together at a more complex, more abstract level.

The necessity of actively engaging in learning by reading material in advance is perhaps most obvious if examples are given from English literature courses. Imagine trying to teach students about interpretations of a novel they have never read. Then imagine the type of test you would set, all the time knowing that many students will either cram the book before a test, or never bother to even read the book with any earnestness. Given the 'no-fail standards' that currently apply in many schools, what type of test would one set that does not fail more than a small percentage of the class? Well, in these circumstances the only viable test would be one that allows students to regurgitate from their lecture notes and what they picked up from a light reading of the material. This type of scenario is reminiscent of the stereotype of the high-school student who relies of Cliff Notes or Coles Notes, but it does not belong in institutions of higher learning worthy of their name, and certainly not in courses that are supposedly part of a liberal curriculum with all of its ostensible transformative potentials.

Now imagine trying to teach large numbers of students – into the hundreds in many classes – how to interpret a highly abstract economic or sociological theory, or grasp the mechanics of a difficult statistical method, knowing that most will not read in advance of the class, and instead walk into the classroom knowing little about the topic at hand. You can spoon-feed these unprepared students by giving them the material from the readings point by point, or you can entertain them with witty stories and various theatrics, two strategies that net the teachers who use them high points on the teacher evaluations. In either case, students are exposed to only a fraction of the material that should be learned if they are to become proficient in the subject, and thus able to critically analyse the material. Students may walk out of academic-lite lectures thinking that they are engaging in 'higher learning,' but this type of learning is really more appropriate for the secondary level, not the tertiary level.

Some readers may think that this situation is only common in large classes at research-intensive universities where professors have the reputation of caring more about 'their research' than 'their students.' However, this scenario can be found even in small, seminar-type classes, if standards of bilateral engagement are allowed to decline.

What needs to be appreciated is that when we speak of 'engagement,' we are not referring merely to 'interest' or 'involvement.' Teachers can simply give their students 'busy work' and achieve this. Those who argue that the new technologies, like 'clickers,' are the key to 'engagement' need to consider this, as we see below in chapter 6.

Educational engagement means more; it means a level of commitment to the role of student and the relationship with the teacher. This student-teacher relationship is a contractual one in which there is a commitment between the student and teacher to meet each other 'halfway':[33] the student contracts with the teacher though the school, and the teacher receives remuneration from the school for that contract. This is not to say that the student is the 'consumer' receiving a product, but rather *the student is both the raw material and the product.* Liberal education is part of this process of intellectual production, as is the identification of the reading material and written/oral assignments required to become proficient at the course level. In this view, the student is a commodity to be transformed in some way by the experience, not a consumer of knowledge or a credential. However, if the student does not uphold his or her end of the bargain, this transformation is less likely to occur, just as the chances for it would decline if the teacher does not prepare a syllabus, show up for class, or grade tests and assignments. This crucial aspect of higher learning is lost on many of the stakeholders of the university system as the basic pedagogical principles of the liberal education are being forgotten.

The term 'engagement' takes on a clearer meaning for most people when it refers more concretely to a marriage engagement, where both parties reasonably expect that the other party will meet them halfway in terms of a long-term commitment. The 'engagement' would hardly transform into a marriage if one or both parties did not live up to their part in the marriage contract (in whatever way that contract is negotiated). Yet, this is precisely what takes places on a daily basis in our universities, and this is why the disengagement problem needs to be taken seriously.

Finally, when the factors producing grade inflation and disengagement are considered together, a mindset of 'entitled disengagement' can be identified. This is an entirely new phenomenon in higher education – both grade inflation and disengagement can be found in previous eras, but this is the first era in which both have combined at such high levels. Many students now feel entitled to high grades, even when they put out little or no effort. For example, a recent study found that one-third of students expect a B in a course merely for attending classes regularly.[34] At the same time, many of these same students do not have the discipline to budget their time, and see nothing wrong with giving their professors excuses for missing class such as 'I had an essay that was due' or 'I had an exam the next day' in another course.

Unreadiness

A precursor to disengagement – in the sense just described where the bilateral contract is not honoured – is a lack of readiness of a student for the rigours of the liberal form of higher learning. The reference point here is learning in which standards require active engagement of the student in the subject matter. This active engagement is not only during class time, but also in preparing for classes in order to partake in meaningful interactions during class time and afterward in out-of-class conversations with classmates and others.

The readiness for active engagement is not only a matter of developing intellectual acuity, which can be broken down to intelligence and prior learning. It also involves motivation, which comprises self-management skills like time-management.[35] Students who self-manage take responsibility for the courses they enrol in to ensure there is a match of their abilities and interests with a course's demands and content. Both of these aspects of readiness – intellectual acuity and self-management – are essential if students are to meet university standards of performance.

Various studies of high-school engagement indicate that this form of readiness continues to decline, and additional evidence is accumulating. Effort has become increasingly optional for high-school students, and consequently little homework is completed by many Canadian and American high-school students, even among those who are university-bound; there are even calls from some quarters to reduce it further. In this context, a recent Canadian study is worth reviewing for what it reveals about how high schools can affect preparation for universities.

Alan Slavin, a winner of five teaching awards and a physics professor at Trent University in Southern Ontario, recently published an article in the *Canadian Journal of Physics*[36] addressing the sharp increase in the dropout rate in the introductory course he has taught since the 1980s (this rate has increased from under 10 per cent to about 30 per cent). He examined dropout statistics from his courses and comparable courses at two other Ontario universities. Slavin's initial concern was that students were dropping out more frequently because of an 'increased reliance on rote memorization over analytical ability that seems to have accompanied the new, more content-intensive, primary and secondary curriculum introduced in Ontario in 1997 and 1998.'[37] However, the students who passed through the system before the implementation of these new curricula evidenced a doubling of the dropout rate in the late 1990s, and so he questioned that explanation and looked more closely at this dramatic increase in course dropout.

In an earlier opinion piece in *University Affairs*,[38] Professor Slavin initially dismissed our argument that student disengagement is affecting the performance of current university students. However, after taking a closer look at the problem and undertaking his own empirical analysis, he revised his view. In one analysis, he examined grade inflation in Ontario high schools, finding that the percentage of As among high-school graduates increased from less than 10 per cent in the 1960s to some 40 per cent by the 1990s, with an overall grade inflation of 9 per cent during that period. Perhaps not coincidentally, several university departments have been using diagnostic tests of key concepts for the past couple of decades to monitor first-year students' knowledge. In Slavin's department, 'the performance of Trent's introductory physics class on an identical first test was 66 per cent in 1996 and 50 per cent in 2006.' Slavin also reports that the mathematics department at his university found a similar drop, as did both the mathematics and physics departments at another Ontario university that he contacted.[39]

To explain the rapid rise in the course dropout rate, Slavin argues 'that a large percentage of students are now going to university, not because they have any desire to learn, but for the credential required for a job. These "disengaged" students do not have the motivation, and often not the work habits, to succeed at university,' and fewer students enrolling in his university-level courses have been taking senior-level high-school physics courses, leaving them ill-prepared in first-year university.[40] He also links this lack of preparation to the Credit Recovery program in Ontario discussed above in chapter 2. Readers will recall that this program makes it easier for students to get credit for courses they are failing, in part by preventing teachers from deducting marks for late assignments and the like.[41]

In support of Slavin's findings, a recent study by the Ontario Confederation of University Faculty Associations (OCUFA) reported that a majority of professors in that province felt that first-year students were less prepared than in the past in terms of both skills and motivations to benefit from the university experience. In terms of skills, professors felt that fewer students had 'requisite written, numeric and critical thinking skills,' and with respect to motivations, professors felt that fewer had the 'capacity to learn independently and be self-motivating,' were less mature, and had greater *expectation of success without the requisite effort*' (emphasis added).[42]

In the United States, problems with student readiness have been a major concern for some time.[43] George Kuh recently commented on this problem on the basis of the extensive research undertaken by the Center for Postsecondary Research, which administers the NSSE, and more recently the High School Survey of Student Engagement (HSSSE).[44] With respect to the level of preparation of American high-school students, Kuh describes the results as 'sobering':

> Although the vast majority of high school seniors (more than 90 per cent) say they intend to go on to postsecondary education, many do not engage in the kinds of educational activities that will prepare them to do well in college ... For example, almost half (47 per cent) study only three or fewer hours per week ... Less than one-fifth (18 per cent) of students in the college-prep track took a math course after their junior year of high school. Only seven of ten high school seniors wrote as many as three papers of five or more pages. Only about half (53 per cent) put a great deal of effort

into their school work; about the same number (51 per cent) said they were challenged to do their best work at school.[45]

At the same time, 'two-thirds of high school students who study three or fewer hours per week reported receiving mostly A and B grades.'[46] These findings reveal the relationship between grade inflation and academic engagement, and how entitled disengagement is institutionally 'enabled,' resulting in high levels of unreadiness – a problem thus rooted in the schools themselves that reward 'bad behaviour.'

Indeed, the results of these studies show that student engagement declines in a linear fashion between the first and the last year of high school. As noted above in chapter 2, this disturbing trend was also recently revealed in research in Canadian schools, where regular attendance decreases to a low of about 40 per cent by the end of high school and only about one-third of students are classified as 'intellectually engaged' throughout the high-school years.[47] Universities continue this 'institutional enabling' by requiring less effort of students than they expect to expend when they begin their first year. As Kuh notes:

> ... about three-fifths expected to spend more than fifteen hours a week studying, but only two-fifths did so. Put another way, they study two to six hours *less* per week on average than they thought they would when starting college.[48]

Kuh concludes from the HSSSE findings

> that many high school seniors are not prepared academically for college-level work and have not developed the habits of the mind and heart that will stand them in good stead to successfully grapple with more challenging intellectual tasks. The senior year in particular seems to be a wasteland.[49]

The issue of readiness has been further examined during the university years through NSSE results. Based on findings that some 40 per cent of American undergraduates complete at least one 'developmental' (i.e., remedial) course, the 2008 annual NSSE report investigated 'first-year students' academic preparation and the relationship between preparation and academic engagement and outcomes,' comparing 'underprepared students and highly prepared students.'[50] Based on a random sample of 10,000 full-time first-year students, they classified

27 per cent as underprepared and 22 per cent as highly prepared, as follows:

> Underprepared students were identified as those who did not pass any high level mathematics, composition, or literature courses while in high school and who took at least one developmental education course in college. Highly prepared students were identified as those who passed at least one high level (e.g., honors) high school course in mathematics, composition, or literature and took no developmental courses in college.[51]

Comparisons of these two groups revealed that underprepared students were less engaged in terms of the benchmarks 'academic challenge' and 'active and collaborative learning,' and were more likely to seek help on their assignments from campus learning centres. They also had lower SAT scores (by over 200 points) and earned lower grades (three times more Cs). Underprepared students were also less satisfied with their school and more uncertain about completing their degree there. These students are clearly in need of extra attention, requiring institutional resources and faculty attention that may not be available to them at certain schools, and which would have been more effectively provided while they were in high school.

Without a doubt, the evidence continues to accumulate that at both the secondary and tertiary levels, a culture of entitlement has emerged, and many teachers are increasingly frustrated that this culture is preventing them from maintaining the standards that would better prepare students academically. In this respect, it is worth ending this section by summarizing for readers the research on the importance of effort in the development of skills as reported by journalist Malcolm Gladwell in his bestseller *Outliers: The Story of Success*.[52]

Gladwell compiles a variety of educational, sociological, and psychological studies to support his thesis that outstanding individual success is due to a combination of *luck* (particularly the era and timing of one's birth), *opportunity* (especially as provided by one's family, school, and community), *ability* (which, he argues, should be understood in terms of thresholds that dictate whether native abilities can be increased through effort),[53] and tremendous *effort* (a minimum of 10,000 hours in the case of the development of high-level abilities). His book is chiefly about people who have become extremely successful, but it can also be read in terms of how societies can maintain mediocrity by not providing opportunities for people – from all economic levels and all segments of society – to expend the large amounts of effort necessary to develop their abilities.

Of particular interest in terms of academic preparation are the studies Gladwell cites concerning the role of families and schools. For example, research on social class origin indicates that low-income families tend to have parenting styles based on a strategy of 'accomplishment of natural growth,' while high-income families raise their children with the 'concerted cultivation' style.[54] These differing styles produce differing results in educational attainment, with lower-income parents assuming that their children will *find their destiny*, while upper-income parents impress on their children that they have to *make their destiny* through effort and self-assertion. This research suggests that the extra effort required by high-income parents of their children in developing their interests and talents is principally responsible for social class differences in school achievement. Yet, Gladwell also shows how schools that place similarly high expectations on low-income students to expend more effort on learning can compensate for this achievement gap in social class.[55]

The primary point to take from Gladwell's many examples and abundant evidence is that schools requiring less effort of their students, in the misguided effort to prevent them from dropping out or in the hope that they will value learning more, are doing exactly the wrong thing if those students are to succeed academically or, just as importantly, find that their interests and talents lie outside of academic pursuits, for instance, in the trades. Gladwell argues that the lessons from the case studies of highly successful people and the research about how the factors of luck, opportunity, talent, and effort combine are 'very simple.'[56] We must move beyond the myth that individual talent naturally develops and rises to the top on its own. Instead, we need to understand the factors that nurture talents, and the ways in which missed opportunities can leave talents to wither on the vine. But, most of all, once identified, talents and interests must be encouraged to develop through sustained effort. To the extent that today's schools are embedded in a 'culture of indulgence,'[57] students who would otherwise flourish will wallow in mediocrity, yet have no idea that they are doing so.

The Teacher / Learning Environment Side of the Disengagement Compact

All three of the student-centred problems identified above have their equivalents with teachers and the learning environments within which teachers interact with students in their role as agents of the educational system. This is a yin-yang, or a complementarity, of roles that is found in structured relationships. For every student who is grade-obsessed in spite of his or her disengagement, there are teachers who have given that student easy grades in a learning environment that condones it. For every disengaged student, there are disengaged teachers operating in learning environments that make allowances for it. And, for every student lacking in readiness for university, there are disengaged teachers who do not prepare their students for future challenges, often because they function in learning environments that do not provide the resources for so doing.

In the final chapter, recommendations are suggested for measures to correct the structural side of the disengagement problem.

The Two-Tiered System: The Spread of the BA-lite in the Credentialist Era

We are ostensibly becoming a 'knowledge society,' yet the university system is becoming a poor preparation for anything but *information-processing* services. The key distinction here is between *knowledge generation*, which has been the purview of universities, and *information processing*, which in its basic form does not require a higher education. The liberal education has been long seen as a means for giving future leaders of society a common language and culture to negotiate social change, and to communicate the means for doing so, but as this degree has become massified, the mission has become increasingly difficult to follow. If the current path toward lower standards is left unaltered, the undergraduate degree of the future will be indistinguishable from the high-school diploma of the past, and most graduates will have been taught only basic information processing.

Many universities are relinquishing a challenging curriculum that would produce future generations of knowledge-producers and leaders who have not only a requisite literacy upon which to engage in higher-level written and oral communication, but also a well-honed ability to conceptualize and effectively research topics (the so-called creative class).[58] Instead, like high schools, they are increasingly producing graduates who struggle to process even basic information and who are uncomfortable exercising the rudiments of written and oral abilities.[59]

A primary source of this problem is that many universities have had to do more with less as enrolments have grown and funding has withered. This has meant that many schools have supplanted written and oral assignments with multiple-choice tests, so that students have increasingly been evaluated in terms of their ability to remember (process) information rather than produce it. Knowing something and being able to communicate that knowledge effectively are two different things, but these things are being confused in mass institutions that are trying to cope with the large numbers of students they now enrol. Liberal education is about developing the ability to analyse information and communicate in written and spoken form. Many hitherto liberal programs have slowly evolved into packages of large courses that are exclusively lecture format, with no tutorials, except perhaps in fourth year.

This expansion of large lecture courses presents professors with obstacles that are insurmountable on an individual basis. Those who assign essays in these large lecture courses, especially without teaching assistants, face a mountain of essays that are typically poorly written, but for which high grades are expected. Add to this the problem of having TAs who are themselves unprepared products of the system and who are unable effectively to evaluate written work. Usually, after experiencing numerous confrontations with students over their grades, these professors drop the essay assignments from their courses, unless it is a specific requirement of that course. In our own program at the University of Western Ontario, only some courses are designated as essay-format. Even in these courses, many professors have stopped providing written comments on papers because they require extra effort and many students either do not read the comments or take offence at being 'criticized.' Increasingly, however, those who require written assignments in non-essay courses encounter complaints from students who prefer the multiple-choice format, presumably because that is what they are used to and their writing abilities are poor.

In many cases, it is too late or not feasible to teach essay-writing skills at university, so that many lower-level university courses no longer require them. Furthermore, those students who make it to fourth year (which used to be a capstone Honours year, but now is increasingly the year in which students scurry to complete the requisite number of courses to qualify for graduation) may suddenly find that all of their fourth-year courses require written assignments and oral presentations. Students who did not learn these skills in high school and develop them further in their early years at university can find themselves way over their heads. When faced with large numbers of such students, professors teaching these courses often have to 'hold their nose' in assigning passing grades. To give low or failing grades at this level can be to deny the student the final step to a degree, and few professors seem willing to do so nowadays. This is also a source of growing academic dishonesty as students panic and increasingly resort to the practices of cheating, buying essays, hiring 'ghost writers,' etc., to assist them in the crunch of the final days or weeks of their 'honours' year.

These trends are not lost on all administrators. A book was recently released in Ontario vigorously arguing that a dual system of universities – research versus teaching universities – is the way of the future.[60] Meanwhile, a number of Canadian universities are developing internally tiered systems in which the idea is for a small percentage of students who are deemed to be prepared for the rigours of a high-quality undergraduate education are admitted into 'élite' streams, while the remainder are left in mass, 'BA-lite' streams. In mass streams, disengagement is apparently condoned, and inflated grades are used to keep students happy with the illusion that they are being well educated. That this practice adds to the stress levels of professors is never openly discussed.

This type of system can be understood in the context of the corporatization of a university system that is based on a for-profit funding model. This model rewards universities for the sheer number of students putting their 'bums on seats' and treats universities like private institutions relying on their marketability (a common situation in the United States, but less so elsewhere), and allots funds accordingly. Regrettably, this two-tiered model can shortchange those students who are handed a BA-lite or a faux-BA, and is deceiving the public and policymakers that the system is 'excellence-driven' in terms of both the process and product of learning.

As explored in the concluding chapter, some people think that a two-tiered system is an inevitable result of the evolution of universities into the mass systems required to include increasing proportions of the population. It is also becoming commonplace to hear that 'the BA is the new high-school diploma,' and that 'the MA is the new BA.' Some observers link this extended education with the prolongation of youth that has occurred over the past few decades, a phenomenon that has reached the public consciousness with adages like 'thirty is the new twenty.'

A longer period of education and maturation, in turn, is sometimes linked with the fact that people are now living longer. This logic erroneously mixes a biological fact (longer lifespans) with two cultural forms. Lifespans have increased in most developed countries, but among those countries there is tremendous variation in the structure of school systems and the extent to which the period of youth is prolonged.

Moreover, this argument fails on three additional grounds. First, to use a later event (longer life) to explain a prior event (prolonged youth) is an error in logic (a teleological argument). Second, it is likely that the extension of educational systems is a chief cause of the prolongation of youth, not a consequence. And third, since the variation in the length of both education and youth, between societies and among those within societies, is far greater than the variation in life expectancies, any correlation between the former and latter would be small to nil.

Besides, this type of argument is a red herring. It diverts attention away from the wisdom of providing the conditions for effective educational systems for those who are in their formative years and hence most likely to benefit from them. Simply delaying the educational process breeds boredom and alienation among the student body, diverts those who are ready to move into adulthood and become productive members of society, and delays those with the academic potential to do well in rigorous university systems.

Conclusion: Preserving Scholarship

The implicit bilateral contract between students and teachers has been slowly eroded to the point where many students expect that all they need to know about a field of study can be related to them in lectures. In addition, many educators have lost sight of the larger issue of education versus training. Both professors and students have certain roles to play, but the expectations for these roles have been lowered as the disengagement compact has spread: fewer students arrive at universities prepared to pursue a truly *higher* education; fewer professors are able or willing to deliver that higher education; students and professors can easily acclimatize to the cultures of disengagement that prevail in many schools; and grade inflation both placates students with false feedback and obscures the implications of the decline in standards to the public and policymakers by giving them false feedback regarding quality-assurance accountability.

Readers have six 'take-aways' from this chapter to reinforce the argument about the decline in quality in many liberal programs.

First, grades must be interpreted as assessments of students' perfor-mances in courses, and not promoted as a basis for judging the worth of people. People have different talents, many of which are not aca-demic, and it needs to be the role of primary and secondary schools to help students discover their strengths and talents and also to recognize their shortcomings and limitations. In many schools, this will require broadening the curriculum at those lower educational levels (rather than waiting for the tertiary level) beyond the academic streams that currently dominate. Pushing most people through academic streams flies in the face of what is known about the ranges of talents and the needs of the economy for those talents.[61]

Second, there are serious misunderstandings about the role of stu-dents in their higher education. The optimal student-teacher relation-ship in university settings involves an implicit bilateral contract in which there is a commitment between the student and teacher to meet each other 'halfway' in terms of the effort put into courses.

Third, the fact that students pay for their university education does not mean that they are 'consumers' purchasing a product; rather, they *are the product*, and they are paying to undergo a transformation. Teach-ing is part of that process of potential transformation. The role of the teacher is to identify the reading material and written/oral assignments required for students to become proficient at a particular course level, and to guide students through the learning process, which potentially transforms the student in some way.

Fourth, when the student is viewed as the product rather than the consumer, the student is more clearly seen as a commodity to be ac-tively transformed by the experience, not a passive consumer of knowl-edge or a credential. Yet, if the student does not uphold his or her end of the bargain (as in disengagement), this transformation is less likely to occur.

Fifth, what happens in class at universities is the 'tip of the iceberg,' not the 'iceberg,' of learning. Most higher learning occurs outside the classroom, when students read assigned material, think and write about that material, seek to see how it applies to the world-at-large in current and past events, and discuss it with classmates and friends. In the lib-eral arts and sciences, classes are to guide students through this process and, optimally, teach them to think critically and independently, so that by graduation they are capable of teaching themselves for the remain-der of their lives in whatever occupational fields they enter, as well as informing themselves in their civil and political engagements. The liberal education is thus an important step in lifelong learning, not the final step in a training process. And, in terms of its contribution to civil society, recall that the origin of the term 'liberal' is the Latin *liber*, meaning 'free,' and that the liberal education is associated with the preservation of freedom, for the person and the society.

And, sixth, these crucial aspects of higher learning are being lost on many of the stakeholders of the university system as the basic pedagogical principles of the liberal education are being forgotten. The more that universities sell themselves as purveyors of marketable credentials, the more they encourage the student-as-consumer model, setting in motion myriad problems associated with entitled disengagement. When administrators, counsellors, parents, and teachers believe that this is the model to follow, students are more likely to fall into the role of being passive vessels to be filled with information and/or consumers entitled to high marks and credentials in exchange for tuition fees; ultimately, in either case, standards slide.

4 Universities: Crisis, What Crisis?

In this chapter, the various stances that can be taken to the question of whether today's universities are experiencing a crisis are examined. This is a thorny area because people vary in their sense of the threshold for what constitutes a 'crisis,' and therefore what needs to be rectified. For some people, a crisis appears to refer only to some impending doom unless drastic action is taken. However, the term 'crisis' has different meanings, ranging from being a dilemma requiring some sort of action – a turning point, as in 'identity crisis' – to a widespread emergency like a natural disaster.

Defining the University's Crisis

In our view, the threshold for defining a problem as a 'crisis' involves the necessity for action at a turning point in dealing with a set of problems, rather than a situation of impending doom. Canadian universities will survive this crisis in some form, but the concern is the form they might take. The university system has developed a set of problems that require some sort of decisive action *now*. The worst thing to do would be to sit back and let it change according to the various contradictory forces identified in chapters 1 and 2, not least of which is the misguided government policy of using the university system as a panacea for labour-market problems.

In broad strokes, this crisis is unfolding as follows: Government policies promoting mass access to universities have addressed the supply side of labour, rather than the demand side of creating more jobs. Consequently, there is an oversupply of university graduates in relation to the demand for them.[1] In conjunction with a decline in funding, universities have attempted to survive by embracing corporate management principles, and these measures, in turn, have helped to create the credentialist approach to universities on the part of both students who are seeking job opportunities and courses of study that are hungry for recruits. In the past two decades, universities have seen an influx of students whose primary purpose for being there is to receive a credential, and they have a less than keen interest in the courses they must take to get that credential. In turn, classrooms have been affected by a culture of disengagement as more students assume the mindset of entitled disengagement: they have paid for their credential and assume that this product will be delivered to their satisfaction. As this culture has taken hold, professors who are sensitive to these changes have reacted in a number of adverse ways that do not bode well for the future of the profession.

For us, the foregoing adequately describes a crisis situation. But, then again, we are directly affected by these circumstances. Indeed, whether someone defines a set of problems as a crisis can depend on how much that person is directly invested in or affected by those problems, and there is clear evidence that the mission drift of universities adversely affects most – but not all – students and teachers.

To provide an analogy, even in the dark days of the global financial crisis at the time of writing (2009), many people are not adversely affected economically. To the contrary, a number of people have benefitted from the lower prices and interest rates that come with this economic downturn. For example, those who are able to buy equities and real estate at low prices before the recovery stand to increase their wealth considerably. For these people, this is a time of opportunity, and they might not favour government interventions to alleviate the problems others are experiencing. Others are looking at a longer historical perspective and see this economic turmoil as welcome evidence that neo-liberalism is coming to an end. Yet others welcome this crisis of consumerism and see it as a turning point toward an economy that is based less on wasteful consumption, with all of its detrimental effects, including climate change (another issue currently under debate in terms of its 'crisis' status).

This subjective aspect of the notion of crisis helps explain why so many people who are not directly affected, such as administrators and researchers who have had no recent exposure to the undergraduate classroom, would be in denial about what those 'on the ground' are reporting.

In light of the ambiguities around the definition of 'crisis,' it is worth considering how the current situation constitutes a crisis for students and teachers requiring some sort action. The crisis for the overall system can then be better understood.

The Crisis Experienced by Students

Many students have a rough time when they attend university. There is ample empirical evidence of increasing stress levels[2] (especially for female students,[3] who now predominate by a ratio approaching 60/40).[4] There is also widespread alienation.[5] The alienation discussed above in chapter 2 is manifested in numerous ways, from a detachment from the (daily) process of learning, to a disdain for the product of learning (the outcomes). The detachment from learning shows up in the disengagement statistics, but can be experienced as an inability to 'be in the moment' and experience university-level learning as an intrinsically gratifying experience that produces a sense of fulfilment. And, alienation can be stressful: being forced to enter or remain in alienating situations can simply compound that stress.

The disdain that many students develop for the product of learning is discernible in the mindset of entitled disengagement. George Kuh similarly characterizes this alienating situation by noting that almost half of students today enter American universities with an 'entitlement mentality,' which goes something like this:

> I have been an A student in high school ... [so] you as faculty member should give me the grade I deserve ... I will put in what I consider to be a reasonable effort and in return expect a good grade. Your job as a teacher is to honor that.[6]

To spend four years detached from an experience that would be a chance of a lifetime in other times and places, and then feel no sense of fulfilment or pride for what should have been a milestone in one's life – to be alienated – can only be described as a monumental waste. We see here how the eclipsing of the liberal education by pseudo-vocationalism is cheating students of a chance in a lifetime to expand their minds and realize certain potentials. Although the students themselves may not recognize this as a crisis for them, those of us who are the stewards of the system certainly should see it as a problem requiring action.

The two university students who were discussed above in chapter 2 voicing their disappointments with their university educations in the print media provide excellent examples of this sense of alienation and waste. As one student made reference to his disappointment in not being taught critical thinking skills, it is worthwhile to pause to consider more precisely definitions of abstract and reflective thinking, or what is more commonly called critical thinking,[7] what transformative experiences critical thinking might engender, and hence what is being denied to those who naïvely register in today's universities believing that there is more to the experience than parties, high grades, and banal tests.

Derek Bok, a past president of Harvard University, used the phrase 'learning how to think' as the title for a chapter in his recent book *Our Underachieving Colleges*.[8] The overall message in Bok's book is that many contemporary universities are squandering the opportunity to provide the quality of education that is within their grasp, falling short of the mark of 'excellence' that often goes with the rhetoric of mission statements and public relations releases. Bok's chapter 'Learning How to Think' could well be titled 'the failure to teach students how to think critically' or 'how universities fail to transform their students intellectually.'

Bok contends that much of the teaching of critical thinking – defining questions and problems, evaluating evidence and arguments, and arriving at a defensible judgment on a matter – is by example, in the assigned readings and lectures. Generally, it is not directly taught in any systematic manner, so that many students can pass through the system without actual practice in exercising critical thinking ever being required of them. He chastises both schools and professors for letting this happen and for not questioning more actively the assumption that they are teaching it.

Bok also suggests that university students are showing less growth in critical-thinking abilities than in the past, citing findings from Ernest Pascarella and Patrick Terenzini's (second) exhaustive review of the evaluation literature on higher education, *How College Affects Students*.[9] Pascarella and Terenzini conclude that 'the evidence from the 1990s ... suggests that [on average] students are making gains in critical thinking skills during college that are appreciably smaller in magnitude than the gains we observed in [1970s and 1980s].'[10]

Specifically, the critical-thinking gains of university students found in the 1990s were about half the magnitude of those found in the 1970s and 1980s. Although they are unable to pinpoint what might be behind this drop, they note that 'not all students develop as critical thinkers' during their university experience. In other words, only some students make gains in this area, and it is possible that fewer students are now doing so. The primary suspect here is effort, which is one of the four crucial factors determining value-added effects of university attendance.[11]

The body of empirical research in this area confirms that the growth of cognitive skills is a direct result of the quality of the effort expended by a student; more specifically, based on the peer-reviewed literature, Pascarella and Terenzini report that critical-thinking skills are enhanced by several effort-based factors, such as the number of hours spent studying per week, number of non-assigned books read by a student, participating in class discussion, and taking detailed notes in class.[12] More generally, intellectual transformations in university are 'a direct result of a student's quality of effort or level of psychological and social involvement.'[13]

The logical conclusion from these findings is that the benefits of a university education, and specifically, learning how to think critically, may be diminishing on average among students as a group because a larger subset of students is not putting out the same effort as in the past, and as a consequence is not developing these skills.

At the same time, while critical-thinking skills are important in all types of higher education, including vocational and liberal, the liberal education also potentially transforms students' overall view of the world – their epistemological assumptions about what constitutes a valid basis for their belief and value systems. Bok also provides a discussion of these potential transformations, distinguishing between critical thinking and 'the epistemic assumptions [people] make in addressing the loosely structured problems, so common in real life, that have no demonstrably correct answers.'[14]

This distinction is important here because of a fundamental difference between training for a profession and undergoing a liberal education. While critical-thinking enhancement is important in training, both critical thinking and epistemic transformations are crucially important if a liberal education is to have any value-added effects. That is, in the training model, teaching involves showing students how to solve problems as well as requiring them to remember procedures and information for which there are correct answers, while the liberal education involves comprehending and evaluating systems of thought for which there are few correct answers beyond factual names and dates. Ideally, teaching in the liberal arts and sciences involves showing students how to develop and defend defensible arguments (vs. unreflective personal opinions).

The literature on epistemic assumptions discussed by Bok distinguishes among three general levels of reflective judgment encompassing seven stages. At the most rudimentary level, 'pre-reflective thinking,' students think that all problems or questions have definite answers, either from an expert or an authority source. Mere opinion is taken as sufficient proof. Students at this level tend to parrot what their instructors say, and feel uncomfortable or confused when multiple views are presented. One way for them to deal with this discomfort is to take the position that all opinions are right.

Only when students transform their thinking beyond this level can they begin to develop analytic skills to reason on their own, including self-criticism. At the intermediate epistemic stages, 'quasi-reflective thinking,' people can conceive of knowledge as being relative and contextual. While this is an advance above authority-based opinion, students can get stuck at this stage, believing that there is no way to judge the validity of different forms of knowledge and opinions about them. As a result, they may adopt a form of dogmatic relativism, retreating to the belief that all opinions are equally valid, regardless of the internal structure and evidence supporting the arguments underlying them.

At the highest epistemic stages, 'reflective thinking,' students come to believe that there are ways to judge the relative merits of complex arguments, in part by acknowledging that those judgments are tentative, awaiting further evidence. In this way of thinking, the way to judge the validity of arguments is to examine the persuasiveness of evidence, the rigour with which it was assembled/collected, and the strength of reasoning involved. Those at these highest reflective levels are willing to accept well-reasoned arguments as substitutes for opinions they may have held in the past, cognizant that these new judgments are themselves provisional, to be evaluated in the future if further evidence or arguments invalidate them.[15]

Although early research was optimistic that most students would reach the highest epistemic level by their senior year of university, recent research suggests that few seniors do so, and the percentage doing so seems to be in decline. What is more, those who do not develop critical-thinking skills do not advance far in terms of reflective judgment. In summarizing these findings, Bok concludes:

Most students at least understand that not all problems have simple right or wrong answers, but they do not see much utility in reasoning carefully about unstructured problems, nor are they convinced that one can critically evaluate the judgements of others.[16]

It follows that students who put little effort into their studies are unlikely to learn critical-thinking skills or develop through the stages of reflective judgment, at least as a result of their exposure to the curriculum. In turn, graduates with a personal history of disengagement will not be prepared by their university experiences for higher levels of functioning in the contemporary world, whether as members of the 'creative class,'[17] as future leaders of society, or as engaged citizens whose voting power and civic engagements can make dramatic differences in the direction of political and economic changes.

So, in terms of the question of whether there is currently a crisis for students, numerous points of stress can be identified that culminate in individual crises, depending on the circumstances of the particular student. Perhaps most importantly, though, the current generation of students is the most financially burdened in history, yet is receiving the least value for its money. Some observers have argued that the university system had quality issues in the past, and therefore we should *not* be concerned about them in the present.[18] Not only does this argument ignore this new financial burden, but by justifying system deficiencies on the basis of past practices, it is also unfair to those students currently being funnelled through the system, often reluctantly. For the sake of current and future students, educators need to be forward-looking and recognize that regardless of past practices, educational quality is important *now and in the future*.

The Crisis Experienced by Faculty

The academic job is the envy of many. It can be a highly rewarding and fulfilling career, replete with high levels of job autonomy and remuneration. Alternatively, it can be a grind requiring long hours of thankless work stretching into evenings and weekends, with little job security, low pay, and continual pressures from students, colleagues, and administrators.

Professors who speak up about job-related problems can expect to be chided for not being grateful for having such a job, as illustrated in the example of the professor who wrote the article 'I'm Leaving,' discussed above in chapter 2. Unfortunately, these types of reproaches are not helpful in terms of the need to improve the university system and take it into the twenty-first century as a vital institution. At their core, these types of reproaches smack of a 'wage-slave' mentality that dictates that workers should not upset their 'masters.' At the very least, this subservient attitude reflects a resignation to the necessity for an authoritarian hierarchy of workers, a system that can breed conformity, mediocrity, and a lack of creativity, all of which are anathema to *knowledge-production*. In reality, professors *are needed* in university systems that claim to produce knowledge rather than just process it. If Canada gives up on this, it will be out of place in a world where most countries are attempting to build or expand their knowledge-production capacities.

If we want a high-quality university system that is internationally competitive in terms of knowledge-production and lives up to the self-accolades of excellence as world leaders in higher education,[19] we need to provide working conditions that will attract the best, brightest, and most creative professors. Regrettably, there are indications that we are moving in the opposite direction, both in terms of attracting the best recruits to the profession and in providing a collegial environment that will keep these recruits in the system and working to their potential.

Prospective recruits to the professoriate necessarily pass through undergraduate programs as students, and what undergraduate students now see is not always pretty. We regularly find that the most promising undergraduates from our department go into professional programs like law, rather than into a graduate program in the discipline that inspires them. One promising sociology major plainly stated her reservations to us a few years ago: 'Why would I want to go into a profession where I have to teach students who don't want to be there?'

In addition to these concerns, many promising students have figured out that the academic profession does not promise the same package of rewards as other professions, especially in view of the necessity of first earning a research degree – the PhD. Earning this research degree can involve a poverty-level existence for a number of years while logging long hours in the process. To come out of the end of it with poor job prospects and little increase in salary beyond a master's degree (as noted above), and especially to face a job that is now rife with stresses associated with undergraduate teaching, is not enticing.[20] Indeed, it appears that PhDs are now being overproduced, in good part because of the inability of the underfunded university system that educates/trains them to, in turn, hire them.[21]

These trends are well underway in the United States, and Canada is taking the same path.[22] Two comments posted on the on-line news source *Inside Higher Ed* in response to the article 'Shying Away from Graduate School'[23] illustrate these feelings. The first is from a lawyer:

> Out of college, I took the LSAT and went to law school. Even today, I wonder if I made the right choice – practicing law at a big firm is gruelling and thankless. But the trade-offs of going into a PhD program make me generally not regret my choice. First, the program lasts 5–7 years. This delays adulthood and financial independence. Second, professors' salaries are *very* low compared to the business sector, especially as we've seen law and finance salaries skyrocket. But most important, job security for professors has steadily declined. More universities are making wider use of visiting, adjunct, and part-time faculty and offering fewer and fewer tenured positions. The only advantage of becoming a professor was the quality of life. Take that away by offering fewer tenure-track positions, and there is no incentive to go the PhD route.
>
> I hope schools soon realize that failing to invest in their faculty, while continuing to build fancy gyms and dorms and student centers, will ultimately bring down the house of cards.

The second is from a nurse, who now works as an instructor on the basis of her accumulated experience in the field:

> I have a MSN and teach in a diploma program. I earn in the 70's with 28 years in nursing and 4 years in teaching nursing. A PhD would cost me 4–7 years, around 50K (more or less) and I could anticipate earning approximately 50K in a collegiate setting. I'd be lucky to find a tenure position and would probably have to move to do so; not to mention the increase in workload. I'd considered a PhD for personal satisfaction, but then I realized I could get that by spending more time with family and friends which would cost me nothing yet provide multiple deposits into the 'emotional bank account.' So, I guess my point is 'what's the point'?

These recruitment problems are exacerbated by a multitude of problems experienced by those who do make it into the professoriate. A 2007 study of 1,500 faculty members at fifty-six Canadian universities found high levels of stress, with 85 per cent reporting workload stress, 22 per cent reporting stress-related psychological and physical symptoms requiring medication, and 13 per cent experiencing 'clinical' levels of distress that could qualify them for a leave of absence.[24] Similarly, a 2006 University of Alberta study found that about 80 per cent of faculty report frequent work-related stress (with females reporting more stress), with 70 per cent of those with more than three years at the university feeling that their stress had increased during that time period. Results from other countries show high levels of frequent stress among faculty members, although not quite as high as in Canada: Australia – 55 per cent, New Zealand – 48 per cent, the United Kingdom – 70 per cent.[25]

Most stressed-out professors apparently just tough it out because there is little offered to them in relief by Canadian and American universities, but a reasonable response to empirical results such as these is to call for measures that address the work environment in ways that make it less toxic. The typical responses from university administrators and outside observers, however, are for professors to just 'suck it up' and be thankful for employment. If we were referring to chemical toxins in the environment, action would more likely be immediate. Lamentably for the professors adversely affected, the hidden nature of these social stressors makes them easy to ignore, and the crisis experienced by these faculty can be denied and dismissed as individual failings.

Professors' stresses can be explained in part by student-teacher tensions, but also in terms of the additional workload required of faculty in dealing with the increasing numbers of students piling into Canadian universities, especially those who are unprepared yet have a sense of entitled disengagement.

The literature from Canada, the United States, the United Kingdom, New Zealand, and Australia is consistent in the finding that professors work between 50 and 60 hours per week. Workload varies over the course of the year, with extremes during fall/winter semesters, especially during exam periods. A study at our university in the mid-1990s estimated a normal workload of 49 hours per week (hpw) averaged over the year, with a high of 52.4 hpw during the fall and 45.6 hpw during the summer.[26] A more recent study at the University of Alberta estimated an average faculty workload of 56.2 hpw.[27] American results come in somewhat higher. The Faculty Survey of Student Engagement (FSSE) reports a range of 55 to 63 hpw, depending on the faculty,[28] while the Stanford University Senate reports an average of 60 hpw.[29] Studies from other countries report similar findings: Australia – 53 hpw, New Zealand – 53 hpw, the United Kingdom – 66 per cent work more than 45 hpw, and 23 per cent work more than 55 hpw.[30]

Some studies have examined differences among types of faculty groups, finding some variation in workload. For example, American research using FSSE data suggests that faculty of colour spend more time on service activities and administration duties, and experience more job stress as a result of these demands, perhaps because these impinge on research time.[31]

Just the same, measuring workload in terms of hours per week tells only part of the story regarding the nature of the work. According to some studies, there is a ceiling effect for most professors at 60 hpw, when more work simply cannot be done during a typical day or week, especially among those who are parents and need to spend time with their children and families.[32] If the demands of the job are such that not all work can be completed by the time the ceiling is reached, several things can happen that require a different type of understanding of workload – *workload unmanageability*[33] and *workload intensity*.[34]

Workload unmanageability refers to the inability to accomplish tasks and reach goals in the time available during a workweek. The University of Alberta study found that 58.7 per cent of faculty report their workload is unmanageable to some degree. A study from the United Kingdom found a similar level, with some 53 per cent of academic staff reporting unmanageable workloads.[35]

Workload intensity involves a lateral compounding of the amount of work or goals accomplished in a unit of time. An example of this would be the prospect of meeting with twenty students during two office hours, as opposed to just four students. If only two hours are available for twenty meetings, each student will need to be dealt with in only five to six minutes, as opposed to thirty minutes for each student. The former situation intensifies the experience, creating greater fatigue and stress, and likely reduces job satisfaction, not to mention the frustration the students might feel, which can be put back on faculty members in their teacher evaluations.

A variety of compromises may need to be undertaken for members to control workload unmanageability and intensity. While these may allow goals to be reached on paper, they do not necessarily allow professional standards to be met, and members may experience reduced job satisfaction and stress associated with the cognitive dissonance produced by taking shortcuts to complete the goals. With respect to teaching workload, these compromises include the following, all of which feed the professorial side of the disengagement compact and reduce the quality of education for students:

- using only tests in courses to evaluate students, and then only multiple-choice tests;
- limiting personal contact with students in discussing material and mentoring them;
- eliminating or reducing e-mail contact with students, and thereby being perceived as unapproachable by some students and receiving lower teacher ratings as a result (and, as noted above, lower teacher ratings threaten job security among untenured faculty and the pay levels of all faculty, which can indirectly increase stress).

In the face of increased enrolments, even those who adopt less time-consuming methods of teaching and assessment may incur a 'cost' in job satisfaction in terms of the job stress resulting from (a) dealing with unhappy students or (b) coping with a sense of dissonance that professional standards are compromised by these assessment methods. This stress and dissonance can reduce job satisfaction and carry over into non-work hours (e.g., general tension and sleeplessness; a desire just to get the term over with). New technologies such as e-mail contact with students, preparing PowerPoint presentations, and posting material to websites generally do not have workplace norms, and tend to be at the discretion of professors, often displacing work that previously would be done in the office during the workday to evenings and weekends at home.

A turning point is available to us with respect to the crisis experienced by university faculty and students. On the teaching side of workload, it involves moving toward a properly funded system in which a reasonable number of students (not exceeding a 15:1 student-teacher ratio) are admitted if they are prepared to meet their teachers halfway in the bilateral contract, and are qualified to learn university-level material without being spoon-fed. Non-academically inclined students should have other options available to them at both the secondary and post-secondary levels. Anything short of this is going to exacerbate the stress levels experienced by faculty members and their students, and continue the downward spiral of standards in universities.

The System Crisis

There is a history of complaint about the university system, although the criticisms are not nearly as extensive as those directed at the primary and secondary systems. This record of complaint should not come as a surprise, given the prominent role of universities in modern societies.

What is of interest is the trend in these complaints; they are becoming more focused on the problems posed by the ongoing massification and corporatization of universities, with the university credential increasingly marketed as a product that everyone should strive to obtain.[36] Accordingly, defenders of the status quo are being illogical when they claim that books criticizing the current system can be ignored because there are so many of them, both now and in the past.[37] In terms of the recent literature, different critics are pointing to different problems with the directions universities are taking.

A key feature of this system crisis is the confusion between education and training. Education, as embodied in the liberal arts and sciences, involves a critical analysis of arguments and the ability to communicate ideas. In contrast, training involves a memorization of facts and procedures. To dismiss this distinction and embrace the confusion between education and training is analogous to confusing an apple with an orange. Both apples and oranges are good in their own right, just as education and training are good in their right. But to shift a liberal education system to a vocational one, and then claim the benefits of the liberal education for pseudo-vocational training is not only mistaken, it is dishonest. If we continue to delude ourselves about this, not only will the system degrade further, but also the mixed system we are developing will diminish further the overall legitimacy of the system in the eyes of stakeholders who count on the quality of liberal arts and sciences graduates and the roles for which they are ostensibly certified.

This confusion is readily apparent in terms of the evolution of grading practices. The liberal education is critical and reflexive. The products of this type of thinking are always open to improvement because the reference point is the unknown limit of the human intellect. In other words, perfection is unattainable and degrees of proficiency are identifiable; hence, the grading distinctions among satisfactory, very good, and excellent in written work and oral presentations.

Vocational training, on the other hand, tends to be passive, descriptive, and regurgitative. The product of training involves meeting expectations regarding procedures and information retention; as such, an outcome of 100 per cent is not only possible in assessments, but is also desirable. It is therefore easy for those who confuse education and training to mistake inflated grade attainment for indications of success in liberal programs.[38] In the liberal educational system, grades are the *criteria*, while personal and intellectual transformations are among the *standards*. In a vocational training system, the standards and the criteria are generally the same – regurgitation of information and imitation of procedure.

Our chief argument in this regard is that with the pressures on undergraduate programs to be marketable, many liberal programs have slowly evolved into pseudo-vocational training programs, at least implicitly. In other words, the training approach is trumping the education approach, and many universities currently have a mixed system in which liberal subjects are often assessed in ways best suited for vocational training (extensive testing of content and procedure). This is causing considerable confusion among stakeholders, especially among students who are told they can convert a BA/BSc into a job, only to find out that there is limited truth to this.

Our own discipline, sociology, has a history of this. The most recent fad in sociology departments is to offer specializations in criminology, in spite of the fact that (a) there are few jobs available in that field[39] and (b) many departments barely have sufficient faculty with advanced credentials in criminology to teach the throngs of students piling into these programs.[40] Apparently sparked by the popularity of TV shows like *CSI New York* and *CSI Miami*, what these sociology programs that 'sell' criminology courses to their students do not tell them is that the very exciting jobs of profiling criminals are usually done by psychology graduates or that the equally engaging assignments tied to the collection and analysis of DNA evidence are normally given to chemistry graduates. A sociology graduate with a specialization in criminology is not a criminologist, and to sell it as such is mendacious.

A good part of the system crisis is due to a loss of understanding of the transformative potential of the liberal education experience. This transformation requires intellectual engagement and emotional commitment. A student cannot just sign up for a liberal program and passively say, 'Here's my money, now educate me.' Liberal education cannot be bought with tuition, and there is nothing magical about spending four years at a university. If there were some magic to it, universities could offer two types of degrees: one for which students take courses; and the other for which they do not take courses, but simply participate in extracurricular activities and heavy doses of socialization with other students while they live in residence. The former could be called a *curricular degree* and the latter a *residential degree*.

Don't laugh. We have tried this idea out on our students in class discussions, and they tell us it is already happening de facto. In fact, as argued in the last chapter, universities are currently awarding bachelor's degrees with three levels of de facto integrity: the traditional BA for the fully engaged student, the BA-lite for the partially engaged, and the faux-BA for disengaged students. Given that only about 10 to 20 per cent of students could be considered fully engaged, it is little wonder that the value of, and respect for, the baccalaureate are in decline.

These system problems need the immediate attention of administrators in institutions thus affected, and they call for policymakers to provide sufficient resources for universities to sustain liberal programs with an appropriate student-teacher ratio (15:1). If addressing these problems needs to be justified by administrators out of a concern for the integrity of their 'brand' and the quality of their 'product,' so be it.

Other stakeholders need to consider the loss of vision and mission that is taking place for the liberal education, and face some questions about what is to be expected from the bachelor's degree in the arts and sciences. Are they satisfied with training programs that appropriate the cachet of a BA/BSc, but in so doing render those baccalaureate degrees meaningless? Do they want undergraduate programs to simply function as proving grounds for graduate and professional programs? Or are they happy with them deteriorating into 'holding pens,' just as high schools have become, for young people who are not welcome in our youth-unfriendly labour market? And, what are the costs to the taxpayer of student disengagement fostered by this dysfunctional system?[41] We believe that it would be better to preserve the liberal education, and provide separate venues for training programs, thereby providing a more functional system.

Not all of the world's university systems have let the mission drift occur to the extent found in Canada. Finland, for example, has endeavoured to maintain educational standards at all three levels, and in so doing is preserving the integrity of the mission of its university system, while providing effective alternatives for those who are not academically inclined.

Beyond the almost universal distinctions among three levels – primary, secondary, and tertiary – educational systems around the world are highly variable when it comes to level-specific organization and practice. Many people have been critical of Canada's shifts away from vocational training at the secondary level toward more general, academically oriented programs through which more and more students have been pushed – what has been called the 'Americanization of education.'[42] The results have included a drop in standards to accommodate those who are not academically inclined or motivated, along with tolerance for both higher levels of academic disengagement and grade inflation, as an ill-fated 'solution' to prevent dropout. It is ill-fated because this 'solution' at the secondary level simply creates problems at the tertiary level, postponing the point at which academically weaker students leave the academic stream of the educational system.

Similar problems can be found in other countries that have massified their educational systems. Still, not all countries have followed this 'academics-for-all' model to the same extent. Of the countries that have not, Finland provides an example regarding how to balance guidance, choice, and options.

THE FINNISH CASE

The Finnish system is certainly not without its problems, but its current attractive features are a result of an openness to admit to problems in the past and a willingness to work to remedy those problems at their source, a process that continues in its third iteration in the past half century. Certainly, some aspects of the Finnish system would be strongly resisted by certain stakeholders in countries like Canada, for reasons discussed in chapter 2, but the Finnish example gives us something concrete to bring to the debate.[43]

The Finns have viewed their educational system as a work in progress for the past few decades, as should be the case in all countries experiencing rapid social and economic change. Indeed, some of the features that warrant close scrutiny from Canadian educators are rather recent additions or reforms to the Finnish educational system, as Finnish society has adjusted itself to contemporary conditions. Table 4.1 shows the three levels of the Finnish system as it is now constituted, along with the typical ages at which people pass through them.[44] Three features of the Finnish system immediately stand out in this table: (1) the late starting age for primary school students; (2) the division of secondary schools into vocational/apprenticeship and academic streams; and (3) the separation of liberal universities from polytechnics. Most germane to the current discussion are features 2 and 3.[45]

Although there is no streaming during primary school, or more specifically 'comprehensive school,' a major streaming takes place when students are sixteen and have completed nine years of formal schooling. Under half go on to upper-secondary schools, which are designed to prepare students for tertiary institutions, and most of the remainder go into vocational institutions and apprenticeships, which are designed for direct labour-force entry. The lack of streaming during

Table 4.1
The Finnish educational system

Starting age (typical duration)	Academic stream	Vocational stream
	Doctorate	
	Licentiate	
(2–3)	Master's (university)	Master's (polytechnic)
20 (3–4)	Bachelor's (university)	Bachelor's (polytechnic)
16	Upper-secondary	Vocational and apprenticeship training
7	Comprehensive (primary)	
6	Pre-primary	

primary school is meant to achieve a more uniform education for all students, regardless of their eventual occupational destination. This helps to reduce social-class reproduction and assure a standard of literacy and numeracy among the Finnish population.[46] During this period, students, teachers, and parents get a good idea of the students' interests and abilities, and the decision is made on this basis regarding which secondary stream is pursued. This is not an irreversible decision, and students graduating from the vocational stream can qualify for tertiary education with additional courses, and by passing an entrance exam.

Most of those who complete the vocational stream go straight into the labour force. Note that in much of Canada, serious vocational training is delayed until the tertiary level, rather than being integrated into the secondary level. Apprenticeships are delayed even further among young Canadians, often not being entered until the person is in his or her late twenties.[47] In contrast, some 65 per cent of young Finns are in vocational/apprenticeship programs in upper-secondary schools (compared to an OECD average of 44 per cent).[48]

Those who complete the upper-secondary stream in Finland can qualify for tertiary education by taking the 'national matriculation examination.' Successful completion of this exam affords entrance into one of Finland's twenty universities or thirty polytechnics.[49] Just as the primary and secondary levels do not require students or parents to pay tuition fees, the tertiary system has no tuition fees, and those who need financial assistance at both the secondary and tertiary levels are eligible. The current polytechnic system was developed in the 1990s, with all of the current schools in operation by 2000. Some polytechnics now offer degrees comparable to master's degrees.[50]

What are the most notable differences in the outcomes of the Finnish system compared to the Canadian one?

First, the dropout rate at the secondary level is lower than in Canada, with 90 per cent of young Finns obtaining secondary qualifications (compare from chapter 2 what the Province of Ontario is doing to hit a target of 85 per cent). About 12 per cent leave vocational schools, but many are simply 'stop-outs' undertaking military service or temporarily doing something else.[51] This lower dropout rate is presumably because more students are involved in educational activities that they find interesting and rewarding, rather than being forced into them, as is the case in Canada and the United States, where these options are not as widely available.

Second, universities are clearly distinguished in their missions from polytechnics. Universities are defined by their 'focus of research and education based on research,'[52] while polytechnics 'train professionals in response to labour market needs and conduct R&D which supports instruction and promotes regional development in particular.'[53] The liberal mission of Finnish universities is kept on track by the National University Act, which specifies that

> universities must promote free research and scientific and artistic education, provide higher education based on research, and educate students to serve their country and humanity. In carrying out this mission, universities must interact with the surrounding society and strengthen the impact of research findings and artistic activities on society.[54]

Thus, the research capacity in the liberal tradition, vital for taking the society and economy into the future, is preserved in Finnish universities, while the immediate labour-market needs of the economy are the focus of polytechnics, as are the earlier-stream vocational and apprenticeship programs. In Canada, these missions have become confused, a conundrum that is being exacerbated as more community colleges across the country are being declared by government fiat to be 'universities.'[55] In turn, liberal pedagogies are being attacked unjustly as not being relevant enough to the job market.

These issues of mission drift are discussed further in the next chapter, where some proposed solutions to student disengagement are considered. However, before moving to a more focused study of student disengagement, it is useful to examine how some people feel they are able to dismiss calls to address the crises experienced by students, faculties, and the system.

Shooting the Messenger

Having clarified the definition of what constitutes a crisis, it is now possible to address several common, but unhelpful, reactions to criticisms of the educational system. These are unhelpful because they are common rhetorical gambits used regardless of the validity of an argument. What they do is deflect a criticism by attacking the critic without engaging the substance of the critique. Generally, the reactions impugn the credibility of the critic as personally biased, and therefore as imagining something that isn't there. These are commonly referred to as ad hominem arguments.

These types of reactions tend to be effective in convincing some of those who already hold positive views of the university system because of what is called 'the confirmation bias.'[56] This bias describes the tendency for people to accept, with little evidence, arguments that confirm their existing beliefs. In contrast, arguments that dispute their existing beliefs are rejected out of hand, or a demand is made for more 'evidence,' far more evidence than would be asked of confirmatory arguments.

Because ad hominem arguments are so common and so readily believed without evidence, they tend to shut down dialogue.[57] It is thus important to identify them and show how they are problematic.

Old-Fogeyism

Perhaps the most common reaction is to dismiss criticism of the university system with the claim that professors have always romanticized the so-called 'good old days' when they were students, when they were engaged, and when they did the right things. Those in denial claim that such professors are to be found in every generation, that their concerns are peculiar to their times, and that they ought not to be taken seriously. The implication is that these criticisms of universities were wrong in the past, and so current ones must also be wrong.

As noted above, books criticizing the university system have a long history, and have taken up a variety of issues, some of which were concerns of the day and some of which are perennial. Yet, solely on the basis of logic, the existence of past critiques does not prove that current criticisms are wrong. Indeed, it is an empirical matter as to whether certain past critiques were wrong on specific factual points, and it is a matter of record how some of these critiques kept the university system on course and corrected mission drifts. It may well be that the higher educational system needs a sort of running critique, so that it improves rather than deteriorates. The preceding section on the Finnish educational system shows the wisdom of this. Remaining open to change and reform is both a political matter of democratic dialogue and a practical matter of institutional reflexivity.[58]

Indeed, Canadian universities have shown institutional reflexivity in the past. For example, a 1957 book titled *Canada's Crisis in Higher Education* published papers from a conference of the same name. The crisis at that time was the urgency of rapidly expanding Canada's university system in the post-war period. In one paper, the president of the University of Toronto wrote:

> There are two watchwords for the universities in the next ten years: flexibility of structure and tenacity of purpose. We must not succumb to what President Harold Dodds of Princeton has called the quantum theory of quality. We cannot meet the country's needs for university graduates by *dropping our standards, taking everyone in and shoving everyone through. That would be simply an attempt to fool ourselves and to cheat the public.* We will have to stand by our standards without standardization, and develop masses of graduates by other than mass-production methods.[59] (Emphasis added)

It appears that solution for the crisis of the 1950s – the urgent need for more universities and increased enrolment – created the crisis that current universities now face, but at the time some foresaw the crisis we now face. But even going back sixty years, one set of concerns remains constant, which – to reiterate the above quote – is that standards must be maintained, not everyone should automatically be admitted to university, and no one should be 'shoved through.'

Other examples could be provided of how crises in higher education have been defined and addressed in the past, but the fact that some educators have voiced complaints in the past on some issue does not prove that current complaints are incorrect, whether on the same or a different issue. Indeed, some past complaints about transformations of the liberal education may well have been correct, especially those made in reaction to the massification and corporatization of contemporary universities, and the drift toward vocationalism. Had they been heeded, the current crisis might have been averted. It appears that these threats to the liberal education have continued over the decades to the point where they have come to a head in terms of widespread entitled disengagement. Accordingly, this type of dismissive reaction is problematic on the basis of logic and ethics.

A variant of this gambit is to claim that adults have always condemned young people, with the implication that any discussion that casts current youth in anything but a positive light continues this form of irrational disapproval. In addition to committing the same logical error, this claim is substantively tenuous. The evidence is usually cherry-picked from surviving written documents, such as those from ancient Greeks like the poet Hesiod or philosopher Plato, but even then, this evidence cannot be taken unproblematically to represent the primary views of these ancients.[60] And even if they could be, such cherry-picked quotations only prove that some evidence can be mustered that some adults at some times have expressed negative views about the 'younger generation' or 'kids these days.' It is implausible that all adults in all eras in all cultures have condemned the moral fibre of young people. Moreover, Hesiod and Plato can hardly be taken as statistically representative of all adults from all times in history in all cultures. Few people throughout history could write, let alone leave documentation of their views. Instead, it is more plausible that inter-generational tensions have ebbed and flowed throughout history among diverse cultures, and that some adults have held more favourable or negative views than others of young people, just as young people have held a variety of views about older people. If the current era is taken as an example, a wide range of opinion about youth can be found, from glorification to vilification.

The curious thing about this rhetorical gambit is that people who would otherwise require rigorous evidence and logic before accepting something as an absolute truth suddenly are willing to accept a claim like this. All the same, it is perhaps expedient for them to do so because they can then feel justified in not pursuing the matter further, and thus not make the effort to adjust their beliefs about the education system and examine their personal stake in holding those beliefs.

Élitism

Some have reacted to the argument that a university education is not for everyone by claiming that it is élitist, apparently believing that the argument is anti-democratic and suggests the endorsement of a de facto hierarchical social system producing first-, second-, and third-class citizens. One response to those who believe that everyone should have a university education is simple, and was noted above: it is élitist of them to believe that those who do not have a university degree are losers or otherwise deficient, as implied by this belief in a 'universal university education.'

There are many other respectable careers that do not, or should not, require liberal arts and science credentials. Furthermore, it is unmerited and irresponsible to disrespect those other careers, which can require talents and ability levels equivalent to those of a good university education.[61]

Chicken Little

Consistent with the social-psychological finding that people do not like negativity, some observers react to critical depictions of institutions as too 'apocalyptic' for their tastes, and charge that these depictions merely represent the negative outlook of the critic.[62] In the case of universities, some people react to criticisms of the system as if critics are predicting impending doom – that the 'sky is falling.' This type of reaction was dealt with in the previous section, where the definitions of various forms of crisis were discussed.

An Imagined Golden Age

Critics of a status quo are also dismissed with an additional gambit, with the defender of the status quo claiming that the critic mistakenly believes that we have left some supposed ideal period to which we must now return.[63] This accusation is so common as to be a cliché, and in the current case is a straw argument – a reconstruction of an argument that presents it in such a weak fashion that it is easily knocked over. We have never claimed there was a Golden Age, but simply that both the content and delivery of a liberal education were better in the past than is now the case. The question of whether the targets (students) of yesteryear were 'better' (by some yet-to-be-specified measure) than those of today is open for debate using empirical evidence.

One implication of the logic of this gambit is that no one can make any comments on potentially negative social change because, unless it can be proved there was 'Golden Age' (whatever that is), there are no reference points to go by. With no reference points, it follows from this logic that anyone who tries to bring some concern to light that does not meet with immediate public approval is to be treated as a Cassandra (whose warnings are to be ignored).

To the extent that attempts to improve social institutions are greeted with this accusation, social change and institutional reform are unnecessarily impeded (in some versions of the mythology, Cassandra's curse was that her *accurate* predictions would always be ignored because she was dismissed as unreliable).

Conclusion: 'Captain, we are off course!' 'Nonsense, you are imagining things.'

The problems facing Canadian universities can be ignored, or they can be deemed important enough to warrant the attention of all educational stakeholders. Attention to these problems – which most observers agree exist – should not be diverted by red herrings and rhetorical gambits, such as whether or not a crisis exists, whether or not there was a Golden Age of 'The University,' or whether the authors have this or that bias. Those who disagree about the nature and severity of these problems should be willing to debate the issues on empirical grounds, not on the basis of irrelevant, ad hominem, or straw arguments.

Debating these issues requires that the parties involved be willing to delve into *all* of the empirical evidence and follow the rules of evidence and logic. Yet those charged with the primary stewardship of the system – administrators and policymakers – apparently prefer preemptory gambits to a thorough examination of all of the evidence. This current moment in the history of the university suggests the analogy of a ship off course. In this case, the deckhands and officers are trying to warn the captain of the ship that they are slowly veering into uncharted waters. But, rather than listen to them and go on deck to see, thereby viewing the situation first-hand, the captain stays below deck looking at charts the shipowners gave him, and calling for more food and ale for himself. He is fine in his cabin, and is lulled by the complacency induced by his preconceptions of the original course and the creature comforts his rank affords him. Meanwhile, the tensions mount among his crew about where they are headed.

5 Students: Is Disengagement Inevitable?

Reactions to evidence of academic disengagement run the gamut, and when taken as a whole are contradictory. Two common reactions are that (1) we all should get used to widespread disengagement because nothing better should be expected from a mass university system; and (2) students have busy lives, and it is unfair to require them to devote more time to their courses. Two other responses contradict these retorts: (1) this is not a characteristic of a *mass* system, but rather has been a feature of *the* university system all along; and (2) there are no disengagement problems at all. Strangely, these claims tend explicitly or implicitly to defend the educational programs condoning disengagement, and as such can be seen as symptomatic of a consensus about the acceptability of a 'lowering of higher education.' Two additional positions also deflect blame from the system: (1) students are smarter today and therefore bored with the old pedagogies; and (2) professors are bad teachers, thereby boring students.

In this chapter, these contradictory claims are sorted out with an examination of the available published empirical evidence, along with a report of the results of our analysis of a data set procured from the NSSE organization. This new data analysis evaluates Canadian/American differences, how much disengagement is 'by necessity' as opposed to 'by choice,' and the relationship between disengagement and academic outcomes.

Get Used to It! It Is Unrealistic to Expect More

Benedikt Hallgrímsson, an associate dean of medicine at the University of Calgary, acknowledges that grade inflation and disengagement are serious problems and that the mass system of higher education has produced them.[1] In his words:

> The real root problem is that we're now teaching a student population that is much more diverse in terms of educational needs and intellectual abilities simply because so many more people now go to university. We in the Ivory Tower have failed miserably to adapt appropriately to this reality, and grade inflation and the disengagement pact that is the subject of the analysis by Drs. Côté and Allahar are simply symptoms of our failure to adapt. The solution, therefore, is not to return grading curves to their state in the 1970s, but to structure our institutions to meet their changing role.

He further argues that 'the rational response is to match the diverse needs of our students with greater diversity in programs and curricula,' including creating two-tiered systems within each university (see chapter 3 for a general discussion of this idea). The top tier would involve

> small 'boutique' undergraduate programs that are selective, challenging and often research-intensive. Several such programs already exist in Canada at the University of Calgary, University of British Columbia and Mc-Master University, among others. Such programs need to be properly resourced and should involve separate sets of small, inquiry-based classes.

The lower tier would, in his words, 'meet the needs of the disengaged majority by providing high quality education at a general level to large numbers of students. Such programs should be focused on achieving a common standard of cultural and technical literacy.' He is not clear how to accomplish 'the task of re-engaging the disengaged student,' except to claim that university professors need to be better teachers. As much as he agrees with our identification of the issues, Hall-grímsson unfortunately misread our book, and believes that we recommended that universities should ruthlessly sort out students:

> Our primary task with these students is not to weed them out from the academic elite and dash their hopes for high level careers, as Drs. Côté and Allahar argue, but rather to provide them with an education commensurate with their abilities that will benefit both them and society.

We do not recommend dashing students' hopes for high-level careers, but do call for providing them with schooling commensurate with their abilities. We see here that Hallgrímsson has confused the ideas of education and training. As we have been at pains to point out, not everyone has the ability to undertake successfully high-level careers. And, by 'high-level careers' he seems to mean fields like his own – medicine. Does he really think that retrained professors could prepare disengaged students for careers in medicine? We think not, so what careers is he referring to that would require a lower-tier bachelor's degree? We think he has the training model in mind when he recommends that 'the renovation required is an expansion of the Tower with many new rooms.' To understand what these 'new rooms' might look like, we can look to an exchange that took place in *Academic Affairs* in 2006-7, which we do in the final chapter, in the section "What Not to Do.'

International Comparisons

Another way to approach this 'inevitability question' is to ask whether the levels of student disengagement observed in Canada and the United States are also found in massified systems in other countries. To answer this question, data from some European studies are examined that have measured students' time use out of class in a comparable way to the NSSE studies.[2] These data come from the Higher Education Policy Institute (HEPI) in Oxford, England.[3]

The HEPI studies, conducted in 2006, 2007, and 2009, found that students in England spent on average about 13 hours per week on 'private study': reading for classes and completing assignments.[4] When added to an average of about 14 hours of class time, the total amount of study time was just over 26 hours, comparable to what Canadian and American students spend according to the NSSE studies – the equivalent of a part-time job (see below in this chapter for more on this).

Study time was also examined in terms of variations among and within universities, with the finding that these averages ranged from under 15 hours per week to over 45 hours at different universities. When different types of programs were examined, it appears that the least effort is put into the liberal arts programs like humanities and social sciences (total time commitments of about 20 hours per week) and the most into professional/vocational programs like medicine and engineering (over 35 hours per week).

However, when compared to other European countries, English students spend on average 15 per cent *less* time on their studies out of class. When time spent in class was added to time preparing for class, students in France spent almost 40 hours per week. Other countries topping 35 hours per week – the equivalent of a full-time job – were Norway, Italy, Germany, Spain, and Switzerland.[5]

After presenting the results for English universities and summarizing these comparisons with other European countries, Bahram Bekhradnia, the HEPI Director, voiced his frustration at how policymakers in England were ignoring these findings, especially the questions raised 'about the possible variation in standards between subjects and universities, and about what it means to have a degree from an English university.'[6] Bekhradnia continued by making the following observations:

> If it is possible to earn a degree in, say, history in one university after studying for just 20 hours a week whereas a student in a different university studying history is required to put in 30 hours each week, then it is reasonable to assume that the student in the latter will, all other things being equal, achieve a higher standard. That is not of course necessarily so. It could be that the former university has found a magic bullet that enables students to achieve the same high standards as a student at the latter – or it could be that the latter is more inefficient than the former. That at least is a matter for investigation and explanation, and so far there has been no apparent inclination on the part of those concerned to investigate whether that is so, and if not, what the implications are for standards in our universities. At the extreme, of course, this may simply be an indication that what students study, and how much they learn, is not the most important thing while they are at university and that the three or four years they spend there are more important for other reasons. If that is the case too, that is something that is worth investigating and concluding on the basis of evidence. What is not acceptable is simply to ignore the issue.

With respect to the unfavourable comparisons of English universities with some continental ones, Bekhradnia concludes 'that students in England appear to devote less time to their studies than students elsewhere in Europe – and that therefore a degree in England can apparently be obtained with less effort than elsewhere.' Given the prospect that English universities 'are not very demanding of their students'[7] – a prospect also faced in Canada and the United States – Bekhradnia contends the following:

> It is inconvenient for us now also to have to demonstrate how students in this country achieve outcomes equivalent to those in other countries

with very different amounts of effort, even within their shorter [3-year] degree courses. It is quite plausible that they might do so, but if the issue is simply ignored, as it has been so far, the presumption will be that degrees in this country are more easily available in some universities and in some subjects than elsewhere in Europe, and that on average our degree standards are lower.

On the positive side, it does appear that some English universities are attending to these problems, but on a negative side, just as in Canada, in England 'the response of the national bodies and those that represent universities collectively has been disappointingly defensive.' Still, the press in England picked up the story, making note of the gender differences, suggesting 'boys are down the pub and the girls are in the library,' as well as the now obvious conclusion that many 'students are enrolled full-time but studying part-time.'[8]

Based on these international comparisons, therefore, it appears that disengagement is not an inevitable result of massification, although it is a distinct possibility if stewards of the system are not watchful. These comparisons of Canada with England, and the issue of stewardship, become relevant again in the final chapter of this book, where the recommendations that Canada imitate the English system are critiqued, especially in its embracing of vocational university educations in its newer 'post-1992' institutions.[9]

Students Have Busy Lives

More than a decade ago, two observers of American higher education noted that about a quarter of students have full-time jobs; consequently, they add, these students 'fit university into their lives, rather than fitting their lives into university.'[10] Just how far has this mentality of 'fitting university in' penetrated the Canadian student body? Some people think it has progressed dramatically, and take this *description* of competing job demands further, turning it into a *prescription*. They actually believe it is unreasonable of educators to expect all students to treat their studies as a full-time endeavour if they have other obligations. The implication is that special accommodation should be made for such students.

While we sympathize with students who feel they have to take on jobs to pay their way through university, or who are caretakers of children or parents, arguments regarding accommodation do not withstand logical scrutiny if the personal and intellectual benefits of a liberal education are viewed as important (as opposed to the university experience culminating in an empty credential, the faux-BA or the BA-lite). Besides, this is what part-time study is intended to address. Holding a full-time job, or even a part-time job requiring long hours, while taking a full course load, is incompatible with benefiting from the transformative effects of a good liberal education, and will likely contribute to further student disengagement and increased teacher stress. Not to recognize this simply confuses the outcome (the baccalaureate) with the process (personal and intellectual transformations). The BA may currently have enough cachet for other post-secondary programs to seek its designation as the 'prize' of their programs, but this will not last long if the public discovers the transformative benefits are lost. This form of credentialism is simply a race to the bottom.

A 'BA-lite' awarded to students who put out little effort, whatever the reason for that low effort – whether it is by necessity or choice – will not magically produce the transformations associated with a deep involvement in academic studies. Those who champion students from disadvantaged backgrounds, for whom they see a university education as an opportunity for upward mobility, need to take stock of this point. Simply handing someone a credential, without the personal and intellectual resources to back it, is to shortchange that person. To add insult to injury, many students from disadvantaged backgrounds have to go deeply into debt to acquire a university credential – in stark contrast to those from advantaged backgrounds. The system is cheating these students (now called first-generation students) if it simply cheers them through four years of BA-lite courses without providing experiences to transform them in ways that might actually produce and sustain the personal and intellectual resources that they could use to strive for upward mobility.

This 'students-are-too-busy-to-learn' argument also demeans the value of the liberal education. Would those who recommend handing off BA-lites to all comers feel as comfortable flying in an airplane with a pilot who cut corners in learning how to fly because she was too busy with extracurricular activities? Would they feel confident with a doctor who skimmed medical texts and crammed for exams while holding down a job so that she would not finish medical school in debt? Would they like to be defended by a lawyer who scraped through law school because taking care of his children took precedence over completing required readings, or driving over a bridge built by an engineer who barely passed his courses because he was the captain of the hockey team? We think not.

Because this 'disengagement-by-necessity' argument seems to be a sticking point for many people, an analysis was undertaken of a data set purchased by us from the Indiana University Center for Postsecondary Research, which administers the NSSE. This analysis rigorously examined this issue of 'disengagement by necessity' (versus 'disengagement by choice') based on a sample of 12,000 Canadian and American students. The results are reported in the latter half of this chapter.

It's Always Been Like This: Historical Considerations

Some people appear to believe that it has always been a norm for university students to be disengaged.[11] Clearly, in the past there have been some minimally engaged students, especially from wealthy backgrounds, for whom the 'gentleman's C' of a bygone era sufficed to keep their bill-paying parents happy. But, they did not expect more in terms of grades and therefore did not have a disengagement compact with professors; nor did they have a sense of entitled disengagement. They simply blended in and did not affect standards in the system. To claim that universities have condoned academic disengagement as a norm is to suggest that higher education has been a fraud for centuries, but most people would not argue this, nor does it withstand empirical scrutiny.

Although there is a shortage of historical research on the topic of student engagement, two sources shed light on this issue. The first is a recent study tracing quantitative surveys of 'study time' back to the 1960s and 1920s,[12] while the second is the book *Campus Life*, which traces the evolution of undergraduate student life in the United States from the eighteenth century up to the time of its publication in the late 1980s.[13]

The first source traces student 'study time' using the recent NSSE surveys, and other large sample sources (NLSY79, 1981; HERI, 1988, 2004), along with data from the 1960s (Project Talent, 1961), showing a very obvious linear decline in student effort. Over that time, full-time students have apparently gone from treating university as a 'full-time job' in the 1960s, involving about 40 hours per week (study time of 25 hours plus class time of 15 hours), to a part-time job in the 2000s, involving about 27 hours per week for study and class time combined. Studies using other methods confirm this trend but extend it back to the 1920s, showing a consistent trend for full-time students to treat university as a full-time job between the 1920s and 1960s, followed by a linear reduction in academic effort from the 1960s to the 2000s.

The authors of this report controlled for a number of factors other than student effort that might have produced these results. For example, they examined 'framing effects' (how the question is worded), whether the definition of 'full-time' student has changed, as well as 'composition' effects. For this latter effect, they examined the possibility that only certain types of students have become less engaged, a favourite argument among those who believe that rising tuition costs have made it necessary for more students to work at outside jobs. However, they found that all types of students have been putting increasingly less effort into their studies since the 1960s to bring us to the new norm of university as a part-time activity:

> No group appears to have bucked the trend. Study times declined overall ... for every subgroup. Working students studied less than others, but study hours fell for students in each category of work intensity, including those who did not work at all. Students with more educated fathers studied more than others; however, study times declined for students in all parental education categories. Similarly, study times declined for all race and gender categories ... Interestingly, women used to study about the same amount as men, but study more than men in recent cohorts. Engineering students studied more than other students and the gap has widened. Study times fell for all choices of major ... Students at liberal arts colleges studied more than other students, but study times fell at all types of colleges ... Lastly, data on SAT scores and school size, available for the later sub-period, show declines in study time for students of all ability levels, and at universities of all sizes and levels of selectivity.[14]

The second source is a social-historical account written in the 1980s by historian Helen Lefkowitz Horowitz, who argues that three distinct undergraduate cultures emerged at different points in the history of American universities. This book provides us with some useful insights into the relationships between students and professors in different eras and their implications for student disengagement that also apply to Canadian universities.

The first undergraduate culture emerged from the expansion of American universities during the 1800s, which depended on the ability of these schools to attract the children of *nouveau riche* parents whose wealth was derived from Southern plantations, mercantile trade, and Northern industrialism. Horowitz calls the culture that emerged through an accommodation of universities with the desires of these young students from affluent backgrounds the 'collegiate culture.' Before this time, those intending to become ministers dominated universities, and they took their studies very seriously. For the sake of sufficient enrolments, and thus their survival, universities of this era played into university attendance as a symbol of social privilege and as a way to help students sustain that privilege by making the appropriate contacts for a future career and marriage. The collegiate culture represented a level of academic engagement that was sufficient to keep both professors and parents happy, along with extracurricular activities and entertainments sufficient to keep students happy. Student resistance to institutional academic norms tended to be implicit and to be kept outside of the classroom. Achievement among students varied mainly in terms of the academic abilities and interests that students brought with them to their undergraduate programs, but the collegiate culture eschewed an obsession with high grades and pleasing professor's demands for excellence.

The second culture, which Horowitz calls the 'outsider culture,' represented those who attended university as a means of upward mobility, beginning in the early twentieth century. These students, who did not have the advantages afforded by wealthy parents, sought to compensate for this by forming close relationships with faculty members and using the university as a stepping-stone to a career at a higher level of status than that of their parents. Horowitz called these students 'outsiders' (to collegiate culture) because they embraced the institutional academic culture rather than eschewing it. Their attitudes and work habits were similar to those who attended because of clerical aspirations, but they quickly outnumbered the clerics-in-training as their ranks included women, minorities (including Jews), and veterans.

The third culture, the 'rebel culture,' also appeared on American campuses in the early twentieth century, and was created by students who valued intellectuality, bohemianism, and a general trade in radical ideas. Horowitz includes people like Walter Lippmann and Margaret Mead in this group of students. Although hard-working, these students were not concerned with grades so much as social justice, and could be as hedonist as the collegiate student, while wanting to play a role in university governance. In spite of this influence, Horowitz argues that the outsider culture eventually came to dominate American campuses as the importance of university credentials spread in terms of gaining access to professional schools and the business world.

Horowitz makes reference to several historically specific norms in these cultures that provide us with a sense of contrast with contemporary university life.

For example, with respect to the norms concerning grades, in one era (the mid-1800s) cheating was considered to be acceptable if it was necessary for a student to stay in school, but it was done on the part of strong students to help weaker students who were at risk of failing. In fact, if a student refused to help a weaker student, it was considered a sign of dishonour. Moreover, it was considered unacceptable for a good student to cheat to better his or her own grades.

In addition, the pressures that contributed to grade inflation apparently began in the 1920s as more students – outsiders – attended universities as an avenue of social mobility. Prior to this, simply passing a course of studies was normally considered sufficient to qualify for post-graduate or professional schools, or entry into the workplace. However, as enrolments increased, so did competition for placements, and grades were increasingly used as a sorting mechanism. This grade-inflation pressure was renewed in the 1970s and 1980s, as more and more students were encouraged through government policies to attain university-level credentials as a means of occupational entry. Horowitz referred to these students as the 'new outsiders' and 'grinds,' and she argues that they came to dominate undergraduate culture, competing with each other for high grades and degrading the sense of common community that had defined campus life in previous eras.

The history of engagement follows a similar pattern. The wealthy collegiate students of the 1800s engaged in a certain amount of distancing from the 'good student' role, maintaining an air of detachment from academic achievement. The 'gentleman's C' is the legacy of this attitude. Later, the outsiders were disdained as 'brown-nosers' because of their hard work in pursuit of high grades.

Extrapolating from these historical trends, since the 1980s it appears that a new student culture has emerged, which we have referred to as a culture institutionalizing a norm of *entitled disengagement*. In no previous era did high levels of disengagement coincide with extreme pressure to attain high grades, as is the case in the current era. This historical evidence supports the argument that disengagement in conjunction with expectations for high grades – entitled disengagement – is a part of a rising tide best described as a *culture of disengagement*.

It therefore appears that this culture of disengagement is coming to dominate many universities, pushing out the 'outsider' culture that Horowitz argues dominated universities of the mid-twentieth century.

This latest historical development is traceable to circumstances unique to the present era of superficial calls for democratization, whereby large numbers of unprepared students from all social classes have been funnelled into universities with the expectation that simply paying tuition and putting out a minimal effort will have a maximal payoff in terms of grade attainment and eventual occupational success. Unlike the past, when those seeking upward mobility did not take for granted their chances of success and therefore valued hard work, those with a sense of entitled disengagement apparently feel that the path has been opened for them and they simply have to follow it.

Finally, apart from this historical perspective, the charge that the current levels of disengagement are justified by the norms established by the children of the wealthy of past generations ignores the fact that a solid education did not likely matter to the future of wealthy students of past eras. Those who would go into the family business, whether mercantile, industrial, or agrarian, or live off a trust, had little stake in the outcome of their undergraduate experience.

In the current era, things are quite different, and a solid education is important for all students, not only those who do not have the benefit of parental patronage, but also for those who do. On the one hand, for those from more affluent backgrounds, it is less common for them to move into a family business (fewer wealthy parents actually own a business enterprise, but instead are employees of corporations that want competent recruits), so that the quality of the credentials these students receive has more of an impact on their occupational attainment. On the other hand, those from less affluent backgrounds are dependent more than ever on the quality of their credentials because of the extreme competitiveness in graduate-employment opportunities, and so more than ever these students need a high-quality education. Whatever might have prevailed in universities of the past is irrelevant to the universities of the future.

There Are No Disengagement Problems

This critique is an outlier that appears to be more epistemological and political than fact-based. One critic rejects the validity of quantitative research in general and thus feels justified in rejecting the findings from studies like the NSSE.[15] An epistemological divide like this cannot be bridged; instead, readers need to judge this critique from the weight of the evidence, including the wealth of *qualitative* evidence, as in the above historical analysis.

Some other critics, who are mainly university administrators, deny that there is any disengagement at their particular schools. Presumably this is a political statement required by their role as public-relations personnel, but this critique will be left with readers to judge for themselves as well. Such statements may seem more defensible in some of the smaller American liberal-arts schools, especially those with a religious affiliation.[16] In this context, we remind readers of Alan Slavin, the physics professor at Trent University, who found from his own research that disengagement is a serious problem among an increasing number of students taking his courses in one of Canada's smaller universities.

Students Are Smarter Now and Just Bored

Some academics have been arguing that people have been 'getting smarter' over the past few decades, and that this change is most noticeable among young people.[17] This notion resonates with those who think that the current system is working just fine, as well as with those who believe that a new generation of 'digital natives' is passing through today's schools, with the implication that those teaching them need to make adjustments to accommodate 'smarter,' more 'savvy' students.[18]

This argument is based on the so-called 'Flynn effect,' named after the psychologist who found that scores on IQ tests increased during the twentieth century.[19] These increases in scores on IQ tests have been found in many countries, so that the 'numbers are there,' as some would say. The problem is with just what the numbers represent, and this is where the consensus ends. We do not want to get sidetracked by the many facets of this debate, but there are numerous reasons for skepticism regarding claims that a monumental shift in human intelligence has taken place, including the fact that IQ scores are affected by numerous factors unrelated to the underlying construct of intelligence (culture, practice with tests, etc.) and that IQ tests have been re-normed since their inception to keep up with the changing knowledge-base in the population (and test scores are weighted so that women do not score lower than men).

The fact is that Flynn himself makes no claims that general intelligence has increased. Rather, the content of questions on IQ tests reflects the general knowledge-orientation of the period in which they were devised, and as more people in the population gain more knowledge in a given area, more people can solve the problems posed by IQ-test items from memory rather than from any innate problem-solving abilities that psychologists call intelligence.[20]

In the view of Malcolm Gladwell, when the logic used by some people in their misunderstanding of the Flynn effect is extended, some ludicrous implications are created about the intelligence of our ancestors and descendants:

> If an American born in the nineteen-thirties has an I.Q. of 100, the Flynn effect says that his children will have I.Q.s of 108, and his grandchildren I.Q.s of close to 120 – more than a standard deviation higher. If we work in the opposite direction, the typical teen-ager of today, with an I.Q. of 100, would have had grandparents with average I.Q.s of 82 – seemingly below the threshold necessary to graduate from high school. And, if we go back even farther, the Flynn effect puts the average I.Q.s of the schoolchildren of 1900 at around 70, which is to suggest, bizarrely, that a century ago the United States was populated largely by people who today would be considered mentally retarded.[21]

At the same time, more recent analyses of IQ test scores suggest that the Flynn effect stalled in the mid-1990s and may even be reversing. Recent evidence from the United Kingdom suggests that IQ scores have dropped between two and six points among British teens, and the finger is being pointed at a dumbed-down youth culture there, exacerbated by less reading and a recent reliance on text-messaging and e-mailing, which apparently require less concentration than other forms of communication.[22]

In short, interpreting whatever might be going on with IQ test scores appears to be a mug's game, but the idea that the general intelligence level of our species has changed is, well, specious.

Thus, while it might be comforting to think that some sort of evolution in human mental capacities is taking place, when applied to educational settings the argument produces discomfort. For example, explaining grade inflation with this claim that 'kids are smarter now' is illogical if we follow the arguments presented above in chapter 3 in the discussion of grading norms. That is, even if students were smarter now than in the past, the reference point should not be the past, but the present. In other words, these ostensibly smarter students should still be graded among themselves in terms of at least the four categories of outstanding, very good, good or average, and below average. Higher grades would only mean that the standards are set too low for this reference group. Indeed, the 'students are smarter' argument can be turned on its head by asserting that many students are bored because standards are too low and high grades are too easily awarded.

Furthermore, the claim that the currently higher grades are produced by smarter students is contradicted by various forms of evidence that compares current scores on substantive tests in math, chemistry, and physics (also mentioned in chapter 3) with past scores on those same tests, which find an F average for current students, whereas the students from a couple of decades ago earned a C average. Indeed, the weight of the evidence is that curriculum is being dumbed down, not 'smarted up.'

An additional explanation for why students express a sense of boredom with schools is that this has always been the case for most students, especially among those who are not academically inclined. As argued by the cognitive psychologist Daniel Willingham,[23] many students do not like school for very predictable reasons that apply to people of all ages, and this is nothing new. Willingham argues that people in general are not 'good thinkers' when it comes to new information. We all prefer to rely on our memory of what we already know instead of making the mental effort to incorporate new information into our mental representations of the world (psychologists refer to people in general as 'cognitive misers' – we would rather explain things with what we already know than spend the time and effort to learn new things).[24] This tendency helps explain not only why students 'don't like school,' but also the reports that students would rather 'co-construct' information with teachers than take lessons from them. Co-constructing allows students to use their memory repertoires more.

Willingham also provides a number of other insights that help us retain a healthy skepticism concerning claims regarding 'new students' in today's schools and help us to keep a focus on the importance of insisting on effort over enabling students to feel justified in slacking off:

- 'Distinct' learning styles do not exist.
  - Students are more similar than different.
- Factual knowledge precedes critical thinking.
  - Proficiency requires practice.

Professors Are Bad Teachers: It's Their Fault

As noted above, some people are pointing fingers at professors as being responsible for student disengagement.[25] To the extent that professors who partake in the disengagement compact do contribute to this problem, this is only a partial explanation and speaks more to the consequences of the crisis in contemporary universities than to the roots of that crisis.

As argued above in chapter 3, for a liberal-learning environment to have a transformative effect, professors need to be met halfway by students as part of the 'bilateral contract.' Anything less than this lowers this form of higher education, reducing its transformative effects: learning that takes place only in the classroom is the 'tip of the iceberg' of learning, especially respecting the various writing, oral, and critical thinking skills, which require independent and repeated practice. Universities that now require only classroom instruction of their students, with little or no class preparation, are little more than glorified grade schools when compared to what they could be.

This claim that bad teachers are responsible for student disengagement can be evaluated by revisiting 'the idea of the university,' its place in society, and the place of teachers and students within it. When this is done, it seems as though so much has changed that we must start from square one all over again. For along with the fact that the university is today seen increasingly as preparing young people for jobs rather than immersing them in its liberal potentials, many students now expect different things from their professors and tend to have few or no demands of themselves. Yet, empowered by the gains of political correctness and being steeped in a culture of entitlement, the aims and ambitions of many such students are no longer seriously questioned by teachers and administrators. Indeed, one hears less about the lack of preparedness of such students and more about students having different 'learning styles' and it being the responsibility of the teacher/professor to cater to those differences.

So, as the tail has come to wag the dog, Kathleen Gabriel has written a book on higher education entitled *Teaching Unprepared Students*.[26] Nowhere in this book does it occur to her that the unprepared student is by definition not ready to be there in the first place. When higher education becomes a right with few, if any, responsibilities, the unprepared must be accommodated, for that is supposedly the democratic way. And in a curious reversal of the old trend, it is increasingly left to the teacher or professor to 'prepare' the student for learning, and in such a schema, it is the professor, not the student, who is at risk of failing. What, then, one may ask rhetorically, is the role of the high-school teacher who has certified these students as prepared for higher studies? With all the literacy *support* teachers and reading *support* teachers in high schools, one might ask what exactly do teachers themselves do? Why do they need all this support? And what did they do before they had it?

Another recent book raises similar questions about the competence of professors. In *What the Best College Teachers Do*,[27] Ken Bain attempts to do what is almost impossible: find a formula for identifying what he calls 'the best' teachers, or what we would prefer to call 'the most effective' teachers. The latter can be understood as those teachers who are able to get students' attention, communicate the message clearly and crisply, and then have the students integrate the learned message into their own world view. Outstanding communicators – those whose messages resonate and remain with the listeners – cannot be reduced to a formula.

Of course, there are good professors/communicators who can get the message across, but the difference is that the message may not go as far and cause students to accommodate a given subject into their pre-existing mental schemas. It does not have to be an earth-shattering, eureka moment, but at least one that resonates with students and remains with them beyond the exam or the semester. It is aimed at elevating understanding over memorization, and serves to transform learners in a meaningful way and move them up a learning curve.

The big question, then, is 'Are effective teachers born or made?' Bain argues for the latter, while lamenting that outstanding teachers are not sufficiently rewarded by the system. So, as they come and go, few traces of their talent and prowess remain. He writes:

> Great teachers emerge, they touch the lives of their students, and perhaps only through some of those students do they have any influence on the broad art of teaching. For the most part, their insights die with them, and subsequent generations must discover anew the wisdom that drove their practices. At best, some fragment of their talent endures, broken pieces on which later generations will perch without realizing the full measure of the ancient wealth beneath them.[28]

It almost seems that finding a solution to prevent the loss of this wealth is what energizes his quest for the formula for great teaching. But in the quest, he makes many unwarranted assumptions. What Bain has in mind is the small school where classes are small; no students and professors are disengaged; administrators are concerned with education and not the bottom line; and the time demands of research and publication are minimal. These are huge assumptions that eliminate most universities in Canada from consideration.

In place of these idealized conditions, what follows are some important points about effective university teaching that we think should be borne in mind.

While Bain has unpacked some of what makes for an effective professor in the classroom, we find that an effective professor needs to do a lot of work outside of the classroom too. Clearly, classroom lectures are important for priming the students, but the engaged ones will come to professors' offices or will be spotted by professors and invited to come. Indeed, some of the most transformative learning can take place during office hours; it is more direct and one-to-one. Once in the office, anonymity is taken away, and the student must be an active contributor to a conversation. Hiding behind the laptop screen in the back row is no longer an option. And this experience is particularly gratifying because it treats teaching and learning as a two-way street.

The effective professor also learns from interacting with students in this way and can incorporate information thus gleaned into her or his lectures, to be more current with examples that combat some of the alienation felt by students that comes with age differences, and to make the crucial link between theoretical insights and empirical reality as defined by the student. In the end, professors need to prepare students for the question that really matters: what did they learn in this course, and how might it affect the way in which they view the world? The ability of the student to articulate an answer to this question in sophisticated language, and even to incorporate a philosophical, moral-ethical, or epistemically refined strand of thought, will tell the effective teacher whether she or he has indeed reached the target.

Variation in Disengagement: New Empirical Evidence

Academic Disengagement: Necessity or Choice?

The NSSE is currently the gold standard for monitoring the state of higher education in terms of several facets of academic engagement. While there is widespread recognition that disengagement is a serious problem in certain programs, as noted above, some observers argue that disengagement should be viewed in different ways, depending on the reasons for the disengagement. These observers argue that much effort-based disengagement is a matter of necessity, arising from the following competing time-demands: (a) many students have to work to pay for their education; (b) some students have family obligations, as in the case of single mothers; and (c) most students have multiple demands on their time in terms other aspects of the collegiate experience, such as co-curricular athletics and clubs.

While these alternative time-demands are legitimate in their own right, it is not clear that they inevitably lead to lower levels of academic effort or performance. It is also not clear how the undergraduate curriculum, especially in the liberal arts and sciences, should accommodate the diminished ability of such students to meet its challenges. For example, as noted above, while most people would not endorse students taking shortcuts in learning how to fly airplanes or practise medicine, many people apparently do not think it is a problem if corners are cut in a liberal education.

In addition, the percentage of students without these alternative time-demands who put little effort into their studies has not been documented. Nor have activities been documented, for disengaged students without alternative time-demands, that are filling the time they would otherwise spend on studying and attending classes.

Because little is currently published in the peer-reviewed literature to address the issue of disengagement by 'choice or necessity,'[29] we procured a data set specifically developed for us from the Indiana University Center for Postsecondary Research.[30] In order to assess the possible role played by school size in enabling disengagement, and to make comparisons between Canadian and American schools of comparable size, we requested a data set that allows for a rigorous examination of the possible correlates of disengagement among small, medium, and large universities in both Canada and the United States.[31] With this data set, we explored the following research questions:[32]

- *Country and school size differences in disengagement*: Do Canadian and American universities differ in terms of the percentage of disengaged students, and are there within-country variations in terms of school size?
- *Disengagement by necessity*: How much time do alternative time-demands 'of necessity' take away from the hours that would be spent preparing for classes?
- *Disengagement by choice*: How much time does socializing take away from the hours that would be spent preparing for classes?
- *The impact of disengagement on academic performance*: How much does academic disengagement affect grade attainment and personal/intellectual development?

Before examining these research questions, a few words are first in order about how to operationalize academic engagement and then about how to interpret the statistical procedures we used in analysing the NSSE data.

Operationalizing academic engagement. The most common effort-based measure of engagement (which we will simply call 'course engagement') is a single question asking students how many hours per week they spend outside of classes on all aspects of class preparation and course completion ('Hours per 7-day week spent preparing for class [studying, reading, writing, doing homework or lab work, analyzing data, rehearsing, and other academic activities].') The NSSE question provides, in addition to a '0 hr/wk' and a '30+ hr/wk' option, six categories with five-hour increments ranging from '1–5' to '26–30' hours per week. Consistent with other characterizations of course engagement levels, we classify those reporting 10 hours or less as 'disengaged,' while those reporting 11–25 hours are considered 'partially engaged.' Those putting in more than 25 hours are coded as 'engaged.'[33]

One logic behind this classification system comes from the 'two-hour rule' mentioned above in chapter 3 – namely, that students should put in two hours of effort for every one hour of class in a course to fully engage themselves.[34] With most courses having three hours of class time per week, students should put in about six hours per class. Accordingly, with a full load of five courses, they should spend some twenty-six or more hours per week engaged *out of class* in their courses.

A more commonsensical logic behind this classification is that the total amount of time spent by full-time students should amount to a full-time job, such that class hours plus study hours approximate 40 hours per week. If an institution is requiring less of its students, it is enabling disengagement; if students put in less than this amount of time, they are squandering the opportunity to benefit fully from the transformative potential of the university experience.

Much of the publicity about the NSSE concerns five benchmarks made up of multiple questions that are added together to give a single score. These benchmarks represent varying degrees and types of person-context interactions – how much the academic environment requires or provides opportunities for involvements, as well as how much effort students expend in these environments. These benchmarks are thus neither pure indicators of how engaging schools are, nor how engaged students are, but a mixture of these in terms of five factors: level of academic challenge, active and collaborative learning, student-faculty interaction, enriching educational experiences, and supportive campus environment.

These benchmarks correlate moderately with each other (the correlations are in the magnitude of about .30 to .60 in our sample), but only academic challenge correlates at this level (+.48) with the course engagement question that is the focus of this section (in part because course engagement is one of the items in the academic challenge benchmark).[35] The other benchmarks correlate at a much lower level (.07–.14) with course engagement, and this correlation does not increase if only senior students are examined, suggesting that the activities making up these scales measure factors that are distinct in important ways from the amount of effort students put into their courses. For example, the amount of student-faculty interaction apparently has little to do with course engagement.[36] For this reason, we use the more direct measure of effort represented by the question on course engagement.

A primer on evaluating statistical associations. One important use of social statistics involves tests that assess the potential relationships among variables. Before presenting our findings, it is useful to give readers a quick lesson on how to understand these types of statistical tests.

In many of the social sciences, studies use relatively small samples as a basis for approximating and therefore generalizing about the population of interest (e.g., university students, voters, Canadians, etc.). In doing so, social scientists use additional tests that estimate the probability that they are making errors in generalizing from the sample to the population. These tests produce probability levels, also referred to as significance levels, of '5 per cent,' for example. When probability levels less than 5 per cent are found, the conclusion can be made that the relationship is 'significant,' in the sense that the observed relationship has less than a 5 per cent probability of being due to chance and a 95 per cent chance that it is 'real' in the population.

However, our sample is so large (12,000 cases) that it has the statistical characteristics of a 'population,' so that the use of probability levels would be misleading in assessing the importance of relationships among variables. With a sample this large, most statistical tests will show significant probability levels, even though the strength of associations may be quite weak and therefore provide little in the way of explanation. In other words, if probability levels were used, it would appear that almost everything is important, even though the strength of the relationship is so weak that one variable does not explain much in another variable, and the relationship in question is trivial. Consequently, tests that assess the *strength* of statistical relationships are utilized below rather than *probability levels*.

Table 5.1
Rule-of-thumb coefficients for interpreting the strength of associations and differences between variables

Effect size	Correlations (r)	Differences between percentages (h)	Differences between means (d)
Trivial	<.10	<.20	<.20
Small	.10	.20	.20
Medium	.30	.50	.50
Large	.50	.80	.80

The tests of the strength of relationships involve the calculation of 'effect sizes.' Effect sizes signify something about the magnitude of the relationship between two variables – whether it be how similar they are or how different they are – rather than whether there is simply a 'relationship' that might be very weak and of little practical value in using scores from one variable to predict scores in another variable. Following Cohen,[37] several rules of thumb can be used in interpreting effect sizes, the calculation of which takes into account (a) the strength of correlations between two variables, (b) proportional differences between percentages, or (c) the magnitude of the mean differences among groups. Effect sizes are considered small, medium, and large. Small effect sizes are not of much substantive importance, while large ones are of considerable importance. Those effects below 'small' are considered trivial. More concretely, if one where to view on paper the actual distribution of responses for two variables, the relationship pattern for a small effect size would hardly be visible, while for the medium effect size the pattern would be observable to the naked eye, and for the large effect size the relationship would be plainly obvious.

Table 5.1 shows the effect size cut-offs proposed by Cohen for the statistical procedures used below. In the description of the data analysis to follow, more details are given about how to interpret the results for the first few sets of findings (e.g., the margins of errors for percentages, and differences between group means), but to avoid repetition only effect sizes are mentioned in subsequent descriptions.

Country and School-Size Differences in Disengagement

The NSSE data set provides equal numbers of students from Canadian and American universities: 6,000 randomly sampled students from the

Figure 5.1 Course engagement categories in Canadian and American universities: percentages

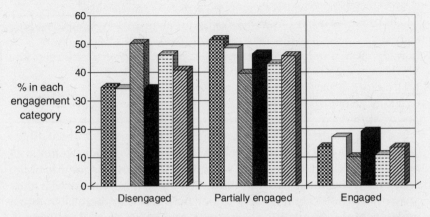

⊠Large - US □Large - CN ◫Medium - US ■Medium - CN ⊟Small - US ▨Small - CN

2006 NSSE data collection from each country, for a total of 12,000 cases. In this sample, three school sizes compatible with the classifications used in the *Maclean's* magazine rankings were equally represented (2,000 students each). Canadian institutions were classified into three groups: 'Small Primarily Undergraduate' (<10K), 'Medium to Large Comprehensive' (>10K to <20K), and 'Large Medical/Doctoral' (>20K). American institutions were classified using the American Carnegie classifications that come closest to the above Canadian classifications: Bac-Div, Bac-A&S, & Masters-S (<10K), DRU-H & DRU (>10K to <20K), and DRU-VH (>20K).

Figure 5.1 compares engagement levels among the three sizes of universities in Canada and the United States for full-time students (all of the results reported below are for full-time students only).[38] The distributions of the three categories of engagement correspond with previous reports of NSSE results. But what is remarkable, albeit now taken for granted by those familiar with the NSSE results, is that the percentage of disengaged students is between two to five times greater than that of engaged students, depending on the category of country/school size. Understandably, many in the general public would assume that these distributions would be reversed and that disengaged students would constitute the smallest category of students, explainable in terms of an inevitable misdirection that a few people experience in their youth. Instead, those treating their studies as a full-time job – engaged students – are the clear minority in contemporary universities, an apparent change from the historical norms examined earlier in this chapter.

A number of other observations are noteworthy in the distributions shown in figure 5.1. First, not taking into account school size, proportionally more Canadian students report course engagement levels of 26 hours or more (16.6 per cent) than American students (11.7 per cent), while more American students report engagement levels of 10 hours or less (43.2 per cent) than Canadian students (36.5 per cent). However, group differences of this magnitude (about 5 to 7 per cent) have trivial effect sizes (h ranges from .12 to .14). Still, these findings of trivial difference between the two counties add a new dimension to the commonly reported results that Canadian universities score lower than American ones on the five benchmark scores.

Second, not taking into account country, the effect size differences among schools of different sizes range from trivial to small. For example, although some 12 per cent of students are classified as fully engaged in small schools, about 15 per cent of students are thus classified in large schools (a trivial effect size; $h = .09$). And, some 44 per cent of students are classified as disengaged in small schools, while 34 per cent of students are so classified in large schools, amounting to a small effect size ($h = .20$). These findings run counter to the common assumption that students in larger schools expend less effort because faculty members are busier with research, or because class sizes are bigger.[39] In other words, the results do not support the assumptions that smaller schools are more demanding of students and that engaged students self-select into small schools.

And, third, as noted, Canadian and American universities show similar patterns in the distributions of the three types of student engagement, with 34 to 50 per cent expending 10 hours or fewer, and 10 to 19 per cent expending 26 or more hours in both countries. Notably, the categories of disengagement and engagement do not even come close to overlapping, even when different sizes of schools in the two countries are examined.[40] The greatest difference is in medium-sized American schools, where 50.3 per cent are classified as disengaged but only 10.2 per cent are classified as engaged (a large effect size; $h = .93$).

Disengagement by Necessity

In addition to the question about course engagement, the NSSE survey asks several questions regarding how students spend their time:

- Hours per 7-day week spent providing care for dependants living with you (parents, children, spouse, etc.)
- Hours per 7-day week spent participating in co-curricular activities (organizations, campus publications, student government, fraternity or sorority, intercollegiate or intramural sports, etc.)
- Hours per 7-day week spent commuting to class (driving, walking, etc.)
- Hours per 7-day week spent working for pay ON CAMPUS
- Hours per 7-day week spent working for pay OFF CAMPUS
- Hours per 7-day week spent relaxing and socializing (watching TV, partying, etc.)[41]

If course disengagement 'by necessity' is caused by a 'displacement effect' of the other activities taking up students' time, there should be *at least a medium effect size* between course engagement and time spent on these other activities. In addition to examining correlations between these variables, comparisons can be made between groups that did or did not work on or off campus, care for others, commute, or engage in co-curricular activities. As we see, for both types of analyses (correlational and group comparison), there is little evidence that these other activities exert anything more than a small effect on the time spent by students on their studies. In fact, there is some surprising evidence in the direction of otherwise busy students putting *more time* into their studies.

Caring for dependants. The correlation between caring for dependants and course engagement shows a trivial effect size for the whole sample, and for the country subsamples ($r < .10$). Yet, contrary to the 'disengagement by necessity' argument, when only those who report caring for others are included in the analysis (3,458 cases, or 31.1 per cent of the sample), the effect size goes from trivial to small for American students ($r = +15$).[42] Because the correlation is positive, the results suggest that many of those caring for dependants *put more time* into their courses out of class.

A shift from the correlational approach to the group-comparison approach shows much the same thing. Although the effect-size is trivial in terms of the difference in course engagement when those who report caring for others are compared with those who report not doing so, the direction of differences in the means of the groups confirms the above positive correlations, suggesting that those who have care-based activities have a slight tendency to be more course engaged.

Thus, there is at best a small effect size between care-based responsibilities and course engagement, and contrary to the displacement-effect hypothesis, it appears that students with these obligations may have a slight tendency to be more engaged in their studies.

Co-curricular activities and commuting. When examining these variables, similar results are obtained to the above care-based activities: there is a positive relationship with engagement, but the effect size is trivial.[43] In other words, there is a very minor tendency toward lower engagement levels among those living in residence (on campus, and therefore not commuting) and not undertaking co-curricular activities (again contrary to the displacement-effect hypothesis).

Working on campus. Again, these findings run counter to the 'disengagement by necessity' thesis, with a trivial effect size.[44] Rather than taking time away from their studies, there may be a very minor tendency for on-campus jobs to enhance students' academic interest or, vice versa, for more academically motivated students to seek work experiences that enhance their educational experiences.

Only two of the activities measured by the NSSE show negative relationships with course engagement: work off campus and socializing. We treat one as a potential factor in 'disengagement by necessity' and the other as a factor in 'disengagement by choice.'

Working off campus. To begin, it must be stressed that only 38.4 per cent of full-time students reported working off campus, and only 12.4 per cent worked more than 20 hours per week. When the analysis is limited to this subsample of working students, the effect size is trivial ($r = -.09$), but the negative correlation is in the direction that corresponds with the 'disengagement by necessity' hypothesis. If all full-time students are included in the correlational analysis, a small effect size is found ($r = -.12$), but this is a questionable statistic given the uneven (non-normal) distribution of this variable (i.e., when all students are included, the category for '0' has 5,700 cases, while the other categories have only a few hundred each).[45]

Shifting from the correlational approach to the group-comparison approach confirms this tenuous evidence that working off campus seriously cuts into study time. Figure 5.2 plots the mean hours worked (along with the number of hours spent socializing, discussed below) against the amount of time spent studying. Along the X axis, this figure shows the number of hours per week spent working (and socializing). Along the Y axis is the amount of time spent studying out of class, where '3' equates to 6 to 10 hours, '4' to 11 to 15 hours, and '5' to 16 to 20 hours. As one would expect, those who do not work report doing

Figure 5.2 Course engagement by working and socializing

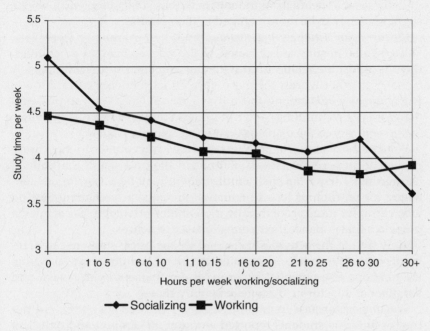

the most studying, with a mean score of 4.47, or about 12–13 hours per week. Following the data points in figure 5.2, the downward trend in study time is evident, but the slope is gradual, with the lowest level at 26 to 30 hours of work, where the mean is 3.83. However, the difference between the highest and lowest means is a small effect size ($d = .37$),[46] amounting to a 3-hours-per-week difference between those who do not work and those who work 26 or more hours.

Contrary to what many people seem to think, it appears that the substantive effect size of working off campus on course engagement is small, and not proportionate to the number of hours worked off campus, so that this 'disengagement by necessity' explanation does not carry weight as an explanation for the levels of disengagement uncovered by the NSSE. There is certainly no reason for us to throw up our hands and say that academic disengagement is inevitable as long as students feel they must work to pay their way through university. In fact, disengagement appears to have other sources than the pressure to work. For example, to give us an idea of how much course engagement professors could expect if they did not have disengaged students in their classes, working or otherwise, when the disengaged group is excluded from the analysis and the study habits of those who work off campus are compared with those who do not, both groups put in between 19 and 20 hours per week on their courses, with a (trivial) difference of only about one hour of course engagement between them.

Disengagement by Choice

Socializing. The correlation between hours spent socializing and course engagement is similar to that reported above concerning working off campus, translating to a small effect size,[47] suggesting that working off campus and socializing have about equally small effects on course (dis) engagement. Then again, as illustrated in figure 5.2, when differences are examined along the axis representing the time spent socializing, a mean difference of about 1.5 points on the scale is observed between the two extremes (5.10 versus 3.62 for the highest and lowest groups). This translates to about 7.5 hours of study time taken up by socializing, a medium effect size ($d = .68$).[48] When viewed in these terms, the effect of socializing on course engagement is twice that of working off campus.

To get a better idea of who is 'disengaged by choice,' full-time students who (a) spent 10 or fewer hours on their studies and (b) did not work off campus were compared as a group with all other students as another group. We call these students the 'hard-core disengaged.'

About one-fifth of the sample falls into the hard-core disengaged category (19.1 per cent). In terms of bivariate relationships, they are more likely to be younger, first-year rather than fourth-year (59.1 per cent are first year) and male (55.9 per cent) (all small effect sizes). They are also more likely to socialize heavily (more than 26 hours per week, but especially more than 30 hours), but are *less likely* to commute or care for others. And, of course, the hard-core disengaged score lower on all five of the benchmarks of engagement.[49]

When these variables are analysed with a statistical technique that simultaneously considers their joint effects (binary logistic regression), most remain statistically significant, but age and gender show the most substantively meaningful effects in terms of what is called the 'odds ratio.' In these cases, age has an odds ratio of 17 per cent,[50] while gender has one of 25 per cent. Commuting (19 per cent) and engaging in care-based activity (5 per cent) also have significant odds ratios in favour of greater academic engagement, while socializing has an odds ratio in favour of hard-core disengagement (8 per cent). All of the benchmarks are significant, but have very low odds ratios when these other variables are controlled (< 1 per cent to 5 per cent). This analysis suggests that those developing interventions to address academic disengagement should target young males living in residence.

Finally, our data set provides additional insights into disengagement by choice because SAT scores are included for American students. As it turns out, hard-core disengaged students in the American subsample do not have significantly lower overall SAT scores,[51] signifying that hard-core disengagement has much more to do with 'attitude' than 'aptitude.'[52]

At the same, the generally high levels of disengagement (40 per cent of the sample overall) may have something to do with the fact that the mean SAT scores for the entire sample are just below those recommended by the College Board in the United States: a total SAT score of 1,180, a verbal score of 580, and a math score of 610.[53] Using these figures to estimate college readiness, over half (60.2 per cent) of the American students included in our NSSE sample do not qualify as ready for university. In this context, the lack of effort in course work for the sample as a whole (at only 12 to 13 hours per week for full-time students) likely has a combination of student and institutional sources: since a majority of students cannot meet higher standards, institutions have lowered the requirements in courses that would make it necessary for students to meet those standards. Hence, we are back to the disengagement compact, but have more insight into it.

Disengagement, Grades, and Personal/Intellectual Transformation

Finally, it is instructive to examine the difference that course engagement might make in terms of such academic outcomes as grades and personal/intellectual development. These analyses give us an idea of the value-added effects of a higher education in terms of its transformative potential.

Effort and grades. According to George Kuh, grades correlate with the benchmarks at low but significant levels, indicating a small effect size.[54] These levels are comparable to those found in our sample.[55] Similarly, in our sample, the specific item measuring course engagement correlates at the same magnitude with grades.[56]

While the observed relationship between effort and grades using the NSSE survey appears to be reliable, one might expect a higher level of association between effort and the rewards universities provide for that effort in meetings their standards. One would *not* expect that great numbers of students who put little effort into their courses would be routinely earning As if university-level learning were set at a high standard. This should be the case even if a disengaged student is high in ability: *a bright student should have to put as much effort into earning an A as a student of average IQ should put into earning a C*.

Yet, common complaints from students include the assertions that they do not have to study much to get good grades, or that it doesn't matter how much they study because they will get the same grade anyway.[57] Additionally, there are inconsistent grading practices among courses, departments, and faculties.[58] Indeed, we suspect this low level of association between effort and grades might shock people who are unfamiliar with current grading practices. In contrast, we know from our previous research and personal experiences that many students are not shocked because they have grown cynical about the reliability of grades.[59]

The tax-paying public would rightly assume that if earned grades were valid indicators of learning outcomes of *higher education*, where all are challenged to do their best and reach their potentials, these grades should be strongly associated with *both* effort and ability. That is, we should find a large effect size for *both* effort and ability on grades (i.e., correlations of at least +.50). The logic for this, in part, is that two variables with large effect sizes should accurately predict the third variable in question (grades, in this case). If trivial, small, or medium effect sizes, and/or unequal effect sizes, are observed in the relationship between effort/ability and grades, something is 'disturbing' that relationship. When we take a closer look at the 'something' behind this small effect size between course engagement and grades, some rather revealing things emerge about current grading practices.

Table 5.2 shows the distribution of grades reported by students completing the NSSE survey. The striking thing about this distribution is the extent to which grades are compressed, such that almost 9 of 10 students report that they most commonly receive As or Bs in their courses.[60]

In terms of country comparisons, while our data indicate that As are over-represented, and Cs under-represented among American schools of all sizes, the differences between American and Canadian grading practices amount to only small effect sizes. Moreover, 84 per cent of grades reportedly assigned in Canadian universities are either As or Bs,

Table 5.2
The compression of grades into the A/B range among full-time students: percentages

Grade	American students	Canadian students	Total
C	10.3	16.0	13.2
B	49.0	54.6	52.0
A	40.7	29.4	34.8
Total	100.0	100.0	100.0

Table 5.3
A cross-tabulation of course engagement with grades: percentages

Grade	Disengaged	Partially engaged	Engaged	Total
C	16.7	11.7	8.6	13.2
B	55.4	51.0	45.3	52.0
A	27.9	37.3	46.1	34.8
Total	100.0	100.0	100.0	100.0

compared to 90 per cent in American schools, which is a trivial effect size ($h = .18$). Evidently, the argument that grade inflation is exclusively an American phenomenon does not hold water empirically in terms of self-reported grades from the NSSE survey.

In spite of this apparent compression, is there evidence of 'fairness' in terms of how grades are doled out – that hard work is duly rewarded and that the weak correlation is a statistical artefact, due to some statistical anomaly like a curvilinear relationship?

Table 5.3 shows the results of another technique involving the cross-tabulation of the three categories of engagement with the three categories of grades. This table shows that while engaged students were more likely to be awarded As, almost one-third of disengaged students were also awarded As, a small effect size ($h = .38$) in terms of the difference between these levels of engagement. Similarly, only about one in six disengaged students were awarded Cs, while about one in ten engaged students were thus rewarded, also a small effect size ($h = .24$). Therefore, the weak correlation discussed above does not appear to be an artefact of that statistical technique or an anomalous statistical distribution: there is simply a weak observed relationship between the two variables such that categories overlap far more than they differ.

In light of these findings, the grading system seems unfair because effort does not appear to pay off for a good number of engaged students, while a substantial portion of disengaged students seem to be able to garner high grades with little effort. The most straightforward explanation for these findings is that universities have low levels of standards in awarding grades, such that it is easy to get high grades with little effort if a student is bright, and only a little more effort is required if a student is of average or above average intelligence. A culture of disengagement in today's universities would tend to neutralize the incentive to work hard in order to achieve higher grades, fostering a sense of entitled disengagement among students. After all, why would someone try harder in their courses when high grades are so easily obtained, especially someone who prefers socializing or making some money on the side?[61]

Effort and ability. The relative contributions of effort and ability were examined with the American students in our sample, for whom SAT scores are available ($n = 1,688$). The (zero-order) correlation between their self-reported grades and SAT scores is +.37, while the correlation between grades and course engagement is only +.22 (in this analysis, the original nine-point question was used in which reported grades ranged from C– to A+). These correlations translate to a medium effect size for SAT scores, but only a small effect size for course engagement. However, when we use a statistical technique that allows us to observe the simultaneous effect of these two variables on grades, a technique that controls for the effect of both variables in predicting grades, the 'part correlation' remains about the same for SAT scores at +.34, but drops to +.16 for course engagement.[62] Consequently, ability explains about twice as much variation in grades than effort, but combined ability and effort only explain 16 per cent of that variance ('variance explained' is estimated by squaring the correlations, and is 11 per cent and 5 per cent, respectively, for ability and effort).[63]

In sum, while it is encouraging that the abilities represented by SAT scores make a difference in the awarding of grades, it is discouraging that this effect is not larger and that effort makes such a small difference. Other factors not related to merit seem to make far more difference in how well someone does in our universities.

Effort and personal transformations. But what about other outcomes of the university experience? If there is not a large difference in grades, are there any other value-added effects of effort in terms of the transformative potential of a higher education?

Table 5.4
Institutional contribution to critical thinking by course engagement: percentages

	Disengaged	Partially engaged	Engaged	Total
A little	3.2	1.8	2.2	2.4
Some	18.4	14.2	10.5	15.3
Quite a bit	41.6	38.6	30.0	38.6
Very much	36.8	45.4	57.3	43.7
Total	100.0	100.0	100.0	100.0

The NSSE data set provides other indicators of outcomes that might shed some light on whether effort really pays off in today's universities. A series of questions are included in the survey about the institutional contributions to a number of forms of personal and intellectual development, such as acquiring a broad general education, speaking clearly and effectively, thinking critically and analytically. The analysis of these questions indicates that effort does predict these forms of development, but the effect sizes are only trivial to small.

One of these outcomes was selected for illustration – critical thinking[64] – where the observed difference among the categories of engagement is greatest. When analysed categorically, as in table 5.4, it turns out that while 57 per cent of those in the engaged category felt that the institutional experience helped them 'very much' to think more critically, so did 37 per cent of those in the disengaged category. Yet, this difference is only a small effect size ($h = .40$).[65] While it is encouraging that course engagement effort does appear to be significantly related to important forms of intellectual development, it is discouraging that the relationship is not stronger.

If effort does not have a great effect on educational outcomes in today's universities, what is its relationship with specific behaviours like preparing for, and asking questions in, class? Sure enough, when these variables are examined, the three engagement groups can be differentiated in the ways one would expect (disengaged students are less likely to prepare for or ask questions in class), but again the effect sizes are trivial to small ($d = .18$ and .44, respectively).

Finally, the answers to one very telling question in the NSSE survey shed light on institutional sources of the disengagement compact. This question asks students how much institutional emphasis there is at their school in terms of 'spending significant amounts of time studying and on academic work.' In contrast to the trivial and small effect sizes noted above on the student side of the equation, on the institutional side the effect size in the comparison of disengaged students with engaged students is large ($d = .84$). Clearly, we need to learn more about the institutional sources of disengagement.

Conclusion: Enough Excuses

Although several arguments can be mustered 'in defence of disengagement,' they do not hold much water when examined logically and empirically.

Logically, the acceptance of disengagement as a way for universities to survive during the present era does not bode well for their future, especially the liberal arts and sciences. The current trend in Canada is for universities to lose their distinctiveness from other forms of post-secondary education (as hitherto 'colleges' are deemed to be universities by government fiat),[66] as well as their integrity as places where the most advanced forms of thought and research are preserved. Regardless of how things might have been in the past – even in someone's imagined Golden Ages – we need to be forward-looking both to serve students who could undergo truly transformative experiences in universities of quality and to serve our society as places where the frontiers of understanding of today's complex world continue to be advanced.

Empirically, the 'disengagement by necessity' hypothesis is a weak explanation for the low levels of effort that are now the norm, while the 'disengagement by choice' hypothesis accounts for where some of the time goes that might otherwise be spent on studies (i.e., socializing). Indeed, the disengagement compact, in which high grades are given for low effort, appears to be the best explanation for the norm of low effort, as evidenced in the low correlations among course engagement, grades, and personal/intellectual transformations. And, in the final analysis, although both students and universities are culpable for complicity in this contract, it is the fiduciary responsibility of the university to terminate the disengagement compact and require students to spend 'significant amounts of time studying and on academic work.'

6 Technologies: Will They Save the Day?

Some observers argue that a variety of new technologies will provide a means by which education will be revolutionized in the twenty-first century, and thereby many of the problems of academic disengagement will be eradicated. The primary obstacle, so the argument goes, is that professors are unwilling to embrace these technologies and the pedagogies they enable.[1] It is important to note that two claims are intertwined in what has been called the 'digital native debate':[2] today's students are disengaged because they are bored with low-tech teaching methods; and professors are at fault for not adopting the high-tech methods their students want. Accordingly, it is claimed, people should stop blaming students for disengagement, and instead blame professors.[3]

Advocates of this techno-revolution position are producing a voluminous literature in the popular press and on blogs, and are garnering considerable interest and support from a number of higher education stakeholders. Despite that, not everyone is willing to jump on the technological bandwagon without first seeing convincing evidence that this is a prudent move. So, a debate has emerged concerning the impact of new technologies, and their potential to reduce student disengagement in the classroom and to provide alternatives for those who find conventional classroom pedagogies boring or alienating.

The technologies that have taken centre stage in this debate are laptops, clickers, and podcasts. In addition, there are calls for a greater use of on-line courses, as well as hybrid courses that utilize some Internet technologies for course delivery as part of regular classroom procedures. Advocates of these technologies argue that they can both revolutionize classroom teaching and enhance on-line courses, the latter of which could possibly supplant classroom teaching (or *should* supplant it, according to some more extreme arguments). Indeed, some schools offer only on-line courses, and various claims – that warrant close scrutiny – are being made about what students can expect to gain by taking them.

Three positions can be identified with respect to the general debate about the impact and potential of new technologies:

- *advocates* who throw their full support behind them
- *cautious skeptics* who are willing to adopt those for which evidence of their usefulness exists
- and a small group of *detractors* who reject their use[4]

We consider ourselves cautious skeptics, and so for the sake of brevity, we focus on the claims of 'tech-advocates' and evaluate the peer-reviewed evidence regarding how these technologies have worked out thus far in classroom settings.

Claims Regarding New Technologies

Tech-advocates constitute a growing and impassioned group that enthusiastically endorse the wholesale adoption of any and all technologies, often with the claim that these will revolutionize university pedagogies.[5] Some advocates even claim that old pedagogies are dead. Unfortunately, these claims often shed more heat than light on exactly how this revolution might take place and what the result would be. Some claims are millennial in flavour, promising a utopian period if people would only have faith in these technologies. And while technological utopianism is not new, a new phase of it is evident in what might be termed 'Web 2.0 evangelism.'

Perhaps the best-known advocate of this approach in Canada is Don Tapscott, who authored *Grown Up Digital: How the Net Generation Is Changing Your World*.[6] In the United States, Marc Prensky is credited with coining the term 'digital native' in 2001.[7] Both of these advocates appear to be evangelical leaders in the new technological utopianism movement.

Other books make similar claims, with titles like *Born Digital: Understanding the First Generation of Digital Natives*,[8] and *Print Is Dead: Books in Our Digital Age*.[9] A trend among these advocates is to mix claims regarding the promise of technologies with claims that a generational shift has taken place with the arrival of 'digital natives' – those who have grown up with the Internet and related communication technologies – into post-secondary institutions and the workplace. Yet, when viewed with a skeptical eye, these generational claims are revealed as seriously flawed by errors in reasoning that raise major questions about other claims regarding the impact of new technologies. The generational argument is dealt with first, to separate it from the issue of the pedagogical value of the new technologies.

The Digital Native Claim

With respect to claims that there is now a distinct generation of 'digital natives' passing through contemporary schools, some clarification is in order. The empirical evidence shows that, although on average there may be more exposure to and use of computer technologies among younger cohorts, especially those who have been born since the introduction of personal computers, not all people in this 'generation' are tech-savvy. Some do not even own a computer, or know how to navigate through even basic programs. We only have to leave the world of the affluent, white, upper middle class, in which tech-advocates live, to see this in our own society among those from lower socio-economic backgrounds. In our own society, we still have a 'digital divide' that is largely socio-economic, but also a 'second digital divide' within each age group comprising those who are not comfortable with computers even if they can afford them, and many of these people grow up with technologies and are studying in today's universities. When we look at the situation in developing countries, the 'global digital divide' is obvious.

From the outset, then, advocates of this position are committing a common error made by those who adopt a generational approach in explaining and predicting social trends. This is the error of homogenization, whereby all members of a given birth cohort are assumed to have the same psychological and behavioural traits. Unfortunately, this conceptual error breeds further errors: over-generalization, exaggeration, selective use of evidence, and ethnocentrism (i.e., ignoring differences among these birth cohorts in terms of social class, race/ethnicity, gender, and nation of origin).[10]

Other skeptics have noted this error as well. For example, Siva Vaidhyanathan published a critique of these claims in the *Chronicle of Higher Education*.[11] Vaidhyanathan, an associate professor of media studies and law at the University of Virginia, teaches courses in digital culture and technology. He writes that he 'shudders' when he reads claims about a so-called 'digital generation.' In his experience,

> every [university] class has a handful of [students] with amazing skills and a large number who can't deal with computers at all. A few lack mobile phones. Many can't afford any gizmos and resent assignments that demand digital work. Many use Facebook and MySpace because they are easy and fun, not because they are powerful (which, of course, they are not). And almost none know how to program or even code text with Hypertext Markup Language (HTML). Only a handful come to college with a sense of how the Internet fundamentally differs from the other major media platforms in daily life.

With respect to the generational claims of tech-advocates, Vaidhyanathan argues that

> today's young people – including college students – are just more complicated than an analysis of imaginary generations can ever reveal. There are far better ways to study and write about them and their interactions with digital technologies than our current punditry offers ... We should drop our simplistic attachments to generations so we can generate an accurate and subtle account of the needs of young people – and all people, for that matter.

A second critique comes from three Australian researchers[12] who in their review of the evidence were unable to find convincing evidence about either the existence of a generation of 'digital natives' or that current students have a preference for technologies as part of their education (at best, they found only about 20–25 per cent of university students could be considered 'tech-savvy' in terms of their usage of technologies).[13] Nor were they able to find evidence for distinctive 'learning styles' among current students. Indeed, certain claims, such as a preference for multi-tasking, are not only unsupported, but research on multi-tasking suggests that it can be counterproductive to learning. On the basis of these and other findings, these researchers conclude:

> Our analysis of the digital native literature demonstrates a clear mismatch between the confidence with which claims are made and the evidence for such claims. So, why have these claims gained such currency? Put another way, why have these arguments repeatedly been reproduced as if they were supported by empirical evidence? An examination of the nature of the 'debate' itself offers some clues.[14]

Borrowing from Stanley Cohen's concept of the moral panic,[15] these Australian researchers note that the public discourse around certain issues 'can achieve a prominence that exceeds the evidence in support of the phenomenon.' Normally, the moral panic concept has been applied to various forms of perceived norm violation, as found in youth subcultures or forms of crime, that evoke a media-driven public reaction of urgency even though there have been no increases in the prevalence of the purported deviance. Similarly, in this case, they note that those promoting the concept of the digital native, along with claiming the need for urgent change in the education system, use 'dramatic language, proclaim a profound difference in the world, and pronounced generational differences.' In addition, tech-advocates evoke 'strongly bound divides: between the new generation and all previous generations; between the technically adept and those who are not; and between learners and teachers.' In this case, the equivalents of the 'deviants' are teachers, who are vilified for putting the education of the young, and the future of society, in jeopardy.

Finally, these Australian researchers note that this moral panic has resulted in open debate being shut down and unsupported claims proliferating in the media. Because the very people who are called upon to change – teachers – are vilified, the likelihood of useful change taking place is diminished. Yet educators 'have every right to demand evidence and to expect that calls for change be based on well founded and supported arguments,' but 'many of the arguments made to date about digital natives currently lack that support.' What the evidence does show, they note, is that there is a complex relationship between young people and technology that is evolving, but there are no grounds to consider the current generation of young people as being 'alien' to older generations. Besides, while the current education system may need to change in some ways, as a group, young people are not rejecting it.

Carrying this notion of moral panic further, the behaviour of certain tech-advocates corresponds to that of the 'moral entrepreneur,'[16] namely, someone who is seeking to create new norms. Moral entrepreneurs can have motives that are either altruistic or selfish. Altruistic moral entrepreneurs would include those promoting altruistic causes (e.g., Mothers Against Drunk Driving), while selfish ones include those who stand to gain personally in terms of their careers. In the case of the tech-advocates examined above, it appears that more career-building than altruism is involved.

The theory of moral entrepreneurship identifies two groups of people involved in the process of norm creation: those who create new norms and those who enforce them. Those who attempt to create new norms are referred to as moral crusaders. If they are to be successful, they must clearly define a problem and a solution. In addition, at a certain point in their crusade they become dependent upon experts who will validate their cause on the basis of scientific evidence. This is the juncture where we currently find ourselves, and it appears that the moral crusade undertaken by tech-advocates will falter on this basis: the evidence is not forthcoming as to the problem or the solution. Meanwhile, these crusaders have made a strategic error in vilifying teachers, because it is teachers who would enforce the new norms of an educational system predicated on the use of technologies.

In sum, there is little evidence for the existence of a distinctive generation defined principally by their relationship with technologies,[17] and tech-advocates are best understood as creating a 'generational myth.' Tech-advocates like Tapscott appear to grant 'young people today' some sort of celebrity status. But, as noted, this stereotype hinges on the belief that all members of this generation are equally 'savvy' in the quality and quantity of their use of these technologies. In contrast, when one takes apart this stereotype, other terms come to mind. For example, rather than referring to baby boomers (the generation that brought most of these technologies to market) as 'digital immigrants,' it seems more apt to refer to *some* in this generation as 'digital elders' or 'digital pioneers.' Indeed, the idea of pioneers evokes images of those who are hard-working, serious, and frugal rather than of those who can use only mass-marketed products requiring little learning or skill, are hedonistic and promiscuous in their use of these products, or mindlessly purchase the latest products regardless of the cost.

To take this wordplay further, the word 'savvy' actually means 'shrewd and adept with practical knowledge.' Given that only about one-quarter of young people are truly well versed in computer hardware/software,[18] then at best only this minority would qualify for consideration as 'savvy,' depending on how much they use these technologies in positive ways that enhance their lives and the lives of those around them. In contrast, large numbers of young people actually seem more 'slavish' to the technologies, feeling insecure when they do not have them within arm's reach. Given the six to eight hours per day now taken up by them (mainly for play and social networking), is this really a 'shrewd' way to spend one's time, especially when healthful, intellectually stimulating, and pro-social activities are displaced?[19] Moreover, would it not be considered *pathological* if a large segment of the population (some 20 per cent) excessively engaged in any activity that seriously undermined such long-term developmental outcomes as school achievement and face-to-face social skills?[20] Because many adults still seem to be awed by these gadgets, their wards are allowed to bypass the type of critical scrutiny that elders might otherwise give them; indeed, many heavy users of new technologies are adulated rather than guided in their prudent use.[21]

Pedagogical Claims

The claim that the new technologies can alleviate the academic disengagement problem is often appended to the charge that professors merely have to embrace the new technologies to adapt to the 'new learning styles' of the current batch of students passing through universities – digital natives – who are bored by old teaching techniques. Note, though, that this claim is ultimately tied to the assumption that so-called 'digital natives' either cannot learn, or are unwilling to learn, through the older techniques, so that the generational myth remains in the background.[22]

On the teacher side of the educational equation, the argument is made by tech-advocates like Don Tapscott that too many professors are Luddites or even 'pre-Gutenberg' dinosaurs,[23] and are too wedded to old teaching techniques like the lecture format. Tapscott further argues that old university 'broadcast' pedagogies like the lecture should be abandoned in favour of collaborative techniques that have been made possible by the Internet, and platforms like Facebook and wikis.[24]

Arguments like this are finding a faithful following among those disenchanted with formal learning, and there is no question that certain technologies can be useful in certain contexts, as shown below. However, technologies are tools, not outcomes; they are means, not ends. This confusion seems to be responsible for some fuzzy thinking about so-called new collaborative pedagogies ostensibly made possible by 'Web 2.0' (interactive) software. While the concept of collaborative learning may indeed sound novel and exciting, in fact this pedagogy is far from new, and so the collaboration the new technologies facilitate is also nothing new, contrary to what Tapscott claims.

To make his case, Tapscott sets up a binary (black and white) opposition that he believes is at the basis of the current problems in the educational system – traditional 'broadcast learning' versus new 'interactive learning' based on 'Web 2.0 pedagogies.' Tapscott identifies four dimensions that he believes represents the contrasts between these pedagogies:

- Teacher oriented vs. learner centered
- One-size-fits-all vs. one-size-fits-one
- Instruction: learning about vs. discovery: Learning to be
- Individualistic learning vs. collaborative learning[25]

The problem with Tapscott's case is that for some time teachers have been doing the very things that he accuses them of ignoring. In fact, it appears that Tapscott has little or no teaching experience himself, so that his prescriptions become little more than empty platitudes generated by someone with little direct experience in the classroom and background knowledge of teaching practices. His recommendation to use Web 2.0 technologies might seem deeply insightful – even trendy – to those with no knowledge of the history of educational theory. Certainly, his vision is replete with a template of uncool 'bad guys' (those anchored in the past) versus cool 'good guys' (those who advocate for the future), which might appeal to people who fancy themselves to be progressive and open-minded.

Contrary to his claims, there is little new in his prescriptions. Take away the new technological gadgets that can facilitate collaborative learning, and you have the same critique of past pedagogies – and prescriptions for new pedagogies that would save the day – that can be traced back to Rousseau (the 1700s), through Dewey (the early 1900s), to Freire (the 1960s). Indeed, these ideas fed the progressive education movement that transformed schools around the world.

If the type of Internet-dependent pedagogy that Tapscott recommends is so useful and important, one would think that his book would be brimming with examples of how the curriculum at various levels has been revolutionized, especially at the university level, given that his book is about those in their age cohort who are now 'grown up.' Yet, after some ten pages of excoriating teachers, whom he portrays as refusing to change their misguided ways and thus causing high dropout rates and student disengagement, the best that we get are two of what he calls 'shining examples' of interactive learning from one university (Cornell). However, neither of these involves Web 2.0 technologies; instead, both rely on old face-to-face techniques and good teaching.

The irony here is that Tapscott merely had to use the Internet to improve his own scholarship by learning about the history of educational

Table 6.1
When teachers are necessary in formal educational systems

	What the student knows	What the student doesn't know
What the teacher knows	Formal education is not necessary	Formal instruction is helpful – students 'don't know what they don't know'; co-construction is possible in certain subjects, but is not necessarily the most useful technique for all students
What the teacher doesn't know	Traditional pedagogies are not necessary/do not work	Co-construction necessary; discovery possible

philosophies. Still, he saw fit to write that 'schools should be places to learn, not teach … now that students can obviously find the facts they're looking for in an instant.'[26] This view is brought to the reader's attention as an object lesson. For example, even if all of the relevant information were on the Internet, which is not the case, how many students would spend the enormous amount of time it would take to learn the history of educational philosophy by surfing it? And without this knowledge of history, how are they going to know what to look for 'in an instant,' as Tapscott would have us believe is now possible on the Internet?[27] And, if certain students already believe they know enough on a subject about which they are absolutely ignorant, how are they going to know where to start?[28]

Table 6.1 provides a way of viewing the issue of when teachers are necessary for student learning and when they are not. Clearly, when students 'don't know what they don't know' teachers can be very helpful, and a variety of pedagogical techniques have been used over the past decades and centuries for helping students to learn what they 'don't know,' including various discovery techniques. Accordingly, if students were left to figure out complex topics only with the aid of the laptop, in most cases educators would not be doing them a favour.

Let's apply this to the case of Tapscott's claims about supposedly new pedagogies. Had Tapscott actually studied educational theory, history, and philosophy, he never would have had the hubris to claim that no one has ever considered what he believes to be revolutionary ideas that will save education. If self-education on complex topics that have steep

learning curves were that easy, he could have found the historical precedents for his ideas 'in an instant.' The fact that he did not undermines
his claims about the revolutionary potential of the Internet in replacing
traditional forms of learning.

Still, the Internet does provide some background on many topics, including the very 'new' pedagogies he promotes. For example, a Google
search would have given Tapscott all sorts of information on the historical precedents for what he claims are now his revolutionary ideas.
Even more ironic is that he could have drawn this information from
Wikipedia.[29] For example, the Wikipedia entry for John Dewey (1859–
1952) states:

> Dewey was a relentless campaigner for reform of education, pointing out
> that the authoritarian, strict, pre-ordained knowledge approach of mod-
> ern traditional education was too concerned with delivering knowledge,
> and not enough with understanding students' actual experiences. Dewey
> was the most famous proponent of hands-on learning or experiential
> education ...

But, of course, one would already need to know that Dewey was an
advocate of progressive education. Even so, from that entry in Wikipedia, he could have clicked the 'progressive education' link, where he
would have found the following:

> The term 'progressive' was engaged to distinguish this education from
> the traditional curriculum of the 19th century ... By contrast, progressive
> education finds its roots in present experience. Most progressive educa-
> tion programs have [a number of] qualities in common ...

These qualities include 'learning by doing,' 'experiential learning,'
'strong emphasis on problem solving and critical thinking,' 'group
work and development of social skills,' 'understanding and action as
the goals of learning as opposed to rote knowledge,' and 'collaborative
and cooperative learning projects.'

Tapscott's claim of an imminent paradigm shift is thus highly suspect. What he refers to is a strong influence in educational practice that
is centuries old. Had he bothered to take a university-level course (e.g.,
the Sociology of Education) on this topic before writing about it, he
would have avoided this egregious error. What is new is the technology
to expedite this type of learning, and we agree that these technologies
should be explored in terms of their utility. We do not agree, though,

that we should rush headlong into a Brave New World where students are coupled all day with laptops, to be at the ready to look up things instantly, instead of reading texts and taking instruction from educated teachers and trained experts. If Tapscott were better informed about the history of educational philosophy and current practices, he would never have made claims such as:

- 'schools should be places to learn, not to teach';
- 'it's not what you know that really counts; it's how you navigate in the digital world';
- 'the scandal of education is that every time you teach something, you deprive a child of the pleasure in benefit of discovery.'[30]

Since Tapscott does not cite any examples at the university level, or review the published, peer-reviewed evidence of the efficacy of various technologies in enhancing learning outcomes and reducing student disengagement, this evidence will be reviewed in the next section.

Nonetheless, readers can take away from this section the recommendation that for those courses whose content and purpose are suited to certain technologies, there is no reason why professors who feel comfortable with them should not incorporate them into traditional lecture techniques. At the same time, it needs to be recognized that most professors have little choice but to use the lecture format as a platform from which to engage in the types of innovations recommended by tech-advocates like Tapscott. Universities use lecture courses as a matter of economy and efficiency, based on the assumption that students will accommodate to them if they are interested in learning from professors (recall the bilateral contract discussed in chapter 3). Classes that have more than thirty to forty students can become unmanageable if the professor has to monitor numerous on-line student collaborations and/or postings on a regular basis, and become impossible to manage when the size exceeds one hundred, a situation that is increasingly common as budgets continue to contract.[31]

The Evidence

Laptops

Schools at all three levels of the educational system that once embraced laptops – even supplied them to students – have been dropping them[32] over the past few years. At the university level, professors have been banning them[33] from their classrooms because they are distractions to other students, to teachers, and to the students using them, who cannot resist playing with their various features.

As systematic evaluations on laptop use in universities are being published in peer-reviewed journals, these concerns are being validated. A recent article in the journal *Computers & Education* found that compared with non-users, laptop users 'spent considerable time multitasking and that the laptop use posed a significant distraction to both users and fellow students. Most importantly, the level of laptop use was negatively related to several measures of student learning, including self-reported understanding of course material and overall course performance.'[34] The 'multi-tasking' involved spending almost one-quarter of the lecture time checking e-mail, instant messaging, surfing the Internet, and playing games.

Apart from the distractions all around, then, the use of laptops is contraindicated because on average they can interfere with the learning process. Some individual students may benefit from their use, as we have found in our classes, but this needs to be determined on a person-by-person basis.

Several articles have examined the role of laptops in learning outcomes. One published in *Computers & Education* found that honours business students did not benefit from laptops in terms of GPAs, and the students voiced a number of frustrations with them, including the steep learning curve to learn how to use them for course work and the distractions they posed.[35] Another article in the same journal reports results that are more positive, but they are based on small groups of third-year civil engineering students (thirty-six students assigned to six groups of six students each) charged with collaborating in designing a hypothetical industrial park. In this case, and depending on the content of what is being taught/learned, it appears that laptops do indeed have a use where the curriculum allows small groups of students to use them to communicate as part of small-scale collaborative assignments, but the laptops were found to not be integral to any learning outcomes.

What is more, it must be noted that not all course curriculum lends itself to group collaboration in problem solving. Many university courses are content-oriented, especially lower-level ones, which also tend to be large, and this content sometimes provides a foundation for learning abstract principles that students can use if they take advanced courses in that area. Only after a certain amount of content is understood, and a number of principles are learned, can students usefully collaborate in solving hypothetical, abstract problems.[36]

Taking these studies as a whole, laptops clearly have their place, but it is not in large lecture classes, except on an individual basis for those students who can truly benefit from their use. In our experience, this applies to very few students with special learning needs. Just the same, this debate may have already been resolved in terms of end-user demand. A recent report notes that 'many students who own laptops do not carry them to class because they are bulky, heavy, and "uncool."'[37]

Clickers

Clickers, also known as audience response systems, have become very popular in some large lecture courses. These devices allow students to select answers in a true/false or multiple-choice format in response to questions usually presented to students on PowerPoint slides. There is much written about them in the press, on blogs, and, increasingly, in academic journals. Those who write about them tend to be positive, and presumably take the time to do so because they are stimulated by their belief that they have successfully used them to increase student engagement, course satisfaction, and learning.[38] Some negative commentaries and academic reports have been published, based on either skepticism about their pedagogical utility[39] or frustrations with the technology, especially in its early forms (e.g., set-up and take-down times at the beginning of each class, software problems, students forgetting their clickers, dead batteries, or clickers not working properly).[40]

Part of the problem appears to be that the technology has been going through growing pains, with earlier versions being cumbersome and time-consuming to set up in each class, and plagued with glitches and reception problems (e.g., interference of fluorescent lights with infrared beams from certain types of clickers; range problems from receivers).

Based on the technical and pedagogical problems reported in the literature, it is not likely that clickers would ever be universally used, especially in liberal-arts courses (as opposed to the so-called STEM disciplines – science, technology, engineering, and mathematics), and would only be widely used if classrooms were permanently wired for them, relieving professors and students of the hassle and expense of their set-up. Just the same, the technology appears to be improving, as is the pedagogy, so that there may be more reason to endorse the use of clickers in certain types of courses if they are used to teach and reinforce how to think about fundamental principles in a discipline.[41]

There is also some literature that helps us understand what students think of clickers. After all, as enthusiastic as a professor may be about clickers, if certain students are not on board, how effective will the clickers be for them? As it turns out, a substantial minority of students, some 15-20 per cent, are not comfortable with clickers,[42] and many have difficulties with simple matters like registering their user-numbers properly and in a timely fashion. Moreover, while just over half of students indicate that they enjoy clickers, a sizable percentage is either ambivalent or downright hostile to them. Our bet is the latter group is largely made up of the more seriously disengaged students.

The key factor affecting the acceptance of clickers by students seems to be whether they are used primarily for the benefit of the instructor (e.g., for taking attendance or easy grading) or for the students; or as one study puts it, whether they are 'compelling or empowering.'[43] This study dug deeper to examine the hard-core group of students with the most negative feelings and found that they generally do not favour any sort of student participation in courses. Consequently, there may not be much to be done to reach these students (this group constituted almost 20 per cent of the sample, and they may be primarily the most disengaged students).

Clickers do seem more suited to pedagogies associated with training students in certain vocational-type skills for which there are clearly correct answers, whether they be content-retention or problem-solving abilities. Be that as it may, there might be room in some liberal-arts courses for the use of clickers in enhancing formative learning exercises that help students understand the tenets of theories and the conclusions that can be drawn from those tenets, as well as to evaluate the validity of arguments in relation to certain types of evidence. For example, questions can be designed for which no response is designated as correct, but responses are instead used to encourage debate.[44]

On the other hand, good teachers using active-learning approaches, such as class discussions that involve students in reasoning through problems, have been able to enhance learning outcomes long before clickers came along. One study investigated this by comparing the same course taught with clickers versus active class discussions of material, finding no difference in learning outcomes.[45]

Finally, the published peer-reviewed research is mixed concerning the effectiveness of clickers in terms of both engagement and learning outcomes,[46] but studies to date have not taken into account students' initial level of general engagement. Student reactions are more positive when clickers are used in ways that they perceive to be in their interest; these involve formative evaluations and active learning of the principles of a discipline.[47] However, the question remains: how much can clickers re-engage seriously disengaged students who seldom attend class, or prepare if they do attend (as noted above, up to 40-50 per cent of students study fewer than 10 hours per week, according to NSSE studies)? Indeed, up to 10 per cent of students will not even buy the clickers when it is part of a course requirement.[48] In fact, seriously disengaged students likely resent the subtly coercive aspects of these devices, and it is unlikely that clickers can actually reduce hard-core disengagement.[49] It is the partially disengaged students who may be the prime beneficiaries of these gadgets, to the extent that classroom 'engagement' compensates for their out-of-class disengagement by raising their grades slightly, especially when the clickers are used to encourage active learning in class. And, fully engaged students may benefit from any type of use of clickers by having their independent learning reinforced in class, thereby helping them move more quickly up the learning curve of the discipline in question.

One study summed up the issues, noting that a certain amount of student engagement must precede the use of clickers, and that clickers cannot produce engagement on their own:

> The clicker itself does not ensure engaged, active students in the classroom, but rather is a tool that may facilitate that process, depending in part upon the expectations that students bring to the large lecture class … If students want to be involved and engaged, they are more likely to perceive clickers positively in terms of both learning and involvement processes.[50]

So, to click or not to click? For professors, it appears to depend on whether one is comfortable using an interactive technology as part of a public performance, and can do so in a way that actively involves students in reasoning through the most difficult principles and theories of one's discipline. For students, it depends on how much one is willing to engage oneself in one's courses and to sincerely attempt to move up the learning curve in each. Unless both professors and students are willing to approach this technology in these ways, there is likely to be some frustration and dissatisfaction on both sides of the lectern.

Podcasts

Podcast technologies present more clear-cut issues than do clickers because they are basically an extra service provided to those students who are willing to view them, either as part of an on-line (or distance) course[51] or in a regular classroom course. Because of this, there is not the implicit coerciveness as in some clicker use. Generally, given that it is reasonable to assume that only keen students would bother to listen to, or view, podcasts, it is unlikely that this technology will address hard-core student disengagement. Disengaged students who do not bother to attend class or pay attention if they do attend are unlikely to take the time to listen to podcasts, at least in any sustained way. In contrast, the promise of this technology seems to be to help serious, engaged students to bone up on material, a supposition supported by the fact that mainly professional schools are using them.[52]

As for students skipping class because they can access a podcast instead, that would depend in part on the quality of the podcast, and measures can be taken to reduce access to podcasts in ways that encourage attendance.[53] At the same time, the research suggests that attendance is not seriously affected.[54] Some podcasts are made only in audio and so would require significant concentration and an attention span not dependent on visual stimulation. Disengaged students would not likely take advantage of this type of podcast because even a boring lecture has to be more stimulating when experienced live, although enhanced audio podcasts may also feature slide images, chapter markers, and links.[55] Podcasts available in video are more enticing (sometimes called 'vodcasts') and, according to one source, are 'absolutely vital' when complex processes need to be illustrated,[56] but good quality ones are expensive to produce, and may require two camera people to film each lecture being 'captured.'[57] Check out YouTube, where numerous lectures can now be accessed, and see for yourself.[58] Better yet, Apple has launched iTunes University, a site where podcasts from entire courses are available to everyone in the world.

Queen's University's School of Medicine uses podcasts, made available to students on an internal website or through iTunes (they helped pioneer iTunes' podcasting of lectures).[59] When just audio podcasts are used, the costs are minimal, and at Queen's the students do the work involved. Each class of medical students from year one through year four appoints a tech rep who is responsible for recording and uploading the course lectures. A 2007 survey of the pilot program found overwhelming support among students in all courses. Students reported that podcasts were convenient to listen to while walking to class, for example, and they thought that they reinforced lecture content. Apparently, some schools are automating podcasting with a resident machine that records the lecture and then uploads it directly to the student server, making the podcast available for downloading as soon as the class ends.[60]

Clearly, podcasts are popular among students in élite professional programs because they are useful in reinforcing lecture content. It must be stressed, though, that this is a highly select group of engaged students, who constitute a very small percentage of initial applicants to these programs. But what does the research indicate about the general undergraduate population? More specifically, how useful are podcasts in liberal-arts courses where integral parts of each class involve class discussion and/or video clips?

To date, little has been reported on their use in general undergraduate courses, but two developments are relevant here. One development involves the use of enhanced podcasts,[61] which can include narrated PowerPoint presentations that students can view in advance of the class, freeing up class time for more interactive forms of learning. The other development is the use of podcasts to enhance a course independent of the lecture. This can be done by professors themselves producing short YouTube-type videos of interest to students, such as video clips explaining assignments, plagiarism, or even 'a day in the life' of a typical prof teaching in a particular discipline.[62]

From what has been published, students appear to be generally happy with podcasts, apparently much more so than with clickers. One source reports that clickers received an evaluation of 3.5 out of 5 in response to a survey question asking students how much the technology helped them learn, while podcasts were given a score of 4.5 out of 5.[63] However, the satisfaction is far from unanimous, with about one-quarter voicing various forms of dissatisfaction.[64] Several articles are reporting success in involving students in the co-creation of 'mashup' podcasts,[65] although given the two digital divides, this would likely only ever be popular among a minority of students, except perhaps in IT and journalism courses.

Indeed, the research reveals that a minority of students are caught in the first and second digital divides. In the first instance, some students do not have iPods or mp3 players, high-speed Internet access at home to download large files, or even home computers or laptops. And, among those who do, some have reported difficulties with simple matters like downloading the podcasts.[66] Finally, those who insist that the current generation of students are all 'digital natives' will be surprised with the finding that only a small minority know about RSS feeds, or would use them to automatically receive podcasts.[67]

With respect to learning outcomes, the few findings reported in the literature are mixed. Some studies find no increased benefits.[68] Several studies have found that podcasts must be regularly used in conjunction with the lecture for enhanced learning ('hybrid learning'),[69] while one study found that they can substitute for the lecture, so long as students are highly motivated and take notes.[70]

The literature on student engagement is likewise thin and non-rigorous. Unfortunately, as was the case with clickers, no studies assess initial differences among students in terms of their general level of engagement in relation to their courses, and those who are among the hard-core disengaged in general would not be inclined to spend time listening to podcasts. One study reported a minor difference in engagement level in a small, seminar-type course in terms of contributing to class discussion, taking more notes, and reviewing notes prior to class.[71] Still, there is reason for skepticism that podcasts would increase engagement in large general lecture courses in terms of 'main effects' (effects averaged over all students). Instead, there may be 'interaction effects,' whereby only certain types of students benefit (e.g., students who have been partially engaged because they do not benefit from straight lecture formats, but for whom the added benefit of the podcast gives them more stimulus to master the material). As noted above, when engagement is not an issue, as in medical programs where students are pre-selected for their ability and motivation, students will benefit because it is a teaching aid that gives them flexibility and reinforcement in their learning exercises.

So, are podcasts worth the cost and effort? Some students may skip lectures when they know a podcast is available, but students often have good reasons for skipping class (sickness, family issues, religious days, etc.) and if a podcast can help these students keep up to date in the course, it is difficult to argue against using them.[72] Besides, as argued, students who are slack in attending lectures are probably not going to spend time taking advantage of a podcast, especially if it is available only in audio, which one source notes is more likely to cause a bored student to doze off than is a video podcast[73] (although improvements are being made.)[74] Unfortunately, because good podcasts are expensive to make, it is unlikely they will be widely used in (underfunded) general programs any time soon.

Could podcasts replace lectures? It is doubtful, any more than did courses available on VHS videotapes or on certain public television stations from previous decades. Podcasts are simply a new generation of technology that can make certain types of learning easier by reinforcing information delivered by live lectures. Most students like and need the structure of live lectures, and the option of interacting with instructors. If students could do without this structure, the lecture system would have broken down long ago: students would simply have gone to university libraries, where most accumulated knowledge has been stored, and read voraciously to educate themselves.[75]

On-line Courses

Through the Internet, universities can now use a large number of specialized programs that can enhance classroom courses or take courses totally on-line. For example, WebCT[76] is a widely used password-protected course-management tool through which student grades and lectures notes can be posted, discussion-groups can take place, collaborative wikis[77] and wimbas[78] can be organized, and the truly virtual classroom can be created in Second Life.[79] These applications can all be of potential benefit in terms of efficiency and ease of use, once professors and students have climbed learning curves to use them effectively.[80]

Unfortunately, there is little published peer-reviewed research literature upon which to evaluate their impact on student engagement and learning outcomes in classroom-based courses. For example, because WebCT can be used to efficiently manage large classes with the posting of grades and lecture notes, one-on-one student-professor interaction, face-to-face or mediated, may actually be reduced. Certainly, there is much information available from the businesses selling these applications, as is the case with the other technologies discussed above, but it should be kept in mind that these companies have a vested interest in promoting their positive benefits and downplaying any neutral or negative features. There is potentially a lot of money to be made with these technologies.

On the other hand, these technologies are undoubtedly a boon to 'distance courses,' which used to be called correspondence courses, and so the evidence will be examined in this section comparing on-line to conventional classroom-based courses.

Some ardent tech-advocates apparently would like to see all university-level instruction go on-line, so that students can learn at their own pace and with their own style, presumably drawing on much of their ancillary knowledge from the Internet.[81] Indeed, on-line university courses and programs are fast becoming a big business in competition with conventional classroom-based ones. On-line courses increased by between 9.7 and 36.5 per cent annually in the United States between 2003 and 2007, as opposed to an annual growth of only about 1.5 per cent per annum for classroom-based courses.[82] About 20 per cent of American students took at least one on-line course in 2007 (almost four million students).[83] In spite of this, not all on-line start-ups have been successful.[84]

In Canada, some fifteen traditional universities offer on-line degree programs, and there are several fully on-line universities now in Canada, including Meritus University,[85] owned by Apollo Group Inc., the parent company of the largest private university in the United States – the University of Phoenix[86] – which, in turn, has campuses in Alberta and British Columbia.[87]

In the United Kingdom, The Open University,[88] a pioneer in distance courses (incorporating lectures broadcast on TV for the past few decades), now offers on-line courses at a low cost to some 150,000 undergraduates and 30,000 graduate students.[89]

Perhaps as a result of its fast growth, the on-line course industry seems to be going through a 'wild west' phase to the extent that accreditation is ambiguous in many instances, and non-existent in others. One American university, Kaplan University, recently launched an aggressive multimedia ad campaign. One of Kaplan's TV ads[90] begins with an authoritative sounding professor 'confessing' to a large lecture class:

> I stand before you today, to apologize. The system has failed you. I have failed you. I have failed to help you share your talent with the world, when the world needs talent more than ever, yet it's being wasted every day, by an educational system steeped in tradition and old ideas. It is time for a new tradition. It is time to realize that talent isn't just in schools like this one. It's everywhere.

As the professor begins to speak, the students look at each other with surprise. As he continues to speak, young people are shown watching and listening to him, not in class, but on laptops, iPods, and other portable devices in living rooms, on subway platforms, and other locations. The professor concludes:

> It's time to use technology to rewrite the rules of education. To learn how you learn so we can teach you better. It's time [that] university adapted to

you, rather than you adapting to it. It's time ... time ... time, for a different kind of university. It's your time.[91]

Founded in 2001, and owned by the Washington Post Company,[92] Kaplan University apparently now has some 50,000 students in more than 100 programs, including law.[93] Unfortunately, as good as this sounds, many students are extremely dissatisfied with the courses, programs, counselling, and the responsiveness of the school to their attempts to communicate with staff there. The website ripoffreport.com[94] had 172 complaint listings as of 6 May 2009, and someone posted a YouTube video titled *Kaplan University Online Is a Ripoff*.[95] Evidently, many students studying law did not read the fine print, which states 'Kaplan University suggests and encourages its students to independently research the licensing requirements in any state where they intend to seek licensure.'[96]

Certainly, there are many good on-line courses provided by accredited universities that offer them as distance courses, and even good courses from universities that offer only on-line courses. On the other hand, as in the case of Kaplan University, the rhetoric is fever-pitched, capitalizing on the hyperbole promulgated by tech-advocates who claim that contemporary students are 'digital natives' who are being cheated by conventional classroom-based educational systems. Resurfacing are claims regarding the 'digital-native generation,' which can take on a life of their own if they are repeated often enough and there is something to be gained by promoting them.

Aside from the caveat emptor nature of the delivery of these types of courses by some schools, and the exaggerated claims made about the value of on-line courses to 'digital natives,' what else should the discerning eye look out for? First and foremost is the fact that on-line courses are by their very nature smaller than most conventional lecture-type courses. On-line courses typically have between twenty and forty students, because beyond forty students, the workload for the instructor becomes unmanageable. This is because by their very nature, in the absence of the efficiency of the lecture hall, instructors must monitor each student and require participation of each student through a series of assignments and postings in discussion groups. Thus, it should not be surprising if research shows that on-line courses 'engage' students more.[97] Without this 'engagement,' students would be learning entirely on their own and simply taking tests. If that were the case, it is doubtful that on-line courses would be very popular.

A recent report by the U.S. Department of Education emphasized this caveat about comparing on-line and classroom-based courses in its exhaustive review of the literature:

> Despite what appears to be strong support for online learning applications, the studies in this meta-analysis do not demonstrate that online learning is superior as a *medium*. In many of the studies showing an advantage for online learning, *the online and classroom conditions differed in terms of time spent, curriculum and pedagogy*. It was the *combination* of elements in the treatment conditions (which was likely to have included additional learning time and materials as well as additional opportunities for collaboration) that produced the observed learning advantages. At the same time, one should note that online learning is much more conducive to the expansion of learning time than is face-to-face instruction.[98]

In other words, a true comparison of on-line and classroom-based courses would require comparing courses of the same size and, to be totally fair, with the same number of assignments and other requirements, yet because this is rarely the case in the evaluation research, the comparison is one of 'apples and oranges.'

A second methodological problem pertains to on-line *distance* courses. According to Ernest Pascarella and Patrick Terenzini,[99] there are fatal methodological flaws that invalidate any attempts to assess differences in outcomes between those who take conventional courses on campus and those who do so from a distance. That is, there is no way to set up true- or quasi-experiments because students 'self-select' themselves into the different types of education, and Pascarella and Terenzini doubt that attempts to control statistically for differences between the two groups would eliminate threats to the internal validity (causal links) of the interaction between this self-selection and learning outcomes. In their words, 'The reasons why students take courses on campus or at distant sites in the first place may represent a constellation of uncontrolled influences that bias the findings on distance learning and student achievement in unknown ways.'[100]

With respect to comparisons of learning outcomes between on-line and classroom courses among students who take conventional on-campus studies, Pascarella and Terenzini argue that the methodological problems are fewer and the results more clear-cut, but that 'the specific medium of instruction has little impact on how much students learn.'[101]

Also focusing on learning outcomes, two Canadian peer-reviewed sources,[102] constituting reviews of reviews, similarly argue that interpretations of studies evaluating the two forms of education are problematic. In general, they found inconsistent results,[103] ranging from no differences between on-line and classroom-based courses, some differences in specific instances, and small positive effects overall in favour of distance education, but with wide variation among the studies (i.e., mixed findings, with at best a trivial effect – 4 per cent – for distance learning overall, but with many studies revealing negative effects).[104]

One study of particular interest found that as students take more on-line courses, thereby gaining more experience with them, they become more cognitively engaged and take more responsibility for their own learning, both of which are general goals of a university education.[105] However, in this case, a self-selection factor may be in effect, such that students who are willing to become more engaged actually do so with practice. It may well have been the case that had they taken smaller conventional courses with more engagement required by written assignments, they would have become more engaged as a result. Again, the potential conflation between medium of instruction and class size has not been addressed.

In contrast to the lack of clear support for the superiority of on-line courses, many educators (and those who sell the supporting technology) still believe that on-line courses are far superior in terms of learning outcomes and engagement. To go beyond this hiatus between clear evidence and unsupported belief, one source evaluated the opinion of expert researchers in Canada on the impact of e-learning technologies (e-learning would include hybrid courses in which classroom instruction includes some on-line instruction). Although finding a degree of consensus, this study concluded that educators are not sufficiently clear about what the most desirable outcomes of higher education are: the goals of education are often not stated, and educators and researchers are often not even able to define them; and when goals are actually discussed, there is little consensus.[106] Once more, some types of educational content and learning may be better suited to distance education than others. It cannot be a panacea.

It is of interest to note that this problem is not limited to the evaluation of different delivery formats, but is also involved in the evaluation of many forms of higher education in general, especially liberal versus applied education programs. Indeed, this is precisely the problem that we are grappling with in attempting to alert people to the problem of mission drift in universities. There is now so little consensus about what universities should be achieving and what teachers should be doing in and out of the classroom, that discussions quickly break down, with stakeholders retreating to defend their interests based on their specific knowledge of the system and their beliefs about how the system should operate to preserve their interests. In the ensuing disputes, the distinction between liberal and applied education gets lost, as in the case of on-line courses, where no studies have compared their relative effectiveness in delivering both types of programs.

Still, it is useful to hear what the direct players in on-line courses – faculty and students – have to say. After all, both the students and the teacher affect the nature of any course. The more each likes a course, the better it is likely to turn out; and from the point of view of teachers and students, the more reasons there are to dislike a course, the worse it is likely to turn out. Since what is at issue here is the medium of instruction, it is helpful to know what students and teachers think about the on-line medium.

Studies show that most students are generally satisfied with on-line courses. One recent study found that students rated factors like convenience and flexibility highly, along with the teachers and reading materials specific to the courses evaluated; but they were less enthusiastic about discussion boards and e-mails among students, even though they missed the socializing aspect of regular classes.[107] Points of dissatisfaction cited by students included feeling isolated because of a lack of face-to-face contact with their classmates and professors, and feeling that there was too much reading and too many assignments (although more than half of the students were satisfied with the workload). Many students also complained about insufficient constructive feedback as well as problems with the technology (concerning both software and hardware). Only one-third of the students surveyed had no complaints.

Unfortunately, this study did not compare these types of responses with experiences in conventional courses, but it is our experience that a certain number of students will always complain about workload, no matter how light it is. It can also be seen from this study how difficult it is to compare courses, even those using the same medium, because of variation in the workload and quality of instruction.

Other studies have found that student dissatisfaction is related to a lack of social interaction, students' own deficits in academic and technical skills, as well as time constraints and technical difficulties in the course delivery. Students who do not achieve grades commensurate with their expectations tend to be the least satisfied, as are students who lack the confidence that they can be successful in these courses.[108]

Faculty satisfaction is obviously very important, because unhappy teachers are likely to produce unhappy students. Indeed, the research suggests that faculty satisfaction with on-line courses is highly correlated with student satisfaction, especially when students perform at higher levels.[109] Faculty are more satisfied when they feel that their students are actively involved, participate at appropriate levels, and maintain effective communication with them.

The satisfaction of professors is also affected by institutional factors, such as recognition and adequate remuneration for their work, opportunity for promotion and tenure within a reward system, adequate tech support, and recognition that on-line teaching is more time-consuming than regular classroom-based courses (including release time for course development).[110]

Faculty who have taught on-line courses have more favourable attitudes toward them, and one study found that 75 per cent of faculty now have positive attitudes toward on-line courses in general.[111] However, in some instances there is suspicion that the move toward on-line courses by an institution is part of a money grab, especially when universities partner with private companies that deliver them.[112] Other faculty view on-line courses as delivering an inferior product if compared to an in-class version of the same course, and yet others regard such courses as a form of slave labour.[113] In many institutions, the growing number of on-line course offerings and the expanding coterie of part-time and contract instructors could be seen as the first warning shot across the bow in the impending war against 'tenure.' As is well known, most on-line course instructors are part-time professors shut out of full-time positions, so that they have to cobble together packages of part-time work to earn a living wage. In addition to the low pay, on-line courses are more time-consuming for instructors than regular courses, both in terms of set-up and monitoring student communication (answering e-mails can be a burdensome task that may have to be completed in evenings and on weekends, or may displace other work to those times).

So, what can be said about on-line university courses? They obviously suit some students and faculty members, and are very useful for distance studies. But, their quality depends upon the effort that both students and professors put into them. This makes many comparisons of on-line with classroom-based courses invidious. Both types of delivery can range from poorly designed and poorly taught to well designed and well taught, so that comparing a poor classroom-based course, or even an average one, with an excellent on-line course makes no sense, but studies have often failed to make appropriate comparisons, even if the courses are of comparable sizes.

Hence, it appears that on-line courses can be just as good, or bad, as classroom-based courses. Good courses in either medium have committed teachers who design the curriculum to engage students and move them up a learning curve, while giving realistic feedback about their achievements in the subject matter and their potential to further pursue it. Good courses also have committed students who are prepared to engage themselves in the subject matter and move up a learning curve, while listening to feedback about their performance and potential to further pursue that subject matter.

Will on-line courses replace classroom-based courses? As with the verdict on podcasts, the answer is no. On-line courses have their place and can provide a quality education for students who are willing to put out the effort under the tutelage of professors who are willing to put out a corresponding effort.

And, can on-line courses eradicate student disengagement? It appears that they can require more engagement by their very nature of requiring regular contributions versus the occasional tests and assignments often found in large classroom-based courses. Then again, the comparison must be fair, because on-line courses are often much smaller than lecture courses, and large lecture courses (without the support of sufficient TAs) cannot realistically employ constant testing and assignments. This issue is one of cost: lecture courses have an efficiency of scale to reduce costs, while on-line courses often reduce costs by exploiting adjunct faculty. If universities were better funded, classroom-based courses would be smaller and be more likely to engage students in more ways and enhance learning outcomes.

Finally, will the rhetoric about on-line courses abate? It is unlikely. Their delivery is becoming a big business, so that those overseeing their delivery have a vested interest in the rhetoric, making statements such as 'students are ahead of faculty on the curve' of this medium of education, an unsubstantiated blanket claim that has been seen with all the forms of technology examined in this chapter.[114] Unfortunately, unless those who would adopt on-line courses critically assess the rhetoric, especially that pertaining to the 'digital native,' it is likely that past mistakes will be repeated. As one source says:

Advocates making claims with little evidence are in danger of repeating a pattern seen throughout the history of educational technology in which new technologies promoted as vehicles for educational reform then fail to meet unrealistic expectations.[115]

Conclusions: Mixed Support and Moral Entrepreneurs

The evidence regarding the efficacy of these new technological educational supplements is still coming in, but what we know thus far is that:

- laptops have not lived up to their initial promise of universally engaging students and increasing students achievement;
- the evidence is mixed regarding clickers, although their effectiveness can depend upon the reason for their use and the skill of the teacher using them;
- podcasts can work very well in reinforcing lectures, although they are expensive and many students would not bother taking advantage of them;
- and the Internet (and technologies whose platforms depend upon it) has assisted in the development of some sophisticated on-line and hybrid courses, which can include (increasingly sophisticated) podcasts of lectures from conventional classroom courses.

In light of these findings, and basic pedagogical principles, calls to reject 'old ways of teaching' need to be carefully scrutinized. The enthusiasm about the application of the new technologies to the university setting has clearly outpaced the empirical evidence regarding their potential to enhance academic engagement and learning outcomes. It is clearly a curious development that so many people are willing to let technology drive the curriculum when it should be the other way around. Otherwise sensible, highly educated people are claiming that professors merely have to listen to the 'wisdom' of young 'digital natives' to learn how to revolutionize the university system with new technologies. In other words, the public is being told that in the span of one generation, the wisdom of numerous centuries of higher education is to be overturned and young people will lead adults to the Promised Land of education with technological gadgets. The susceptibility to technological evangelicals is also out of character for otherwise cautious people.

Unfortunately, some well-meaning professors and administrators may get caught up in the 'moral panic' noted above, and certain tech-advocates will step in as 'moral entrepreneurs' to take advantage of this panic. Contrary to their claims, technologies will not save the day in eradicating student disengagement. The solutions lie elsewhere.

The take-aways from this chapter are that the new technologies can facilitate learning, but they do not replace teachers. Evangelicals have it wrong: *the Internet is a library, not a teacher*, a distinction lost on people like Marc Prensky, whom Tapscott quotes as claiming that 'teachers are no longer the fountain of knowledge; the Internet is.'[116] In spite of these types of excessive claims, some of these technologies can enhance engagement, but not likely among 'hard-core' disengaged students. For many young people, including university students, these technologies are best used for the *fun* of learning concrete, personalized material (e.g., popular culture), not for the *work* of developing critical thinking skills, and learning how to deal with abstractions in written and verbal forms. And, in and of themselves, they are clearly not the best means for reaching the liberal-arts goals of developing advanced writing and oral skills and honing critical thinking skills. In fact, some believe that they can have the opposite effect.[117]

PART THREE

The Way Forward into the New Millennium

7 Recommendations and Conclusions: Our Stewardship of the System

What to Do

Our Recommendations

We begin by itemizing our recommendations for high schools and universities to combat grade inflation and disengagement – and therefore entitled disengagement – and to increase student readiness for a rigorous liberal education:

- Funding formulae need to be changed to allow schools to present university students with sufficient faculty contact and guidance to facilitate the transformative processes for which the liberal education is known;
  - Forcing universities to accept funding on the basis of number of students rather than program needs is unacceptable, and simply leads to watered-down programs;
  - The target should be a student-teacher ratio of 15:1 (for full-time professors in all departments, not an institutional average) for liberal programs;
- High schools and universities need to develop a system-wide standard of grade distributions for non-vocational programs following a reasonable approximation of the normal curve, with an appropriate calibration of at least four levels of performance;
  - All schools should publish their grade distributions on readily accessible websites;
- Standardized university entrance exams should be developed to ensure a minimal level of literacy and numeracy among students applying to enter baccalaureate programs;[1]

- University program exit exams should be implemented in each academic discipline to ensure that a minimum level of proficiency is attained by students in different schools ostensibly acquiring the same degree (similar to exams used in professional schools);[2]
- Teaching evaluations should target engagement levels, intellectual transformation, and learning outcomes, rather than student satisfaction and teacher popularity;[3]
  - In the absence of this, teaching evaluations need to be de-emphasized in performance evaluations, and departments should have mechanisms established so that evaluations are unaffected by the grading practices of individual teachers (e.g., if a teacher assigns more As than the grade distribution guidelines allow, a comparable proportion of the highest students' ratings of that teacher should be deducted from the teacher's evaluations);
- The liberal arts and sciences should be promoted as part of lifelong learning and made more accessible to those of all walks of life, instead of being sold as status symbols and credentials primarily to young people from more affluent backgrounds;
- All stakeholders should discuss and debate the mission of the contemporary university and the role of the liberal arts and sciences within it, with an eye to ensuring high-quality delivery;
  - A national enquiry should be established with the distinction between liberal and applied educations as its guiding principle;
- Administrators (who have emerged from the ranks of the professoriate) should be required to spend some time teaching as part of their stewardship of university standards. For example, all senior university administrators should teach introductory- and senior-level courses in their discipline. This would ensure that administrators are academics and not bureaucrats;
  - Similarly, at the secondary level, in jurisdictions where principals no longer teach because they have been legislated as full-time administrators, this should be reversed, and they should teach at the freshman and senior levels.

Association of American Colleges and Universities Recommendations

In the United States there are far more schools with just a few thousand students than is the case in Canada. In theory, therefore, these schools can attend more closely on a student-by-student basis to a liberal arts and science curriculum. Apparently, however, many schools, small or large, are not doing so. To address this, the Association of American Colleges and Universities (AAC&U; with some 950 institutional members) has issued statements intended to keep these schools 'on mission.'

Their 2004 statement, *Our Students' Best Work: A Framework for Accountability Worthy of Our Mission*, reiterates the commitment of the organization 'to ensuring that every student experiences the benefits – intellectual, economic, civic, social, and intercultural – of a well-designed and intellectually challenging liberal education.'[4] They acknowledge the transformation of the liberal education from the nineteenth century, when the 'liberal education primarily served young men who were preparing for leadership positions, often in the clergy, medicine, and law,' through the twentieth century, when it endeavoured 'to be inclusive and to provide an empowering education to widely diverse students.'[5] At the same time, they also recognize the threat of the pseudo-vocational logic creeping into many schools, noting that the pubic has come 'to contrast liberal education with professional education and to regard it as, by definition, not "practical."'[6] Moreover, they identify this as false dichotomy, asserting that the

> opposite of liberal education is narrow, situation-specific training. While situation-specific training has many good uses, by itself it is insufficient preparation for a world characterized by complexity, conflicting judgments, and accelerating change. Even students in technical fields, therefore, need and deserve the complementary benefits of a liberal education to help them make sense of the social and environmental contexts in which they will use their skills, and to prepare them for lifelong work rather than just an initial job.[7]

In order to keep universities 'on mission,' the AAC&U report identifies five key educational outcomes for which liberal programs should strive to keep themselves on high-quality missions, thus avoiding pseudo-vocationalism:

1. **strong analytical, communication, quantitative, and information skills** – achieved and demonstrated through learning in a range of fields, settings, and media, and through advanced studies in one or more areas of concentration;
2. **deep understanding of and hands-on experience with the inquiry practices of disciplines that explore the natural, social, and cultural realms** – achieved and demonstrated through studies that build conceptual knowledge by engaging learners in concepts and modes of

inquiry that are basic to the natural sciences, social sciences, humanities, and arts;

3. **intercultural knowledge and collaborative problem-solving skills** – achieved and demonstrated in a variety of collaborative contexts (classroom, community based, international, and online) that prepare students both for democratic citizenship and for work;

4. **a proactive sense of responsibility for individual, civic, and social choices** – achieved and demonstrated through forms of learning that connect knowledge, skills, values, and public action, and through reflection on students' own roles and responsibilities in social and civic contexts;

5. **habits of mind that foster integrative thinking and the ability to transfer skills and knowledge from one setting to another** – achieved and demonstrated through advanced research and/or creative projects in which students take the primary responsibility for framing questions, carrying out an analysis, and producing work of substantial complexity and quality.[8]

We wholeheartedly endorse the AAC&U outcome-quality objectives[9] and draw readers' attention to their call for grading rubrics to 'summarize levels of student achievement across different academic fields and institutions and for particular groups of students in terms of [four levels of] student achievement: advanced, proficient, basic, and below basic.'[10]

What Not to Do: Managing the Line between Mass and Élite Universities

Massification

Specifying the courses of action universities should *not* take is more complex, given the number of directions that can be taken by different schools in diverse jurisdictions. Accordingly, what we can do in this section is present a case study of a 'discussion' of approaches that have been tried elsewhere and are now being recommended for Canada. We will critique what has been suggested for Canada and see how these approaches have turned out elsewhere.

In December 2006, Clive Keen, director of lifelong learning and enrolment management at the University of Prince Edward Island, and Ken Coates, dean of arts at the University of Waterloo, published an opinion piece in *University Affairs* titled 'Universities for the 21st Century,' with the caption 'It's time for universities to face the challenges of mass education.'[11]

Keen and Coates have some useful suggestions directed at helping universities maintain their enrolment levels, and they advance the aspect of the debate regarding how much universities should embrace vocational training, especially that already provided by other post-secondary institutions like community colleges (in some regions) and poly-technical institutions.

Theirs is a matter-of-fact solution that rejects the idealism of those of us who want universities to maintain liberal curricula and higher-educational standards. Their argument is essentially that the variously unprepared, unmotivated, and disengaged students should not be expected to meet their learning environments halfway; instead, their learning environments should do all the stretching in programs that students will enjoy, with teaching methods that will get them through to graduation, and programs that will lead them directly into jobs. Universities, they argue, 'are in the business of mass education' and will do better at it once they 'admit to the facts.' But, based on what we have been arguing, instead of mass education, we have actually been providing mass certification, and the large numbers of certified 'graduates' are not enriching the economy or society in ways that might be expected.

Similar to Hallgrímsson (discussed above in chapter 3), their solution is a multiple-tiered university with liberal programs for those who can handle them; for others, vocationally oriented programs would be provided, taught with methods geared to students who lack academic motivation and ability.

In March 2007, Andrew Park, a biology professor at the University of Winnipeg, responded with his own opinion piece titled 'Heck No, You Shouldn't Go,' with the caption 'Despite our best efforts to help struggling students, there are some who really shouldn't be there in the first place.'[12] He presents a position close to ours, noting evidence for the poor preparation of many students, along with their poor outcomes. He goes on to identify three types of students he has not been able to reach, in spite of taking 'great pains to professionalize [his] teaching, address [himself] to different learning styles, produce challenging assignments, make lectures available online, and reach out to students of all abilities.'

According to Park, two of these three groups have no interest in biology (yet take his courses) and are 'not shy to say so on course evaluations.' The third group is enthusiastic, but unable to handle course requirements, either because of a lack of preparation or because they are too busy with other activities. He disagrees with Keen and Coates that remediation will help these students, and he rejects their call for a two-tiered system, arguing that the 'idea amounts to boutique education for some and devalued "Walmart" degrees for the rest.' The fairer solution, he insists, is to counsel 'students far more carefully before they enter university and, when necessary, turn them away for their – and our – own good.' He also points out viable alternatives to university for job training, which are eschewed because of the persistence of 'the myth that university is the only route' to high-paying jobs 'in the minds of parents and students alike.'

Keen and Coates responded to Park by arguing that he is being too idealistic, and should acknowledge the inevitable task of dealing with disengaged students, whom they designate as the bread and butter of contemporary universities:

> The tempting route, when faced with the disengaged, unmotivated and ill-prepared students he describes so well is 'Just exclude them all from universities. They shouldn't be here.' That's fine, as long as we are prepared to live with the consequences.
>
> We agreed with [Park's] main point – that many students come to universities without the requisite level of commitment, preparation or curiosity. But his solution – leaving them out – would be fine if we don't mind closing down half our universities and displacing very large numbers of our faculty and staff. Save for the highly selective universities, our campuses are financially dependent on these same students who seem so ill-suited for the kind of education many faculty would prefer to provide.[13]

Not only do Keen and Coates explicitly acknowledge that universities are businesses (delivering products that are inferior by traditional standards), they go on to contend that because mass access is a 'political imperative,' universities would not be allowed to exclude disengaged students. Indeed, echoing our earlier comments about superficial calls for democratization, they tacitly acknowledge that a decline in standards has taken place to the extent that 'the public has much the same expectations of access to university that they had in the 1950s about high-school education.' In view of this education inflation, they argue that universities must find ways to engage and motivate these students, even if it means they become more 'polytechnic-like' (read: pseudo-vocational). They then evoke the rhetoric of the '21st century' university, asserting that the '19th and 20th century curriculum is at the heart of the problem,' and intimate that many twenty-first century learners will not engage with it. In assessing these claims, readers should bear in mind the examination of the rhetoric about '21st century learners,' or 'digital natives,' in chapter 6, where much of it was found to be baseless.

One of us had the opportunity to discuss Keen's views with him as part of a symposium titled 'Strategic Options in a Changing Enrolment Landscape,' sponsored by the Maritime Provinces Higher Education Commission (MPHEC), where Keen and Côté were panellists presenting 'two diametrically opposed paths for universities.'[14] As it turns out, our views are not entirely different. Instead, our views vary mainly in *what* should be done to reform universities as well as *how* those reforms should be undertaken, but not *why*.

The 'why' for Keen is similar to that offered by Charles Murray in his recent book *Real Education*, which is discussed in the next section. Keen's 'why' reasoning is based on evidence that the average student in current mass systems has less academic aptitude than did/does the average student in pre-massified university systems and in more selective institutions still found in some countries. Currently, it is argued, the more able students who would have prevailed in earlier systems are now a minority. Consequently, it is unrealistic to expect high levels of engagement in the liberal arts and sciences from average students today: as they do not have the intellectual ability to engage deeply in reading and discussions, and are not interested in developing those abilities, no manner of teaching approaches will reach them. Keen argues that we must change the curriculum to address this. In contrast, we argue that these students must be targeted earlier to develop the 'habits of heart and mind,' to quote George Kuh once again,[15] to appreciate the value of higher learning.

It is commonsensical that if students coming to universities were better prepared for the university-level curriculum, far more of them could handle it. The evidence provided above in chapter 5 that mass universities in many European countries can maintain adequate levels of student engagement, supports this argument. Yet, this would also require that Canadian students be accustomed to a non-inflated grading system that accurately assessed their abilities, and be willing to put out the effort to meet higher educational standards. This would require that the stigma be reversed and removed from the C grade throughout the entire system at all levels. De-stigmatizing the C grade would allow for it to return to its position as the modal, or most common grade assigned. If this were accomplished, as discussed above, students of average academic ability, who are adequately prepared, could pass courses with a C or better if they expended sufficient effort. In view of the fact that C has traditionally designated a satisfactory performance, there should be no shame in this achievement if the standard is such that the C assessment represents a 'good' or 'adequate' performance, as represented in good writing abilities, for example.

With appropriate feedback, if students aspired to improve their grades on, say, written assignments, they could attempt to do so and find their potential in terms of the written communication of ideas. Academic abilities can improve with effort, but if students are given false feedback and told that minimal effort is good enough, this crucial aspect of higher education goes unrealized (recall from chapter 2 the student's complaints published in the *Globe and Mail* about being over-rewarded and therefore under-challenged). Universities could thus sustain their current enrolment levels, and indeed might increase enrolment, as more of these academically developed students come to believe that there are viable opportunities for personal and intellectual development if they attend university, even if they are 'C students.' Of course, to do this properly, faculty complements would have to be increased to achieve the 15:1 student-teacher ratio identified in the last section.

Keen does not address this wider need for reform of both the secondary and tertiary systems, and he instead argues that the public should accept the poor preparation and lack of motivation of would-be students as an unchangeable given. Hence, for him, the route to reform is for the system to finally give in to the mentality of the alienated student. He quotes an alienated student as proof that this is the best way for us to go:

> Students do not come to school to learn ... we come because a university education is deemed socially and economically necessary ... We have been brainwashed into a game, whereby we memorize vast amounts of material, regurgitate it onto paper in a crowded room, and then forget about it. The academic environment has trained us to perform. Revolutionize the system! Start now. And make society, and academia a more productive and positive learning and living environment.[16]

In a paper titled 'Male University Transition Problems: A Guilt-free Explanation,'[17] Keen makes the case that North American universities should follow the example of those in the United Kingdom and Australia by offering courses that are of intuitive interest to males, who are more likely to be disengaged in high school, and therefore to have less interest than females in academics. He asserts rather boldly that

> North American universities will need to become more polytechnic-like, changing not just their curriculum but their pedagogy. They will have to realize that they suffer from incredible self-delusion in telling young males that they should spend two hours in private book-study for every hour spent in class. Perhaps that happened when universities dealt with the gifted and intellectually curious. Repeating this expectation for today's average young males is to live in cloud-cuckoo-land.

The programs that he argues could be offered, and which now can be found in British and Australian universities, include:

- BSc Disaster Management and Emergency Planning
- BSc Pollution Control
- BSc Ethical Hacking and Countermeasures
- BA Crime and Social Order
- BSc Computer Forensics
- BSc Computer Games Technology
- BA Adventure Recreation
- BSc Cruise Operations Management
- BA Resort Management
- BSc Robotics and Automated Systems
- BSc Security Technology
- BSc Property Development
- BA Sports Journalism
- BSc Science and The Media
- BSc Mobile and Wearable Computing

He adds a further program – a BSc (Hons) in Surf Science – which he quips 'shows how very far British universities have come from the stodgier days.' This degree is advertised at the University of Plymouth as 'a rigorous academic study of the scientific, technical and business aspects of the international surfing industries.' Keen argues this program 'would surely be a lure to some sixteen-year old males who would otherwise be first in the dropout queue.'

In reacting to Keen's suggestions, we do not object to universities offering vocational programs so long as they are clearly differentiated from liberal programs, and designated as parts of separate faculties (say, a Faculty of Applied Studies, as is currently the case in some schools). These vocational programs are obviously capitalizing on the cachet of the bachelor's degree, but if developed in universities, we would prefer that the programs culminated in a degree with a different name to avoid confusion and further dilution of the value of the BA/BSc. However, the biggest obstacle to Keen's prescriptions may well be the community colleges (in parts of Canada) and polytechnic institutions that would likely strenuously object to this poaching of their students.

Additionally, it would be more beneficial to the educational system as a whole to introduce such programs as part of an upper secondary school curriculum, similar to that found in many European countries (like Finland, above) and the CEGEP system in the Province of Quebec. CEGEP offers a three-year 'career program' stream and a two-year 'pre-university' stream.[18] In this way, the unmotivated high-school students to which Keen refers could be inspired at the point where they might otherwise be tempted to drop out of the system.

More generally, though, when viewing the interests of the entire post-secondary system, recommendations for universities to take on explicit vocational training would set in motion zero-sum competitions for students among publicly financed institutions. In other words, given that the public purse subsidizes secondary and post-secondary education in Canada, there is not much to gain collectively from this attempt to capture the 'disengaged student market.' Our solution is to provide better high-school preparation for those who would benefit from a liberal education, and let those who want applied programs go to upper secondary programs, colleges, or polytechnics, where teachers who do not conduct independent research have the time and training to instruct them.[19]

This more reasoned solution should also produce more – not fewer – students who want to pursue some form of post-secondary education. But this is a long-term solution, and not a quick fix done out of a fear of enrolment declines in the pursuit of 'bums-on-seats' government funding. Moreover, it is not evident that there are enough qualified teachers for such vocational programs, and enough jobs available for their graduates. For instance, how many jobs in Surf Science can there be, and what are the graduates of those programs in the United Kingdom really doing for a living? Without assurance on both points, we believe it would be unwise to proceed down this path.

Indeed, when what has happened in the United Kingdom as a result of the expansion of their universities in a pseudo-vocational fashion is examined, it is apparent that little has been accomplished to address access concerns in terms of social class backgrounds. Andy Furlong and Fred Cartmel argue that a three-tiered system has emerged in the mass higher education system that has been put in place in the United Kingdom over the past couple of decades.[20] The bottom tier comprises universities built since 1992 that target those of lower socio-economic backgrounds (45 per cent from working-class backgrounds) who respond to marketing strategies stressing the schools' '"down-to-earth" and accessible image,'[21] their catering to different 'learning styles,' their approachable staff, and their teaching the types of vocational subjects listed above by Keen.

Middle-tier universities constitute those that are somewhat older than 1992, and many were formerly colleges and polytechnics, but these are clearly differentiated in status from the 'Russell Group,' the twenty larger research-intensive universities, including Oxford, Cambridge, and St Andrews, which draw 85 per cent of their students from the middle and upper classes. These élite universities have held vocationalism at bay, in favour of high-quality liberal programs, with the exception of professional programs like law and medicine, and continue to do so.

The lesson from the U.K. experience is that you can 'build them and they will come,' but little may be accomplished in terms of a social agenda such as democratizing access and ensuring that those from lower socio-economic backgrounds compete on equal grounds. Furlong and Cartmel summarize this situation as follows:

> The separation of the old and new universities (and the more subtle distinctions that mark status within each of these broad categories), result in a class-based set of experiences that ultimately represent clear channels between unequal family origins and unequal labour market positions. Within institutions (especially the older ones) there are clear divisions between prestigious and less prestigious courses and restricted patterns of interaction between students. There is little evidence that working-class students are becoming absorbed into the assumptive worlds of the established middle classes or developing the sorts of networks that smooth access to traditional graduate careers.[22]

Back to the Canadian context, a recent book written by several senior academics for the Higher Education Quality Council of Ontario (HEQCO) recommends transforming some universities into the vocational-like institutes recommended by Keen.[23] Their recommendations for transforming Ontario universities are based on the premise that the model of the research university as a way of delivering a university education to all comers is now too expensive. These authors call for a number of changes that would have the effect of creating multiple tiers, including creating three-year and 'pre-professional' degrees, and locking more professors in 'teach-only' contracts.

While some of their ideas might have merit, especially in diverting academically disengaged students who are simply in search of jobs to explicitly vocational programs, the authors do not distinguish between education and training, and thus fail to acknowledge the pedagogical differences between a liberal education and a pseudo-vocational course of study. Consequently, these recommendations might only hasten the eclipse of the liberal education by pseudo-vocationalism. What we do not find in this book is a call for more money to fix the seriously underfunded Ontario university system.

Our other disappointments with the recommendations in this book include the following:

- Major issues like student disengagement, grade inflation, unreadiness, and underemployment get the usual bureaucratese, which 'talks around' each problem rather than directly addressing it;
- The human capital model is the only framework (implicitly) recognized, and corporatization is not critiqued;
- Government policies that could be directed at enhancing demand in the youth labour market, linked with vocational training at the secondary level, are not considered;
- The wisdom of the continuing growth of universities is never questioned, nor is the role played by neo-liberalism in the retreat of governments in properly funding them;
- There is no consideration of returning some of our smaller schools to their originally intended sizes with adequate funding to carry out respectable liberal missions;
- The possibility that the three-year teaching universities they recommend creating will simply be 'glorified high schools' is not considered.

At the very least, we would have hoped that these senior academics would have helped develop a vision of how to take us into the future in ways that do not excuse governments from investing more money into our grossly underfunded universities. These authors apparently had a good run in their university careers, and they seem rather complacent about closing the doors behind them to deny future generations the benefits they enjoyed. It is becoming far to common for those who grew up in the post-war affluence of the 1950s and 1960s to see little obligation to 'pay their advantages forward' to future generations.

Élitism

Charles Murray, infamous in some circles for his work on the policy implications of IQ research, especially in *The Bell Curve*,[24] has some interesting things to say about what might be done to rescue the liberal education from its imminent decline into pseudo-vocationalism. Although he doesn't use the latter term, his description of what is happening in the United States is similar to ours for Canada. However, reminiscent of the distinction between the old Right and old Left discussed above in chapter 1, Murray holds many of the views typically found among the old Right in lamenting the passage of the education of an élite for the 'good of society.' In contrast, our views correspond more closely with the old Left.

Our agreements with Murray pertain to the value of the liberal education and the range of abilities that educational systems, freed from political partisanship, must recognize and nurture. Our disagreements involve his deterministic view of IQ and associated beliefs that only the 'gifted' can benefit from exposure to a liberal education. Also, we argue that a liberal education must now embrace more than the Eurocentric classics.

First, with our agreements:

We recommend that educators take seriously Murray's discussion of Gardner's seven different types of abilities in relation to the education system. Only three of these abilities are measured by IQ tests and contribute to what are recognized as academic abilities: spatial, logical-mathematical, and linguistic. The other four abilities are found in people regardless of their academic skills but also constitute the potentials at the basis of competence in a variety of occupations for which an academic education provides little preparation. These abilities are musical, bodily-kinesthetic, interpersonal, and intrapersonal. We agree with Murray's argument that many students who become disillusioned with schools and do poorly academically have talents that lie within these other ability domains, and not with the academic ones; yet, many educational systems are forcing these students to forego the development of abilities upon which they (would) excel in favour of activities for which they have less potential. People would do well to remember the simple lesson known to earlier generations as the futility of trying to fit square pegs into round holes. We also agree to some extent with Murray's critique of 'educational romanticism,' by which he means the erroneous belief 'that every child can be anything he or she wants to be.'[25] Clearly, certain levels of native ability, along with extensive effort (see especially chapter 2, above), are crucial in people's accomplishments.

Now with our disagreements:

In our view, Murray espouses an overly deterministic view of IQ in relation to higher learning. He believes that only the academically 'gifted' – those with IQs above 115 (some 16 per cent of the population)[26] – can benefit from exposure to a liberal education. His rationale for this is that it takes this level of intelligence to master key elements of the liberal arts and sciences, such as advanced calculus or the literary analysis of complex texts. Based on these IQ assumptions, Murray argues that American universities are over-enrolled by two to three times.

A problem with Murray's argument is that he seems to have in mind students who would excel in their courses and then go on to become professionals in a given field. In contrast, we believe that a larger number of students who were properly prepared for university-level studies would benefit from exposure to a liberal education. As noted in the last section, this would require better preparation at the primary and secondary levels, including a valuing of knowledge as an end in itself (and Murray recommends that primary and secondary schools provide more grounding in liberal curricula), as well as re-instituting the full range of grades as an acceptable form of evaluation – including de-stigmatizing the C grade. If everyone accepted that they are average at most things (and excel in few), whether it be playing hockey, playing a flute, or solving math problems, this stigma could be eradicated. Under these circumstances, those of average ability in reading comprehension, say, could benefit from an exposure to the structure and content of literary analyses or the processes involved in undertaking advanced statistical analyses, even if they are not going on to teach and research these topics.

Murray wants to preserve universities for an intellectual élite who all score as gifted on IQ tests. He believes that this is the best way to educate the future leaders of society in a broad knowledge of culture, philosophy, the arts, sciences, and history. Well, societies need leaders at all levels, and these leaders do not have to be gifted in the liberal arts and sciences for this broad knowledge to play a role in their worldly involvements. We believe that a range of students with varying ability levels can benefit from the type of educational system we have advocated in this book. The key to such a system is a student body committed to effort, honesty, and humility, supported by a curriculum that rewards these things.

Finally, Murray provides examples of the curriculum to which the IQ-blessed future leaders would be exposed, and these all involve European classics. These Eurocentric choices are odd in a globalized world, where a liberal education should be as much forward-looking as backward-looking, embracing the best of all human civilizations.

Conclusion

Action needs to be taken, and soon. Unless it is, the current generation of adults will be responsible for the ultimate demise of the liberal education for all but the very wealthy, and its replacement by pseudo-vocationalism for the masses, replete with a high-school mentality toward teaching and learning. In the latter case, universities will pretend to teach students at a level of higher education, and students will pretend to learn at that level, but the truth will be that universities are simply providing empty degrees that are little more than expensive 'fishing licences' for lower-level white-collar jobs.

Notes

Introduction

1 Debating the role of universities is further complicated because it involves different understandings that often follow the political Left/Right and/or progressive/traditionalist spectra of opinion that have historically swung educational practices back and forth on an ideological pendulum. Although our argument does not neatly fit into either pole of these continua, some people have attempted to pigeonhole us into these extremes, thereby fostering further misunderstandings. For an example of this, see Joseph Galbo, 'Anxious Academics: Mission Drift and Sliding Standards in the Modern Canadian University,' *Canadian Journal of Sociology* 33.2 (2008): 418–20, http://ejournals.library.ualberta.ca/index.php/CJS/article/view/1991/1412; for rejoinders to Galbo see http://ejournals.library.ualberta.ca/index.php/CJS/article/view/1992 and http://ejournals.library.ualberta.ca/index.php/CJS/article/view/4548/3694 (accessed 7 Dec. 2009).

2 A book with a similar title was released as we were finishing this book. *The Lowering of Higher Education in America: Why Financial Aid Should Be Based on Student Performance* (Santa Barbara, CA: Greenwood Press, 2010), by Jackson Toby, is focused entirely on the United States and is in concurrence with our analysis of many problems such as grade inflation and student disengagement. However, Toby's focus is more on solutions to these problems associated with financial aid systems specific to the United States, where he argues that the low effort expended by many students could be addressed by pulling various levers of economic incentives and disincentives.

3 Out of necessity we will repeat some of the points made in our previous book, but will not continually reference it when we do so.

1. A History of a Mission Adrift: The Idea of the University Subverted

1 Hugh Chisholm, *Encyclopaedia Britannica: A Dictionary of Arts, Sciences, Literature and General Information*, Vol. 27 (Cambridge: Cambridge University Press, 1911), 748.

2 Gerard Delanty, 'The Sociology of the University and Higher Education: The Consequences of Globalization,' in *The Sage Handbook of Sociology*, ed. Craig Calhoun, Chris Rojek, and Bryan S. Turner (Thousand Oaks, CA: Sage, 2005), 530–45.

3 Cf. ibid.

4 The distinction between 'scholar' and 'academic' is to highlight that modernists generally adhere to standards of scholarship in which objectivity is held as an ideal, even if it proves ultimately unattainable. In contrast, postmodernists may take up an academic position but not use any measures to limit their biases; to the contrary, prejudgments are often celebrated and drive their work from start to finish. The public is generally unaware of the postmodernist academic's approach and may mistake his or her work as reflecting modernist scholarship. For an unabashed rejection of modernist standards governing plagiarism, see Susan D. Blum, *My Word! Plagiarism and College Culture* (Ithaca, NY: Cornell University Press, 2009). For a review of this book, see, James Côté, 'Student Cheating, Relativism, and Standards of Scholarship: Where Are We Going, and What Are We Doing in This Hand Basket?' *Academic Matters (Online)*, http://academicmatters. ca/current_issue.article.gk?catalog_item_id=3586&category=/web_ exclusive/articles/current (accessed 2 Jan. 2010).

5 John S. Brubacher, *On the Philosophy of Higher Education* (San Francisco: Jossey-Bass, 1977), 24.

6 James E. Côté and Anton L. Allahar, *Ivory Tower Blues: A University System in Crisis* (Toronto: University of Toronto Press, 2007), 128, 133–4.

7 For some useful analyses of the long-standing conflict between the liberal education and vocationalism, see Derek Bok, *Our Underachieving Colleges* (Princeton: Princeton University Press, 2006); Harry R. Lewis, *Excellence without a Soul* (New York: Perseus Books, 2006); and George Fallis, *Multiversities, Ideas, and Democracy* (Toronto: University of Toronto Press, 2007). Fallis provides an excellent summary of the history of the first millennium of the university, and the dual role of liberal arts knowledge for its own sake as well as for indirect economic uses, a tension that can be traced to the inception of the liberal education.

8 Côté and Allahar, *Ivory Tower Blues*, 171. But, of course, the issue of cause and effect is difficult to sort out here, as is the influence of third variables that might produce spurious correlations.

9 This is C. Wright Mills's famous notion of the 'sociological imagination' that every student learns in introductory sociology courses (C. Wright Mills, *The Sociological Imagination* [New York: Oxford University Press, 1959]).

10 Thorstein Veblen, *The Higher Learning in America: A Memorandum on the Conduct of Universities by Business Men* (New York: B.W. Huebsch, 1918).

11 Cited in J.M. Cameron, *On the Idea of a University* (Toronto: University of Toronto Press, 1978), 15.

12 Antoine Nicolas de Condorcet, 'The Progress of the Human Mind,' in *Classics of Western Thought Part III: The Modern World* (enlarged edition), ed. Charles Hirschfield (New York: Harcourt, Brace, Jovanovich, 1964), 213–14.

13 Kern Alexander, 'The Object of the University: Motives and Motivation,' in *The University: International Expectations*, ed. E. King Alexander and Kern Alexander (Montreal: McGill-Queen's University Press, 2002), 4. Compare these hopes with current claims that new media of knowledge transmission – the new technologies discussed in chapter 6 – will empower people by merit of the technology's inherent potentials. Mass empowerment did not happen then and will likely not happen now in the context of the current political economy of social class relations.

14 John Henry Newman (Cardinal), *The Idea of a University Defined and Illustrated* (London: Longmans, Green & Co., 1925), 183.

15 Ibid., 99–112.

16 Cameron, *On the Idea of a University*, 13.

17 Leo Strauss, 'Liberal Education and Mass Democracy,' in *Higher Education and Modern Democracy: The Crisis of the Few and Many*, ed. Robert A. Goldwin (Chicago: Rand McNally & Co. 1967). Also available at http://www.ditext.com/strauss/lib2.html (accessed 7 Dec. 2009).

18 Max Weber, *The Protestant Ethic and the Spirit of Capitalism* (New York: Charles Scribner's Sons, 1958), 183.

19 Alexander, 'The Object of the University,' 6.

20 Strauss, 'Liberal Education and Mass Democracy,' http://www.ditext.com/strauss/lib2.html, para. 49 (accessed 7 Dec. 2009).

21 Simon Marginson, 'Putting the "Public" Back into the Public University,' *Thesis Eleven* 84 (2006): 44–59, 48.

22 Bill Readings, *The University in Ruins* (Cambridge: Harvard University Press, 1996), 21.

23 Ibid., 25.

24 Ibid., 22.

25 Cameron, *On the Idea of a University*, 9.

26 Randall Collins, *The Credential Society: A Historical Sociology of Education and Stratification* (New York: Academic, 1979); Randall Collins, 'Credential

Inflation and the Future of Universities,' in *The Future of the City of Intellect*, ed. Steven Brint (Stanford, CA: Stanford University Press, 2002).

27 Craig Calhoun, 'The University and the Public Good,' *Thesis Eleven* 84 (2006): 7–43, 9.

28 Ibid., 8.

29 Roger Kimball, *Tenured Radicals: How Politics Has Corrupted Our Higher Education* (Chicago: Ivan R. Dee, 1998), 14.

30 Bruce Smith, Jeremy Mayer, and A. Lee Fritschler, *Closed Minds? Politics and Ideology in American Universities* (Washington, DC: Brookings Institution Press, 2008), 67.

31 Dinesh D'Souza, *Illiberal Education: The Politics of Race and Sex on Campus* (New York: The Free Press, 1991), 229.

32 A team of authors wrote two self-professed polemics in the '80s and '90s designed to stir up interest in Canada's universities over problems that they saw with 'leftist' gains such as unions and tenure, and the lower standards associated with catering to political correctness. See David Bercuson, Robert Bothwell, and Jack. L. Granatstein, *The Great Brain Robbery: Canada's Universities on the Road to Ruin* (Toronto: McClelland and Stewart, 1984); and David Bercuson, Robert Bothwell, and Jack. L. Granatstein, *Petrified Campus: The Crisis in Canada's Universities* (Toronto: Random House, 1997).

33 Todd Gitlin, *The Twilight of Common Dreams: Why America Is Wracked by Culture Wars* (New York: Metropolitan Books, 1995).

34 For discussions of postmodernism and the culture wars, and the machinations of the Left and Right in the '80s and '90s, see Peter C. Emberley and Waler R. Newell, *Bankrupt Education: The Decline of Liberal Education in Canada* (Toronto: University of Toronto Press, 1994); and Peter C. Emberley, *Zero Tolerance: Hot Button Politics in Canada's Universities* (Toronto: Penguin, 1996).

35 Consider, for example, the Rogers School of Journalism at Ryerson University, or the involvement of the University of Western Ontario with the testing of ballistic materials for the manufacture of military vehicles for the Pentagon, or even McGill University's experiments in perfecting torture techniques and related research into 'sensory isolation' and 'white noise.' And this does not even deal with the proliferation of corporate fast-food outlets on campuses, designer clothing, music, and computer stores, banks, state-of-the-art gymnasia, and beauty salons, sun-tanning booths, and spas. To all of this, Bill Readings would use a U.S. reference and comment: 'When Ford Motors enters into a partnership with The Ohio State University to develop "total quality management in all areas of life on

campus," this partnership is based on the assumption that "the mission(s) of the university and the corporation are not that different"' (*The University in Ruins*, 21). Though U.S.-based, this example is equally instructive in Canada, where the language of business (total quality management or TQM) is increasingly at home on campuses and can be seen as the extension of the calls for democratization, transparency, and accountability.

36 Adrienne S. Chan and Donald Fisher, eds, *The Exchange University: Corporatization of Academic Culture* (Vancouver: University of British Columbia Press, 2008).

37 Max Weber, 'Science as a Vocation,' in *From Max Weber: Essays in Sociology*, ed. Hans Gerth and C. Wright Mills (Oxford: Oxford University, 1958), 145.

38 John Ellis, *Literature Lost: Social Agendas and the Corruption of the Humanities* (New Haven: Yale University Press, 1997), 7.

39 Stanley Fish, *Save the World on Your Own Time* (New York: Oxford University Press, 2008), 10.

40 Gregory S. Prince, Jr, *Teach Them to Challenge Authority: Educating for Healthy Societies* (New York: Continuum, 2008), 35.

41 Smith et al., *Closed Minds?* 151.

42 Ibid., 140.

43 Prince, *Teach Them to Challenge Authority*, 62.

44 Smith et al., *Closed Minds?* 107.

45 Shelby Steele, *The Content of Our Character: A New Vision of Race in America* (New York: St Martin's Press, 1990), 132.

46 Kimball, *Tenured Radicals*, 14.

47 Weber, 'Science as a Vocation.'

48 For example, one conservative claims that 'the general crisis of the humanities today is caused by the collapse of a genuinely moderate center in the face of ideological pressure from a Leftist extreme. In the last few decades, he argues that we have witnessed the occupation of the center by a new academic establishment, an establishment of tenured radicals' (Kimball, *Tenured Radicals*, 215).

49 Smith et al., *Closed Minds?* 2–3, 5–7.

50 Ibid., 46.

2. Stakeholder Relations: The Educational Forum

1 See Toby, *The Lowering of Higher Education in America*, who cites evidence that only about one in five of those who require extensive remediation actually completes a degree within eight years.

2 Joseph Berger, Anne Motte, and Andrew Parkin, eds, *The Price of Knowledge*

2008: Access and Student Finance in Canada Fourth Edition (Montreal: Canada Millennium Scholarship Foundation, 2009).

3 Not all stakeholders can be discussed here because of space limitations. Those not discussed are clearly important in the debate, but their influence is often more indirect, and thus more difficult to gauge, as in the case of the media.

4 An annual exit survey at our own university, which prides itself as providing 'the best student experience' in Canada, finds that only about two-thirds of graduating students rate their learning experience as 'intellectually challenging' (Office of the Provost and Vice-President [Academic], *Report on the Survey of Graduating Students: 2006-07* [London, ON, 2007]). It is interesting that those graduating from the Faculty of Education, and thus moving into the ranks of primary- and secondary-school teachers, give one of the lowest ratings regarding intellectual challenge: less than 50 per cent of graduates rate their learning experience in that faculty as intellectually challenging. This low score is interesting in light of the extremely high grades required for admission into the Faculty of Education and the very high grades awarded in courses there.

5 Mary Woodward, 'My Best Marks Were in Partying 101,' *Globe and Mail*, 6 Sept. 2006, A18.

6 James Watson-Glaze, 'Reflections on a Damaged Education,' *Psynopsis* 29.3 (Summer 2007): 12.

7 John Smith, 'I'm Leaving.' *Inside Higher Ed*, http://www.insidehighered. com/views/2008/10/31/smith (accessed 4 Oct. 2009).

8 http://www.mended.ca/about/ (accessed 4 Oct. 2009). After this book went to press, the website was closed down, with the group apparently taking a hiatus.

9 http://www.societyforqualityeducation.org/index.php/ (accessed 4 Oct. 2009).

10 http://hslda.ca/index.php?option=com_content&view=article&id=95&Ite mid=156 (accessed 23 Dec. 2009).

11 Canadian News Wire (CNW GROUP), 'Study Shows Home-Educated Become Model Citizens,' 2 Dec. 2009, http://www.newswire.ca/en/ releases/archive/December2009/02/c7005.html (accessed 23 Dec. 2009); Deani A. Neven Van Pelt, Patricia A. Allison, and Derek J. Allison, *Fifteen Years Later: Home-Educated Canadian Adults* (London, ON: Canadian Centre for Home Education, 2009), http://www.hslda.ca/cche_ research/2009StudySynopsis.pdf.

12 Apparently, Alberta tried doing without province-wide standardized teaching in the 1970s but encountered too much grade inflation using

teacher-assigned grades. In 1983, diploma exams were reintroduced in grade 12 to cover core subjects, and are weighted as 50 per cent of students' final grades. Students applying from Ontario to Alberta universities are given a handicap to make their grades more compatible with the graduates of Alberta's high schools (Michael Woods, 'Making the Grade,' *Queen's Journal* [19 Sept. 2008], http://www.queensjournal.ca/story/2008-09-19/features/making-the-grade/ [accessed 19 Sept. 2008]).

13 Of course, in past generations, leaving high school before graduation was not defined as a problem. It was simply accepted that not everyone had the interest or ability to stay in school that long (e.g., in the 1950s, only about half of those in their late teens were in school). The common-sense notion was that there was little point in trying to fit 'a square peg in a round hole.' In more contemporary social-scientific terminology, this would be expressed in terms of a 'goodness of fit': since people's characteristics interact differently with social contexts, a one-size-fits-all approach to social adjustment is ill-advised. But, at the same time, job prospects were better in those pre-credentialist days, and since the collapse of the youth labour market in the 1980s (and with no government policies to correct the collapse), the commonsense view today is to stick it out in school even if you hate it.

14 The memo, signed by Ben Levin, a University of Toronto (OISE) professor seconded to the Ministry of Education as a deputy minister, was first circulated as an e-mail attachment to school boards, and then posted on the following address, which may not stay current: http://cal2.edu.gov.on.ca/may2009/StudentAssessment.pdf (accessed 1 June 2009).

15 Jon Cowans, 'Why Johnny Can't Fail,' *Education Forum* 32.3 (2006): 16–9; Jon Cowans, 'Credit Integrity: How Johnny Can Succeed,' *Education Forum* 33.2 (2007): 18–21; Joanne Laucius, 'Pressured to Pass: A Roundtable Discussion,' *Ottawa Citizen*, 25 April 2009, http://www.ottawacitizen.com/travel/Pressured+Pass+Roundtable+Discussion/1523493/story.html (accessed 25 April 2009).

16 Moira Macdonald, 'Our Kids Are Smart ... Really but Some Teachers Are Frustrated, Calling Growing Graduation Rate a Product of "Pseudo-Credits,"' http://www.torontosun.com/comment/columnists/moira_macdonald/2009/05/19/9496746-sun.html (accessed 20 Dec. 2009).

17 OCUFA, 'Students Less Prepared for University Education,' http://www.quality-matters.ca/QualityMatters/docs/Students_less_prepared_April_6_2009.pdf (accessed 20 Dec. 2009).

18 CBC's *Cross Country Checkup* devoted the show to the issue on 12 April 2009, http://www.cbc.ca/checkup/archive/2009/intro090412.html; see

also *The Sunday Edition*, 10 May 2009, http://www.cbc.ca/radioshows/THE_SUNDAY_EDITION/20090510.shtml (accessed 18 Dec. 2009).

19 J. Douglas Willms, Sharon Friesen, and Penny Milton, *What Did You Do in School Today? Transforming Classrooms through Social, Academic, and Intellectual Engagement*, First National Report (Toronto: Canadian Education Association, 2009), 17.

20 J. Douglas Willms, *Student Engagement at School: A Sense of Belonging and Participation* (Paris: Organization for Economic Cooperation and Development, 2003).

21 Malkin Dare, President, Society for Quality Education, e-mail communication with J.E. Côté, 12 May 2009, www.societyforqualityeducation.org.

22 See the following websites from the Ontario Quality and Accountability Office: http://www.eqao.com/NIA/PIRLS/PIRLS.aspx?Lang=E and http://www.eqao.com/NIA/TIMSS/TIMSS.aspx?Lang=E (accessed 26 May 2010).

23 Robert Rosenthal and Lenore Jacobson, *Pygmalion in the Classroom* (New York: Rinehart and Winston, 1968).

24 See the discussion of abilities in the concluding chapter, below, along with the concept of 'educational romanticism' coined by Charles Murray in *Real Education: Four Simple Truths about Bringing America's Schools Back to Reality* (New York: Crown Forum, 2008).

25 See, for example, Malcolm Gladwell, *Outliers: The Story of Success* (New York: Little, Brown and Company, 2008).

26 Underemployment is documented in *Ivory Tower Blues*, including the replicated finding that some 50 per cent of BA/BSc graduates are in jobs not requiring a university credential two years after graduation (pp. 174–7).

27 A minor voice in education economics recognizes that certain credentials have more of a social than an economic function; see, for example, Ana Ferrer and W. Craig Riddell, 'The Role of Credentials in the Canadian Labour Market,' *Canadian Journal of Economics* 35 (2002): 879–905.

28 J.R. Walsh, 'Capital Concept Applied to Man', *Quarterly Journal of Economics* 49.2 (1935): 255–85, 256.

29 Ibid.

30 Gary Becker, *Human Capital* (Chicago: University of Chicago Press, 1964).

31 David Walters, 'The Relationship between Postsecondary Education and Skill: Comparing Credentialism with Human Capital Theory,' *Canadian Journal of Higher Education* 34 (2004): 97–124, 117.

32 Ibid., 116.

33 See, for example, George C. Leef, 'The Overselling of Higher Education,' 5 September 2006, www.popecenter.org (accessed 21 Dec. 2009)

34 Alex Usher made this error in the report *A Little Knowledge Is a Dangerous Thing: How Perceptions of Costs and Benefits Affect Access to Education* (Toronto: Education Policy Institute, 2005), www.educationalpolicy.org/pdf/littleknowledge.pdf. (accessed 16 July 2007).

35 See Doug Lederman, 'College Isn't Worth a Million Dollars,' *Inside Higher Ed* (7 April 2008), http://www.insidehighered.com/news/2008/04/07/miller (accessed 21 Dec. 2009).

36 See Robertson Education Empowerment Foundation, *The Biggest Gamble of Your Life (Is College Worth It?)* (6 Dec. 2006), http://www.aboutreef.org/is-college-worth-it.html (accessed 4 Jan. 2010).

37 Statistics Canada, 'National Graduates Survey,' *The Daily*, 22 April 2009, http://www.statcan.gc.ca/daily-quotidien/090422/dq090422a-eng.htm (accessed 10 Dec. 2009).

38 The collapse of the youth labour market is undisputed among experts in the sociology of youth, and is common knowledge among the public, especially young people and their parents. As we see later in this chapter, however, many of those feeding the Canadian government with educational research appear oblivious to it, blinded by the ideology otherwise known as 'human capital theory.' For descriptions of this collapse see, for example, James Côté and Anton Allahar, *Critical Youth Studies: A Canadian Focus* (Toronto: Pearson Educational Publishing, 2006); Andy Furlong and Fred Carmel, *Young People and Social Change: New Perspectives* (Milton Keynes: Open University Press, 2007).

39 For example, see Richard Brisbois, Larry Orton, and Ron Saunders, *Connecting Supply and Demand in Canada's Youth Labour Market*, Pathways to the Labour Market Series – No. 8, CPRN Research Report, April 2008 (Ottawa: Canadian Policy Research Networks Inc., 2008).

40 William Rees, 'Science, Cognition and Public Policy,' *Academic Matters*, April–May 2008, pp. 9–12.

41 Ibid., 10.

42 See, for example, Lucie Nobert, Ramona McDowell, and Diane Goulet, *Profile of Higher Education in Canada – 1991 Edition* (Ottawa: Department of the Secretary of the State of Canada, 1992).

43 Julian Betts, Christopher Ferrall, and Ross Finnie, *The Transition to Work for Canadian University Graduates: Time to First Job, 1982–1990*, Analytic Studies Branch Research Paper Series, No. 141 (Ottawa: Statistics Canada, 2000).

44 Mario Lapointe, Kevin Dunn, Nicolas Tremblay-Côté, Louis-Philippe Bergeron, and Luke Ignaczak, *Looking-Ahead: A 10-Year Outlook for the Canadian Labour Market (2006-2015)* (Ottawa: Human Resources and Skills Development Canada, 2006), 27. The HRSDC does put the standard caveat

on this publication that views expressed may not necessarily reflect those of the HRSDC, but their Labour Market and Skills Forecasting and Analysis Unit released it.

45 HRSDC, *HRSDC Policy Research and Survey Plan: Directions for the Next Three Years* (Ottawa, 2005), 2.

46 Ibid., 20.

47 Ibid., 58.

48 HRSDC, 'Can a Supply of Highly-Qualified Labour Create Its Own Demand?' (RFP), http://www.merx.com/English/Supplier_Menu.Asp?WCE =Show&TAB=1&State=7&id=121566&hcode=7FzlCQxAyXgV3nL8Rn4a ZA== (accessed 19 July 2006).

49 The Province of Ontario recently established the Higher Education Quality Council of Ontario (HEQCO), whose mandate is 'to evaluate the post-secondary education sector, report to the Minister on the results of the evaluation and make the report available to the public' (Higher Education Quality Council of Ontario, *Second Annual Review and Research Plan* [Toronto, 2008]). After reviewing the studies that it has summoned through its tenders, as well as other selective literature, the report states the following, using the predictable bureaucratic dodge of claiming that 'more research is needed':

> The objective of this section is to attempt to evaluate learning quality in PSE in Ontario … The general picture that emerges is confusing and contradictory. Using per capita funding as an indicator, quality of Ontario universities appears to lag behind that of peer institutions in other provinces and particularly that of US counterparts. No US comparisons are possible for Ontario colleges, but their per-capita funding compares poorly to their counterparts in other provinces. However, other indicators, such as student and graduate satisfaction scores or NSSE engagement scores, paint a different picture. Ontario's universities compare favourably to those in other provinces, but less so to their US counterparts. Clearly, considerably more research is needed before we can make any definitive statements about educational quality in Ontario. (71–2)

50 Christopher Lubienski, 'School Choice Research in the United States and Why It Doesn't Matter: The Evolving Economy of Knowledge Production in a Contested Policy Domain,' paper presented at the Institute of Advanced Studies conference 'The Globalization of School Choice?' University of Western Australia, December 2006, p. 3. See also a special issue of the journal *Educational Policy* (Janelle Scott, Christopher Lubienski, and Elizabeth DeBray-Pelot, 'The Politics of Advocacy in Education,' *Educational Policy* 23.1 [2009]: 3–14), including the article by Christopher Lubienski,

Peter Weitzel, and Sarah Theule Lubienski, 'Is There a "Consensus" on School Choice and Achievement? Advocacy Research and the Emerging Political Economy of Knowledge Production,' 161–93; and the recent book by Jeffrey R. Henig, *Spin Cycle: How Research Is Used in Policy Debates – the Case of Charter Schools* (Thousand Oaks, CA: Sage, 2008).

51 Education Policy Institute, http://www.educationalpolicy.org/aboutEPI/ourmission.html (accessed 29 Nov. 2009).

52 Education Policy Institute, http://www.educationalpolicy.org/aboutEPI/whatisepi.html, (accessed 29 Nov. 2009).

53 Alex Usher, 'Back to the Future,' *University Affairs*, November 2009, pp. 30–3.

54 Alex Usher, 'Campus Navel Gazing: Two Insider Books Ponder the Future of the University,' *Literary Review of Canada* (December 2007), http://reviewcanada.ca/reviews/2007/12/01/campus-navel-gazing/ (accessed 29 Nov. 2009).

55 This is a pre-recession–based estimate. If we use current, recession-based estimates, the figure is higher. Based on the denominator of some 4.4 million people in this age group, of whom almost one million are in university, if the approximately 50 per cent of university students who are disengaged suddenly sought jobs, this half million person influx into the labour market would more than double the number registered as unemployed (some 437,800 people at the end of 2009). When added to 15.9 per cent for this age group already registered as unemployed, some 30 per cent of young Canadians would then be registered as unemployed; see Statistics Canada, *Labour Force Information November 8 to 14, 2009* (Ottawa, 2009), 23.

56 Côté and Allahar, *Critical Youth Studies*, 49–51.

57 Côté and Allahar, *Ivory Tower Blues*, 171–4.

58 Usher, 'Campus Navel Gazing,' 2.

59 Côté and Allahar, *Ivory Tower Blues*, 22–4.

60 Jon Cowans, 'Left Out in the Cold: Making School Administrators Accountable,' *Education Forum* 33 (2007): 20–2, 43–4.

3. Standards: Schools without Scholarship?

1 For detailed reviews of these benefits and the methodological issues associated with studying them, see Ernest T. Pascarella and Patrick T. Terenzini, *How College Affects Students: Findings and Insights from Twenty Years of Research* (San Francisco: Jossey-Bass, 1991); and the second edition, Ernest T. Pascarella and Patrick T. Terenzini, *How College Affects Students, Volume 2: A Third Decade of Research* (San Francisco: Jossey-Bass, 2005).

2 James Côté, Rod Skinkle, and Anne Motte, 'Do Perceptions of Costs and Benefits of Post-Secondary Education Influence Participation?' *Canadian Journal of Higher Education* 38.3 (2008): 73–93.

3 As noted above, the extent of this earnings advantage has been recently questioned.

4 According to Pascarella and Terenzini's, *How College Affects Students* (2005), the research is conclusive that effort is key to intellectual transformations.

5 For example, many of those seeking admission to medical schools are now obtaining a master's degree to add to their portfolio, along with a wealth of volunteer work and other résumé items to help them to stand out. The competition for medical programs is fierce, with only a very small percentage of applicants typically accepted.

6 Maritime Provinces Higher Education Council, *Five Years On: Survey of Class of 1999 Maritime University Graduates* (Fredericton, 2006).

7 Ibid., ii.

8 The following website provides extensive historical and comparative data on grade inflation in the United States: Stuart Rojstaczer, Grade Inflation at American Colleges and Universities, http://gradeinflation.com/ (accessed 27 Dec. 2009).

9 http://www.stopgradeinflation.ie/links_uk.html (accessed 27 Dec. 2009).

10 Network of Irish Educational Standards, http://www.stopgradeinflation.ie/aboutus.html (accessed 27 Dec. 2009). Their statement of this problem is as follows:

> Extensive research conducted and published on this website shows that there has been significant grade inflation in both the University and Institute of Technology sectors in the Republic of Ireland. In 1994 the percentage of first class honours awarded across the Universities was 7%. By 2005 that figure had jumped to 17%. In the Institutes of Technology over the same period, despite a steep decline in the CAO points of entrants, there was a 52% increase in the award of first class honours degrees. Thus, weaker and weaker students have been entering the sector, only to receive ever improving grades ... Grade inflation in Irish higher education has been driven by institutions prioritising student numbers and growth at the expense of educational standards ... Grade inflation undermines the status of qualifications and misleads the stakeholders in education, such as students, employers and policymakers. It inevitably results in a continuing decline in the quality of education, with serious long-term implications for the competitiveness of the Irish economy.

11 See, for example, Michael Woods, 'Making the Grade,' *Queen's Journal* (19 Sept. 2008), http://www.queensjournal.ca/story/2008-09-19/features/

making-the-grade/ (accessed 19 Sept. 2008). In this article, the associate university registrar of undergraduate admission at Queen's University is quoted as saying: 'If there is grade inflation – and I'm not saying there is or there isn't – but if there is, the pool would be inflated, so we're still looking for the top-performer students to come to Queen's.'

12 As we saw in chapter 2, this has happened in many high schools where principals no longer teach but attend only to administrative duties decreed by their boards and ministries.

13 A useful general grading rubric for assessing written material is available from the Critical Thinking Community: Foundation for Critical Thinking, http://www.criticalthinking.org/resources/HE/college-wide-grading-standards.cfm (accessed 27 Dec. 2009). Clear differences are obvious in the rubric among the grading categories, and can be adjusted to the level of the students being evaluated, taking into account the differing complexity and specificity of the material. For example, more rigorous expectations should be used for undergraduates over high-school students and graduate students over undergraduates.

14 Cooperative Institutional Research Program (CIRP), *The American Freshman: National Norms for Fall 1999*, UCLA Graduate School of Education and Information Studies, Higher Education Research Institute, http://www.gseis.ucla.edu/heri/norms_pr_99.html (accessed 12 Sept. 2005).

15 Because the ECTS is based on a distribution of grades for those seeking to transfer between universities, the F grade is not relevant. Obviously, adjustments to the distribution would need to be made when the entire range of student performances is assessed.

16 See chapter 5 for further discussion of NSSE data and these types of findings.

17 Robert Runté, *Conceptual Difficulties in Establishing Whether There Is Grade Inflation*, http://people.uleth.ca/~runte/inflation/confusion.pdf (accessed 30 Jan. 2009).

18 The causes of grade inflation have been debated, and following this issue in detail diverts our attention from dealing with its consequences. Two things can be culled from the literature on its causes: (1) it has been a concern in the past, and efforts can be found to wrestle with it, especially when universities first massified in the 1950s through 1970s (Lewis, *Excellence without a Soul*); and (2) high schools are now under continual pressure to inflate grades to gain their students access to university, while at the same time universities are now under continual pressure to gain their students access to graduate and professional programs (cf. Helen Lefkowitz Horowitz, *Campus Life: Undergraduate Cultures from the End of the Eight-*

eenth Century to the Present [Chicago: University of Chicago Press, 1987]). However, the current competition among schools to give *their* graduates a special advantage is a metaphorical 'arms race' in which the larger system loses.

19 For a discussion of the various facets of grade inflation, such as grade compression, see Lester H. Hunt, ed., *Grade Inflation: Academic Standards in Higher Education* (Albany, NY: State University of New York Press, 2008).

20 American universities have struggled with this problem for the past decade or so, especially Ivy League schools. Harvard found itself awarding honours grades (As and Bs) to over 90 per cent of its students, qualifying them for the 'Dean's List.' The Dean's List made sense in the past when only about 20 per cent of students qualified, as in the 1920s. The Dean's List was dropped in the early 2000s, but with grades so compressed at the A level at Harvard, the designation of *summa cum laude* is now limited to the top 5 per cent of grades, but this requires a cut-off at 3 decimal places! (Lewis, *Excellence without a Soul*). Harvard might as well use a lottery to determine the top honours because the distinction between, say, 92.456 and 92.457 per cent is obviously meaningless.

21 Polly Young-Eisendrath, *The Self-Esteem Trap: Raising Confident Kids in an Age of Self-Importance* (New York: Little, Brown and Company, 2008), 15.

22 In fact, much research has tested this belief that giving higher grades leads to future increases in achievement, mediated by gains in self-esteem. The best scientific evidence finds that this relationship is dubious, or at best the relationship is statistically very weak. See, for example, Roy Baumeister, Jennifer Campbell, Joachim Krueger, and Kathleen Vohs, 'Exploding the Self-Esteem Myth,' *Scientific American* 292.1 (2005): 84–91; James E. Côté, 'Identity and Self Development,' in *Handbook of Adolescent Psychology*, 3rd edn, ed. Richard M. Lerner and Laurence Steinberg (New York: Wiley, 2009).

23 Robert Laurie, 'Setting Them Up to Fail? Excellent Marks Don't Necessarily Lead to Excellent Exam Marks.' *Atlantic Institute of Market Studies*, 3 May 2007, http://www.aims.ca/library/Gradeinflationvfinal_cc.pdf (accessed 2 Feb. 2009).

24 Ibid., 5.

25 These results are for francophone schools in New Brunswick. The same results were found in anglophone schools in New Brunswick, as well as schools in Newfoundland and Labrador, but the data set is most complete for francophone schools in New Brunswick.

26 Ibid., 5.

27 Ibid.

28 See, for example, William Damon, *The Path to Purpose: Helping Our Children*

Find Their Calling in Life (New York: Free Press, 2008); Young-Eisendrath, *The Self-Esteem Trap*, 119–24.

29 See the efforts by UK Youth to establish a movement promoting the recognition of non-formal learning as a means of combating 'social exclusion': http://www.ukyouth.org/whatwedo/News/Vision+not+Division+Conference.htm (accessed 21 Dec. 2009).

30 For a discussion of the various possible functions of grading in different disciplines, see Hunt, ed., *Grade Inflation*.

31 Workload may spike during exam periods, although there are no data for this, but without classes to attend, the total time devoted to studying may not be any greater than during the regular term. Besides, if students keep up with their courses by preparing on a weekly basis, studying for exams should not be onerous because learning is more effective and long-term than is the case if students cram for exams. Compare Daniel Willingham, *Why Don't Students Like School?* (San Francisco: Jossey-Bass, 2009).

32 Willingham, *Why Don't Students Like School?*

33 James Côté and Charles Levine, 'Student Motivations, Learning Environments, and Human Capital Acquisition: Toward an Integrated Paradigm of Student Development,' *Journal of College Student Development* 38 (1997): 229–43.

34 Ellen Greenberger, Jared Lessard, Chuansheng Chen, and Susan P. Farruggia, 'Self-Entitled College Students: Contributions of Personality,' *Journal of Youth and Adolescence* 37 (2008): 1193–204.

35 Côté and Levine, 'Student Motivations, Learning Environments, and Human Capital Acquisition.'

36 Alan Slavin, 'Factors Affecting Student Drop Out from the University Introductory Physics Course, Including the Anomaly of the Ontario Double Cohort,' *Canadian Journal of Physics* 86 (2008): 839–47.

37 Ibid., 843.

38 Alan Slavin, 'Has Ontario Taught Its High-School Students Not to Think?' *University Affairs* (10 Sept. 2007), http://www.universityaffairs.ca/has-ontario-taught-its-high-school-students-not-to-think.aspx (accessed 10 Sept. 2009).

39 We can see here the need for centralized data collection to determine how widespread this problem is – whether it applies across Canada – and whether it might be a precursor to the situation in the United States, where fewer American students are completing their degrees.

40 Slavin, 'Factors Affecting Student Drop Out,' 843.

41 See, for example, Cowans, 'Why Johnny Can't Fail,' and 'Credit Integrity: How Johnny Can Succeed.'

42 OCUFA, 'Students Less Prepared for University Education,' http://
www.quality-matters.ca/QualityMatters/docs/Students_less_prepared_
April_6_2009.pdf (accessed 9 June 2009).

43 American research suggests many faculty feel the same as in Canada, with
41 per cent of professors surveyed believing that most of their students
lack the basic skills necessary for a higher education. See Cooperative
Institutional Research Program (CIRP), 'More Than One-Third of College Faculty Believes Most of Their Students Lack Basic Skills Needed for
College,' UCLA Graduate School of Education and Information Studies,
Higher Education Research Institute, http://www.gseis.ucla.edu/heri (accessed 3 May 2009). Over half of the professors who report they deal with
underprepared students also report that doing so is stressful for them.

44 George Kuh, 'What Student Engagement Data Tell Us about College
Readiness,' *AAC&U peerReview* (Winter 2007): 4—8.

45 Ibid., 5.

46 Ibid.

47 Willms, Friesen, and Milton, *What Did You Do in School Today?* 17.

48 Kuh, 'What Student Engagement Data Tell Us about College Readiness,' 6.

49 Ibid., 5.

50 National Survey of Student Engagement (NSSE), *Promoting Engagement for
All Students: The Imperative to Look within 2008 Results* (Bloomington, IN:
Center for Postsecondary Research, 2008), 18.

51 Ibid.

52 Gladwell, *Outliers: The Story of Success.*

53 Gladwell provides a number of convincing arguments about how
intelligence on its own is not enough to guarantee outstanding accomplishments. For example, Einstein had an IQ of 150, but many less
accomplished geniuses have scored much higher, including a man he
interviewed who has an IQ of 200, but has spent his life working in odd
jobs like bouncer and carpenter. This man had the misfortune to be born
into a troubled, low-income family and did not encounter educational
opportunities that would help him develop and socialize his talents (e.g.,
was forced to drop out for financial reasons, partly because of unsympa-
thetic administrators). Gladwell argues being 'smart enough' is sufficient
if it is supplemented with the opportunity to develop those smarts, citing
evidence that IQ scores alone above 120 do not predict achievement.

54 Ibid., 104–5. He is citing the work of sociologist Annette Lareau (*Unequal
Childhoods: Class, Race, and Family Life* [Berkeley: University of California
Press, 2003]).

55 Ibid. He discusses the KIPP (Knowledge Is Power Program) schools in the

United States, which take inner-city (overwhelmingly Black and Hispanic) children who are at risk of very low school achievement, accept them through a lottery system (because of the high demand, it is deemed the only fair admissions standard), and nurture them to develop academic interests and talents that result in high educational achievement, with 80 per cent eventually going on to university. In addition to innovative teaching practices, this result is achieved largely by requiring far more effort of students than does a typical American public school, including extensive homework, Saturday classes, and short summer breaks.

56 Ibid., 268.
57 William Damon, *Greater Expectations: Overcoming the Culture of Indulgence in America's Homes and Schools* (New York: Free Press, 1995).
58 Richard Florida, *The Rise of the Creative Class: And How It's Transforming Work, Leisure, Community and Everyday Life* (New York: Basic Books, 2003). See his 2009 report on the Ontario economy: http://www.martinprosperity. org/research-and-publications/publication/ontario-in-the-creative-age-project (accessed 10 Sept. 2009).
59 Mark Bauerlein, *The Dumbest Generation: How the Digital Age Stupefies Young Americans and Jeopardizes Our Future* (New York: Penguin, 2008).
60 Ian D. Clark, Greg Moran, Michael L. Skolnik, and David Trick, *Academic Transformation: The Forces Reshaping Higher Education in Ontario*, Queen's Policy Studies Series (Montreal and Kingston: McGill-Queen's University Press, 2009).
61 Murray, *Real Education*.

4. Universities: Crisis, What Crisis?

1 Meanwhile, the trades cannot find sufficient numbers of recruits. See, for example, the Skilled Trades website: http://www.careersintrades.ca/ media/default.asp?load=faqs01 (accessed 3 Jan. 2010).
2 Richard Kadison and Theresa Foy Digeronimo, *College of the Overwhelmed: The Campus Health Crisis and What to Do about It* (San Francisco: Jossey-Bass, 2004). According to these authors, in addition to developmental issues experienced by all young people of the normal attendance age (18–22), today's students experience tremendous pressure to bring home high grades for their parents (and many experience a major grade-drop from the highly inflated grades they received in high school), and often face financial strains that can contribute to a variety of psychological disorders associated with a general set of malaises described by these authors as a 'crisis of hopelessness and helplessness' (especially depression and

anxiety disorders). One study followed the incidence of students seeking university-counselling psychological assistance in 1998 and 2001, along with a mid-point between these two points in time, finding that depression and suicidal thoughts doubled; situational crises triggering distress jumped from 22 per cent to 58 per cent; and students with A or B averages sought assistance more than those with lower grades.

3 Cooperative Institutional Research Program (CIRP), *The American Freshman: National Norms for Fall 1999*, UCLA Graduate School of Education and Information Studies, Higher Education Research Institute, http://www.gseis.ucla.edu/heri/norms_pr_99.html (accessed 12 Sept. 2005).

4 See, for example, Elizabeth Church, 'Who's in the Know: Women Surge, Men Sink in Education's Gender Gap,' *Globe and Mail*, 7 Dec. 2009, http://www.theglobeandmail.com/news/national/whos-in-the-know-women-surge-men-sink-in-educations-gender-gap/article1390902/ (accessed 27 Dec. 2009).

5 Côté and Levine, 'Student Motivations, Learning Environments, and Human Capital Acquisition.'

6 From *Declining by Degrees: Higher Education at Risk* (DVD); see 'Meet the Experts' interview with George Kuh on the DVD's website: www.decliningbydegrees.org/meet-experts-3-transcript.html (accessed 11 Nov. 2006).

7 See also http://www.criticalthinking.org/index.cfm (accessed 27 Dec. 2009).

8 Bok, *Our Underachieving Colleges*.

9 Pascarella and Terenzini, *How College Affects Students, Volume 2*. These authors are considered the foremost authorities on the effects of the university experience. This book reports the peer-reviewed literature from the 1990s, whereas their first book (published in 1991) reported the literature from the 1970s and 1980s.

10 Ibid., 158.

11 See, for example, Marilyn Montgomery and James E. Côté, 'The Transition to University: Outcomes and Adjustments,' in *The Blackwell Handbook of Adolescence*, ed. Gerald Adams and Michael Berzonsky (Oxford: Blackwell, 2003).

12 Pascarella and Terenzini, *How College Affects Students, Volume 2*, 186.

13 Ibid., 159.

14 Bok, *Our Underachieving Colleges*, 113. See also Patricia M. King and Karen S. Kitchener, *Developing Reflective Judgment: Understanding and Promoting Intellectual Growth and Critical Thinking in Adolescents and Adults* (San Francisco: Jossey-Bass, 1994); Pascarella and Terenzini, *How College Affects Students, Volume 2*, 36–8, 160–7.

15 Parenthetically, these levels of reflective judgment roughly approximate the advancement of human thought from moral absolutism to ethical universalism, and from fundamentalist religion to modern science.

16 Bok, *Our Underachieving Colleges*, 116.

17 Florida, *The Rise of the Creative Class*.

18 See, for example, Lewis, *Excellence without a Soul*.

19 It cannot be ignored that Canada's apparent world-leading status, as deemed by OECD reports, may be in part due to the need for the OECD to 'fill in' information. Apparently, Canada provides only 57 of 96 indicators for the OECD's annual *Education at a Glance* report, the worst reporting record of all the countries involved (CAUT, 'Education International Says OECD Promoting Privatization, Not Access,' *CAUT Bulletin* 54.8 (October 2007).

20 Hiring is almost at a standstill in relation to the growth in the student population. In Ontario alone, some 10,000 new hires – in addition to retirement replacements – are necessary to bring student-faculty ratios to those found in the United States (OCUFA, *Trends in Faculty Hiring at Ontario Universities*, http://notes.ocufa.on.ca/HETrends.nsf/trends_v1n2.pdf?OpenFileResource (accessed 10 Dec. 2009).

21 See, for example, Louis Groarke and Wayne Fenske, 'PhD: To What End?' *University Affairs* (November 2009), http://www.universityaffairs.ca/phd-to-what-end.aspx (accessed 10 Dec. 2009).

22 Part-time and limited-term staff now comprise sizable portions of the faculty complement in many departments, teaching about half of the courses in many cases (e.g., Clark, Moran, Skolnik, and Trick, *Academic Transformation*). More recently, a move is afoot to institutionalize positions for 'teaching professors,' who will likely be required to earn the (research degree) PhD, but who will spend their careers teaching undergraduates, without time release for research or, presumably, access to graduate students. The consequences of this are not clear, but when it is done merely to more efficiently process more students though 'universities,' it hardly looks like a step forward.

23 Scott Jaschik, 'Shying Away from Graduate School,' *Inside Higher Ed*, http://insidehighered.com/news/2008/12/08/gre (accessed 10 Jan. 2009).

24 Vic Catano, Lori Francis, Ted Haines, et al., *Occupational Stress among Canadian University Academic Staff* (Ottawa: CAUT, 2007). Although one might find similar stress-medication levels among the general population (which are estimated at lower rates of 15–20 per cent), professors are a select sample of high-functioning professionals, like doctors and lawyers, whereas the general population includes people from the entire spectrum

of functioning, so that one would not expect comparable rates. See, for example, Kristinn Tmasson, Helgi Tmasson, Tmas Zoëga, Eggert Sigfsson, and Tmas Helgason, 'Epidemiology of Psychotropic Medication Use: Comparison of Sales, Prescriptions and Survey Data in Iceland,' *Nordic Journal of Psychiatry* 61 (2007): 471–8.

25 Marianne Sorensen and Jennifer de Peuter, *University of Alberta Workload / Work Life Study for the Association of Academic Staff: University of Alberta*, 29 June 2006, http://www.uofaweb.ualberta.ca/aasua//pdfs/ AASUAworkloadReportJune30.pdf (accessed 7 Aug. 2007). Results for other countries are taken from this source.

26 Douglas Baer, David Bellhouse, Regna Darnell, et al., *Faculty Workload Study: Summary Report* (London, ON: University of Western Ontario and University of Western Ontario Faculty Association, 1996), http://www. uwo.ca/western/workload/workload.html (accessed 21 Dec. 2009).

27 Sorensen and de Peuter, *University of Alberta Workload / Work Life Study*.

28 Faculty Survey of Student Engagement, *FSSE 2006 Selected Results: Faculty Time*, http://fsse.iub.edu/index.cfm (accessed 7 Aug. 2007).

29 Stanford University Senate, *To the Members of the Academic Council, Thirty-Sixth Senate Report No. 4: Summary of Actions Taken by the Senate*, 4 Dec. 2003, http://academiccouncil.stanford.edu/2003_2004/minutes/ 12_04_03_SenD5528.pdf (accessed 8 Aug. 2007).

30 Sorensen and de Peuter, *University of Alberta Workload / Work Life Study*.

31 George Kuh, Thomas F. Nelson Laird, and Paul D. Umbach, 'Aligning Faculty and Student Behavior: Realizing the Promise of Greater Expectations,' *Liberal Education* 90.4 (2004): 24–31.

32 Jerry A. Jacobs and Sarah E. Winslow, 'Overworked Faculty: Job Stresses and Family Demands,' *Annals of the American Academy of Political and Social Science* 596 (November 2004): 104–29; Mary Ann Mason and Marc Goulden, 'Marriage and Baby Blues: Redefining Gender Equity in the Academy,' *Annals of the American Academy of Political and Social Science* 596 (November 2004): 86–103.

33 Sorensen and de Peuter, *University of Alberta Workload / Work Life Study*.

34 Jacobs and Winslow, 'Overworked Faculty.'

35 Sorensen and de Peuter, *University of Alberta Workload / Work Life Study*.

36 Scott Davies, 'A Revolution in Expectations? Three Key Trends in the SAEP Data,' in *Preparing for Post-secondary Education: New Roles for Governments and Families*, ed. Robert Sweet and Paul Anisef (Montreal and Kingston: McGill-Queen's University Press, 2005).

37 William Barker, president of University of King's College in Halifax, is quoted by Jay Teitel as claiming that 'one of those [books] comes out every other year' ('Failure to Fail,' *The Walrus* [April 2008]: 40–9, 44). The author

of this article attempts to find someone who has been flunked out of McGill University – or any university in Canada for that matter – but finds no cases (students do drop out, but universities apparently no longer go out of their way to flunk them out, giving second and third chances). This search began when his son told him about his idea of developing a reality TV show called *The Bum's B.A.* in which contestants vie to do the least amount of work in their courses and still pass their year. The idea was based on the son's experiences at McGill University, where he witnessed widespread 'idleness and duplicity' (p. 40).

38 For an example of this confusion resulting from an incomplete understanding of the relationship between grades and standards, see Shouping Hu, *Beyond Grade Inflation: Grading Problems in Higher Education* (ASHE Higher Education Report, 2005).

39 See, for example, Daniel McCabe, 'The CSI Effect,' *University Affairs* (November 2005), http://www.universityaffairs.ca/the-CSI-effect.aspx (accessed 10 Dec. 2009).

40 See, for example, Scott Jaschik, 'Sociology Jobs Plentiful, but Do They Match?' *Inside Higher Ed* (23 June 2008), http://www.insidehighered.com/news/2008/06/23/socjobs (accessed 10 Dec. 2009).

41 In addition to the personal debt incurred by students, which can be compounded if disengagement prolongs the time of the degree, taxpayers are still paying for about 60 per cent of the costs for educating each student. To the extent that academic disengagement squanders educational opportunities for a student's personal and intellectual development, it also squanders taxpayers' money.

42 According to Ken Roberts, the decline of secondary-level vocational training and its creep into the tertiary level of academia is a worldwide trend following the American model, with some unfortunate consequences (*Youth in Transition: Eastern Europe and the West* [New York: Palgrave Macmillan, 2009]).

43 A delegation from the United States, with representatives from the Department of Education and the National Education Association, recently visited Finland to examine its system (Ellen Gamerman, 'What Makes Finnish Kids So Smart?' *Wall Street Journal* [29 Feb. 2008], W1, WSJ.com [accessed 24 March 2009]).

44 Ari Antikainen, *Transforming a Learning Society: The Case of Finland* (Bern: Lang, 2005). One feature that is not indicated in this table is the wider age range at the tertiary level, with one-third of university students older than thirty, reflecting a commitment to lifelong learning in Finnish educational and labour policies.

45 Finnish students do not begin primary school until age seven. Prior to this

age, a variety of options are available, including a year of 'pre-primary education' for six-year-olds. Meanwhile, several other features of Finnish social and educational policy prepare young Finns to begin a formal education. High-quality, universal, free daycare is provided from the time when maternity-leave benefits end, when the child is nine months old, until pre-primary school, when the child is six years old. Pre-primary school is kindergarten year, which is more socially than academically oriented, teaching children how to self-reflect, cooperate, and accept personal responsibility (Open Education, 'Several Lessons to be Learned from the Finnish School System,' http://www.openeducation.net/2008/03/10/several-lessons-to-be-learned-from-the-finnish-school-system [accessed 24 March 2009]).

This practice of beginning formal education at age seven is supported by evidence of a significant change in the 'readiness to learn' between age five and seven, especially for boys. Introducing children into formal learning structures when they are better prepared developmentally is one way to influence favourably their attitude toward learning, and it subsequently makes teachers' jobs much easier in terms of engaging students (Leonard Sax, *Boys Adrift: The Five Factors Driving the Growing Epidemic of Unmotivated Boys and Underachieving Young Men* [New York: Basic, 2007]).

46 For example, PISA test results show fewer socio-economic status differences in the various proficiency scores among fifteen-year-old Finnish students than in other countries (Ilse Julkunen, *Early School Leaving in Finland – A Problem Solved?* n.d., http://www.injuve.mtas.es/injuve/contenidos.downloadatt.action?id=206483288 [accessed 25 March 2009]).

47 The median age of apprentices in Canada is in the 25-9 age range, with only a small percentage of those aged 15-24 in an apprenticeship (4-6 per cent), compared to 18 per cent in Germany (where about 40 per cent of 18-year-olds were in apprenticeships in 2002) and 15 per cent in Australia (Andrew Sharpe and James Gibson, *The Apprenticeship System in Canada: Trends and Issues* [Ottawa: Centre for the Study of Living Standards, 2005], http://www.csls.ca/reports/csls2005-04.pdf [accessed 22 Dec. 2009]). See also Willms, Friesen, and Milton, *What Did You Do in School Today?*

48 OECD, *Education at a Glance 2008: OECD Indicators*, www.oecd.org/edu/eag2008 (accessed 22 Dec. 2009). Jon Cowans ('Credit Integrity') notes that at one time the academic/vocational stream split was 60/40 in Ontario; Murray (*Real Education*, 149–50) argues that in the United States the ratio should really be more like 60/40 in favour of Career and Technical Education (CTE), but that the 'college-for-all' mentality stigmatizes these programs and deprives them of funding.

49 Finnish Ministry of Education, *Studies and Degrees*, http://www.
   minedu.fi/OPM/Koulutus/ammattikorkeakoulutus/opiskelu_ja_
   tutkinnot/?lang=en (accessed 24 March 2009).

50 Finnish Ministry of Education, *Polytechnic Education in Finland*, http://
   www.minedu.fi/OPM/Koulutus/ammattikorkeakoulutus/?lang=en
   (accessed 24 March 2009).

51 Julkunen, *Early School Leaving in Finland*.

52 Finnish Ministry of Education, *Education System in Finland*, http://www.
   minedu.fi/OPM/Koulutus/koulutusjaerjestelmae/?lang=en (accessed
   24 March 2009).

53 Finnish Ministry of Education, *Polytechnic Education in Finland*, http://
   www.minedu.fi/OPM/Koulutus/ammattikorkeakoulutus/?lang=en
   (accessed 24 March 2009).

54 Finnish Ministry of Education, *University Education in Finland*, http://
   www.minedu.fi/OPM/Koulutus/yliopistokoulutus/?lang=en (accessed
   24 March 2009).

55 See, for example, Clark, Moran, Skolnik, and Trick, *Academic Transformation*, ch. 6.

56 See, for example, Margit E. Oswald and Stefan Grosjean, 'Confirmation
   Bias,' in *Cognitive Illusions: A Handbook on Fallacies and Biases in Thinking,
   Judgement and Memory*, ed. Rüdiger F. Pohl (Hove, UK: Psychology Press,
   2004); Raymond S. Nickerson, 'Confirmation Bias: A Ubiquitous Phenomenon in Many Guises,' *Review of General Psychology* 2.2 (1998): 175–220.

57 Check the comments sections of news articles and blogs on the educational
   system to witness the vitriol that can emerge among commentators or
   be directed at the author of an article/post, as in the examples we have
   provided above. The flak that Mark Bauerlein, the author of *The Dumbest
   Generation*, attracts is particularly telling (for the archive of his posts on the
   Chronicle of Higher Education, see http://chronicle.com/blogAuthor/Brain-
   storm/3/Mark-Bauerlein/77/ [accessed 22 Dec. 2009]).

58 Scott Davies and Neil Guppy argue that with respect to the general critique of public education, 'today's reformers have another critique that is
   very different from those of yesterday's progressives: that today's public
   schools are underperforming, and increasingly mediocre' (*The Schooled Society: An Introduction to the Sociology of Education* [Toronto: Oxford University Press, 2006], 143).

59 Sidney E. Smith, 'Educational Structure: The English Canadian Universities,' in *Canada's Crisis in Higher Education*, ed. Claude T. Bissell (Toronto:
   University of Toronto Press, 1957), 19.

60 See Robert Epstein, *The Case against Adolescence: Rediscovering the Adult in*

Every Teen (Sanger, CA: Quill Driver Book, 2007). Epstein argues that such arguments are ill informed. In the case of Aristotle, Epstein contends that while harsh portrayals of the young can be found in his works, such as *Rhetoric*, even harsher portrayals of old people can be found. But, this cherry-picking methodology misses Aristotle's point of 'creating caricatures of the young and old simply for didactic purposes' (p. 386) to make his point that age is a poor basis for pre-judging people. In Aristotle's words, 'It is superfluous … to distinguish actions according to the doers' ages, moral stages, or the like; it is of course true that, for instance, young men do have hot tempers and strong appetites; still, it is not through youth that they act accordingly, but through anger or appetite' (Epstein, p. 387).

61 Murray, *Real Education*.
62 Allan Hutchinson, an associate dean at Osgood Hall Law School, wrote a review for the *Globe and Mail* (25 Aug. 2007, D10) in which he stated that he reacted to our depiction as if we were claiming that universities 'will simply disappear down [a] bottomless and standardless drain.'
63 See, for example, Usher, 'Campus Navel Gazing.'

5. Students: Is Disengagement Inevitable?

1 Benedikt Hallgrímsson, 'Repairing the Ivory Tower: What's Broke and How Do We Fix It?' *University Affairs (Online)*, 10 Sept. 2007, http://www.universityaffairs.ca/repairing-the-ivory-tower.aspx (accessed 28 Jan. 2009).
2 The question asked in the HEPI studies was worded as follows: 'In an average week during term-time, roughly how many hours have you spent on private study? Please include time spent reading, researching, writing essays and reports, doing unsupervised laboratory work etc.' (Tom Sastry and Bahram Bekhradnia, *The Academic Experience of Students in English Universities*, Higher Education Policy Institute, September 2007, http://www.hepi.ac.uk/466/Reports.html [accessed 18 Dec. 2009], 30).
3 See also the report *Eurostudent 2005: Social and Economic Conditions of Student Life* for results from a project coordinated by HIS Hochschul-Informations-System, Hanover, Germany, 2005, http://www.his.de/Eurostudent/report2005.pdf (accessed 18 Dec. 2009).
4 Bahram Bekhradnia, *The Academic Experience of Students in English Universities: 2009 Report*, Higher Education Policy Institute, September 2007, http://www.hepi.ac.uk/466/Reports.html (accessed 18 Dec. 2009).
5 Ibid., 7. The *Eurostudent 2005* estimates are a bit lower for European countries, with most recording between 30 to 35 hours per week, and a high of 41 hours for Portugal (pp. 132–3). These differing estimates among studies are likely due to question wording.

6 Bekhradnia, *The Academic Experience of Students in English Universities: 2009 Report*, 6.

7 Ibid., 8.

8 BBC NEWS, 'Students in England "Work Less,"' http://news.bbc. co.uk/2/hi/uk_news/education/7011121.stm (accessed 19 Dec. 2009). Males put in an average of 11.7 hours per week in private study, while females put in 13.3 (Sastry and Bekhradnia, *The Academic Experience of Students in English Universities*, 9).

9 Students in the older schools in the Russell Group put in more hours than those in the newer schools, and students in Oxford and Cambridge Universities put in the most hours of all schools (Sastry and Bekhradnia, *The Academic Experience of Students in English Universities*, 10).

10 Arthur Levine and Jeanette S. Cureton, *When Hope and Fear Collide: A Portrait of Today's College Students* (San Francisco: Jossey Bass, 1998).

11 The suggestion that students 'have always been disengaged' was made by David Strong (President, University Canada West, a small private university in British Columbia) on CBC's *Cross Country Checkup*, on 16 Sept. 2007, http://www.cbc.ca/checkup/archive/2007/intro070916.html (accessed 22 Dec. 2009).

12 Philip S. Babcock and Mindy Marks, 'The Falling Time Cost of College: Evidence from Half a Century of Time Use Data,' Working Paper 15954, National Bureau of Economic Research, Cambridge, MA, April 2010, http://www.nber.org/papers/w15954 (accessed 4 May 2010).

13 Horowitz, *Campus Life*.

14 Babcock and Marks, 'The Falling Time Cost of College,' 15-16.

15 Rebecca Coulter, *The Agenda* (TVO), 7 Sept. 2007, http://www.tvo.org/ cfmx/tvoorg/theagenda/index.cfm?page_id=7&bpn= 779015&ts=2007-09-07%2020:00:00.0 (accessed 22 Dec. 2009).

16 In the United States there are proportionately far more small schools than in Canada. According to the Carnegie classification system (www.carnegiefoundation.org/classifications), the average size of their listing of 4,391 American degree-granting colleges/universities is about 4,000 students. When small religious schools and those granting only associate degrees are excluded, average school size is about 8,000 students, and about 40 per cent of schools have enrolments under 2,000 students – these are essentially liberal-arts settings without the graduate programs. Four-year liberal arts universities with fewer than 2,000 students are rare in Canada. In Canada, the average university size is almost 20,000 students, and only about one-quarter of universities have enrolments under 10,000 students.

17 Charles Ungerleider, *The Sunday Edition*, 10 May 2009, in a panel discussion involving James E. Côté and Carolyn Orchard, a high-school math

teacher of thirty-four years who circulated the petition concerning Credit Recovery discussed in chapter 2, http://www.cbc.ca/radioshows/THE_ SUNDAY_EDITION/20090510.shtml (accessed 18 Dec. 2009).

18 Keri Facer, *Educational, Social and Technological Futures: A Report from the Beyond Current Horizons Programme*, www.beyondcurrenthorizons.org.uk, June 2009, http://www.beyondcurrenthorizons.org.uk/wp-content/up-loads/final-report-20092.pdf (accessed 17 Dec. 2009).

19 For his most recent book, see James Flynn, *What Is Intelligence? Beyond the Flynn Effect* (Cambridge: Cambridge University Press, 2009).

20 Ibid.

21 Malcolm Gladwell, 'None of the Above: What I.Q. Doesn't Tell You about Race,' *The New Yorker*, 17 Dec. 2007, http://www.newyorker.com/arts/critics/books/2007/12/17/071217crbo_books_gladwell#ixzz0Zz2I7ro7 (accessed 17 Dec. 2009).

22 Brainstorm, *Chronicle of Higher Education*, 18 May 2009, http://chronicle.com/blogPost/the-young-british-mind-going-down/6902 (accessed 17 Dec. 2009).

23 Daniel Willingham, *Why Don't Students Like School?* (San Francisco: Jossey-Bass, 2009).

24 One characterization of the 'cognitive miser' concept is as follows:
    A mental characteristic in which the least amount of attention and mental effort needed to process information is used. This concept assumes that humans are limited in their capacity to process information and, therefore, make use of automatic processes (mental shortcuts, formally referred to as cognitive heuristics) that simplify complex problems.
    In other words, all other things being equal, we are motivated to use relatively effortless and simple mental shortcuts that provide rapid but often inaccurate solutions rather than effortful and complex mental processing that provides delayed but often more accurate solutions. (Jeffry Ricker, *An Introduction to Psychology: The Science of Mind and Behavior* [glossary entry], http://www.scottsdalecc.edu/ricker/psy101/readings/definitions/cognitive_miser.html [accessed 20 Dec. 2009])

25 Benedikt Hallgrímsson, 'Repairing the Ivory Tower.'

26 Kathleen F. Gabriel, *Teaching Unprepared Students: Strategies for Promoting Success and Retention in Higher Education* (Sterling, VA: Stylus, 2008).

27 Ken Bain, *What the Best College Teachers Do* (Cambridge: Harvard University Press, 2004).

28 Ibid., 3.

29 Prior to the establishment of the NSSE research program, very little was known about the characteristics of students who expend effort on their studies that is considered by educators to be less than optimal. How-

ever, the NSSE has stimulated interest in this topic and provided a useful database for studying it in a way that can help to rectify it. Studies are now being published that look to both the characteristics of students and their learning environments. See, for example, George D. Kuh, 'Assessing What Really Matters to Student Learning: Inside the National Survey of Student Engagement,' *Change* 33.3 (2001): 10–17, 66; and George D. Kuh, 'What We're Learning about Student Engagement from NSSE,' *Change* 35.2 (2003): 24–32.

30 Funding for this data set was provided by the Social Science and Humanities Research Council of Canada (SSHRC), grant #R1756A11.

31 The data set includes random samples of 1,000 first-year and 1,000 fourth-year respondents (equally represented by gender) from each of three types of Canadian and American institutions drawn from the 2006 NSSE data set of cases represented by these types of schools ($n = 32,242$) for a total sample size of 12,000 students.

32 We have attempted to keep the discussion of this analysis as non-technical as possible while still providing statistically knowledgeable readers with sufficient information for them to judge the validity of our statistical procedures. Accordingly, our presentation is not as technical or detailed as it would be in an academic journal. We plan to publish more technical analyses in peer-reviewed journals.

33 One study comparing different ways of reporting study time suggests that the NSSE may actually overestimate the amount of time per week students spend on out-of-class academic activities. See Babcock and Marks, 'The Falling Time Cost of College.'

34 National Survey of Student Engagement (NSSE), *Engaged Learning: Fostering Success for All Students: Annual Report 2006* (Bloomington, IN: Center for Postsecondary Research, 2006), 19–20.

35 Other items in this benchmark scale are indicators of the effort required in courses, such as the number of readings and essays, and how much coursework emphasizes analysis, synthesis, evaluation, and application of course material.

36 An examination of the items constituting those scales shows why four of the benchmarks of engagement are not strongly related to course engagement. For example, some items enquire about things like computer skills and ethnic relations. We suspect that this lack of strong association is an artefact of a culture of disengagement, in which effort devoted to courses is not key to certain outcomes.

37 Jacob Cohen, *Statistical Power Analysis for the Behavioral Sciences*, 2nd edn (Hillsdale, NJ: Lawrence Erlbaum Associates, 1988).

38 When only full-time students are included, the sample size is 5,383

students for Canadian schools and 5,076 students for U.S. schools. With a sample this large, the margins of error for the percentages reported are very small, at less than +/- 1 per cent. When the sample is broken down into subsamples, this margin of error increases, such that if there are of 1,000 students in a group under consideration, the margin of error is about +/–3 per cent.

39   Cf. Galbo, 'Anxious Academics.'

40   The margin of error of both of these overall percentages is very small, given that the 40 per cent figure is based on about 4,000 cases and the 14 per cent figure is based on about 1,400 cases. The effect size is medium ($h = .60$).

41   This wording is from the NSSE codebook. In the actual questionnaire, the wording of the stem is: 'About how many hours do you spend in a typical 7-day week doing each of the following?'

42   The correlation is +.09 for all full-time students and +.15 among American full-time students (among part-time students the correlation is zero).

43   The correlations range from +.05 to +.09 for full-time students.

44   Correlations are small but positive (reaching +.08 among Canadian students), revealing a very minor tendency among those working on campus to put more time into their courses.

45   For part-time students, the correlation is -.18 if students are included regardless of work status, but only increases to -.19 if only working part-time students are included, showing a small effect size for part-time students. Country differences are trivial.

46   For those who want to verify this, the standard deviations of the means for all of the categories average at 1.8, with a range from 1.62 to 1.87. Category sizes range from 305 to 5,698 cases.

47   The correlation is about -.12.

48   The average standard deviation of the means for all of the categories is 1.8, with a range from 1.65 to 2.45. The category sizes range from 80 to 2,913 cases.

49   When we look at what is commonly thought to be a risk factor for post-secondary educational success, we find that first-generation students (those with parents who did not gain post-secondary experience themselves) are actually *less likely* to be among the hardcore disengaged, but the effect is significant only among Canadian students and only when both parents are without post-secondary experience.

50   Odds ratios give an estimate of how much the dependent variable differentiates among categories of the independent variable, controlling for the other independent variables in the equation. In the case of age, this means

that respondents have a 17 per cent greater chance of being in the hardcore disengaged category with each of the age categories (<19, 20–3, 24–9, 30–9, 40–55, >55).

51 Total SAT scores for the hardcore disengaged are1,121 versus 1,125 for other students. Their math and verbal scores are, respectively, 571 vs. 583 and 562 vs. 572.

52 Cf. James E. Côté and Charles Levine, 'Attitude versus Aptitude: Is Intelligence or Motivation More Important for Positive Higher-Educational Outcomes?' *Journal of Adolescent Research* 15 (2000): 58–80.

53 These cut-offs define college readiness in terms of SAT scores, predicting a 65 per cent probability of getting a first-year grade point average of at least a B-minus (Murray, *Real Education*, 69).

54 The correlations range from +.10 to +.17 (George D. Kuh, *The National Survey of Student Engagement: Conceptual Framework and Overview of Psychometric Properties* [Bloomington, IN: Center for Postsecondary Research, 2004]). The question wording for grades is: 'What have most of your grades been up to now at this institution?'

55 For full-time students in our sample, the correlations range from +.09 to +.23.

56 The correlation is +.15.

57 We often hear this in discussions with students. The PBS documentary *Declining by Degrees*, based on a book of the same title, has footage of American students saying the same things (http://www.decliningbydegrees.org/ [accessed 28 April 2010]; Richard H. Hersh and John Merrow, *Declining by Degrees: Higher Education at Risk* [New York: Palgrave, Macmillan, 2005]).

58 James Côté and Anton Allahar, 'Grade Inflation: A Tale of Three Western Faculties,' *Western News*, 25 March 2010, 5; see also a variety of papers covering the various issues in the grade inflation 'debate' in Hunt, *Grade Inflation*.

59 See, for example, Côté and Levine, 'Attitude versus Aptitude.' This study found that students become more alienated between first and third year university, in the sense that they see less merit in putting out higher levels of effort. This effect is especially pronounced among bright students (those with IQs greater than 120).

60 Part of this compression may be due to an under-reporting of lower grades by some respondents, who may have a tendency to present themselves in a favourable light on surveys. However, our comparison of NSSE grades with institutionally recorded ones shows that the disparity in reporting methods is small; see *Ivory Tower Blues*, 197–8.

61 This imbalance is not quite as bad in Canadian schools, but the same pat-

tern is found there: about one-third of disengaged students report that they regularly earn As, and more than half earn Bs. One might hope that this pattern differed in fourth year – that first-year 'mercy grading' might be responsible for first-year results, but that is not the case. Nor does it differ by the gender of the student.

62 This is a multiple regression analysis that 'partials out' the shared variance between independent variables, which in this case is .18.

63 This multiple regression was also run with an interaction term for total SAT score by course engagement, but it was not significant and the part correlation was -.03.

64 The NSSE has been criticized on a number of grounds, one of which is whether students can really provide valid ratings in areas such as their own critical thinking capacities. An obvious problem is that different students would define this differently, and many may not really understand what it means. See, for example, Mark Schneider, 'Assessing NSSE,' http://www.insidehighered.com/views/2009/11/24/Schneider, 24 Nov. 2009 (accessed 28 April 2010).

65 Similarly, in response to the question regarding how they felt their university experience helped them to speak clearly and effectively, while about 30 per cent of engaged students indicated 'very much,' so did about 20 per cent of disengaged students (also a small effect size; $h = .23$).

66 See, for example, Clark et al., *Academic Transformation*, ch. 6.

6. Technologies: Will They Save the Day?

1 Don Tapscott, *Grown Up Digital: How the Net Generation Is Changing Your World* (New York: McGraw-Hill, 2009).

2 Sue Bennett, Karl Maton, and Lisa Kervin, 'The "Digital Natives" Debate: A Critical Review of the Evidence,' *British Journal of Educational Technology* 39.5 (2008): 775–86.

3 For example, in a recent exchange on one of the authors' blog postings (James Côté, 'Academic Engagement: A Bi-lateral Contract,' http://www.academicmatters.ca/bloggers.blog_article.gk?catalog_item_id=2468&category=/blogger/artandscience [accessed 22 Dec. 2009]), Paul Axelrod, past dean of education at York University, wrote the following in response to a posting on academic engagement:

Unlike many of their professors (though perhaps not unlike their younger teaching assistants), they are steeped in the world of new technology – they consume information differently, they multi-task on line, and they may well have different ways of processing and creating knowledge, a subject that also requires more study. I spoke to a retired public school administrator recently who said that educators will not successfully repress students' use of cell phones in schools, any more than professors can effectively control students' use of laptops etc in university classrooms. Instead, teachers and faculty should be learning how to use these devices as educational tools – seeking to achieve their educational goals in new ways.

4 For example, in *The Dumbest Generation*, Bauerlein contends that these new technologies undermine education, displacing more serious intellectual activities that would engender a greater sense of cultural literacy and world knowledge.

5 See, for example, the story by Steve Kolowich, 'Hybrid Education 2.0,' *Inside Higher Ed*, 28 Dec. 2009, http://www.insidehighered.com/news/2009/12/28/Carnegie (accessed 28 Dec. 2009) about the on-line programs under development at Carnegie Mellon University that could 'could teach a college course without a classroom or a professor.'

6 Tapscott, *Grown Up Digital*.

7 'Digital Natives, Digital Immigrants,' *On the Horizon* 9.5 (2001): 1–6. He recently published the book *Don't Bother Me, Mom – I'm Learning: How Computer and Video Games Are Preparing Your Kids For Twenty-first Century Success – and How You Can Help!* (Saint Paul, MN: Paragon House Publishers, 2006). A review from *Scientific American* reprinted on the Amazon. com page advertizing this book states: 'Prensky presents an opinionated argument filled with anecdotes, a few studies, and quotes pulled from published news stories. There is no evidence too specious' (Aimee Cunningham, 'Review,' http://www.amazon.com/gp/product/1557788588/sr=1-2/qid=1137584499/ref=pd_bbs_2/104-5009678-2698352?_encoding=UTF8).

8 John Palfrey and Urs Gasser, *Born Digital: Understanding the First Generation of Digital Natives* (New York: Basic Books, 2008).

9 Jeff Gomez, *Print Is Dead: Books in Our Digital Age* (New York: Macmillan, 2007).

10 See, for example, Bennett et al., 'The "Digital Natives" Debate.'

11 Siva Vaidhyanathan, 'Generational Myth: Not All Young People Are Tech-Savvy,' *Chronicle of Higher Education*, 19 Sept. 2008, http://chronicle.com/free/v55/i04/04b00701.htm (accessed 31 March 2009).

12 Bennett et al., 'The "Digital Natives" Debate.'

13 Another study of university students found that most overestimated their skill level for basic applications like Word, PowerPoint, and Excel. Their perceptions were worst for Excel, where most (69 per cent) rated them-

selves average, but could not even perform basic operations. For Word, '75 per cent of students perceived a high skill level, and could on average perform 12 out of the 13 basic tasks, like changing the font and making text bold or italic. But these students could perform only five out of the 10 moderately difficult tasks, like performing word counts or justifying paragraphs, and none of the advanced tasks, which included copying and pasting items from the clipboard' (Erica R. Hendry, 'Students May Not Be as Software-Savvy as They Think, Study Says,' *Chronicle of Higher Education*, 22 July 2009, http://chronicle.com/blogPost/Students-May-Not-Be-as/7276?utm_source=at&utm_medium=en [accessed 28 Dec. 2009]).

14 Bennett et al., 'The "Digital Natives" Debate,' 782.

15 Stanley Cohen, *Folk Devils and Moral Panics* (London: MacGibbon & Kee, 1972).

16 The term 'moral entrepreneur' was coined by Howard Becker in *Outsiders: Studies in the Sociology of Deviance* (New York: The Free Press, 1973).

17 See Ellen Johanna Helsper and Rebecca Eynon, 'Digital Natives: Where Is The Evidence?' *British Educational Research Journal* 36 (2010): 503–20. These advocates have (mis)appropriated a sociological concept without exercising the caution that normally accompanies the use of this concept. Sociologists who study generational change are aware of the limitations of the concept of generations, recognizing it as a conceptual tool whose utility is limited by the arbitrary boundaries that are used to define age cohorts. Without some associational ties, such as are found in social movements cohered by moral bonds, the concept of 'generation' is of limited potential in terms of explaining or predicting social change.

18 Bennett et al., 'The "Digital Natives" Debate.'

19 Cf. Bauerlein, *The Dumbest Generation*.

20 Gary Small and Gigi Vorgan, *iBrain: Surviving the Technological Alterations of the Modern Mind* (New York: Harper Collin, 2008)

21 For cautions about the uncritical acceptance and imprudent use of Web 2.0 technologies, see Jaron Lanier, *You Are Not a Gadget: A Manifesto* (New York: Knopf, 2010). Lanier is a 'visionary' computer scientist who is known as 'the father of virtual reality technology' (dust-cover quote).

22 For instance, Tapscott quotes a source in *Grown Up Digital* as saying 'they want to learn, but they want to learn only when they have to learn, and they want to learn in a style that is best for them' (p. 130), which he claims is almost exclusively via the Internet.

23 As Tapscott would have it in *Grown Up Digital*, 128.

24 Tapscott also co-wrote, with Anthony D. Williams, *Wikinomics: How Mass Collaboration Is Changing Everything* (New York: Portfolio, 2006), claiming

that the key to success for businesses of the future is 'mass collaboration' via the Internet.

25 Tapscott, *Grown Up Digital*, 133.

26 Ibid., 134.

27 Much more is currently available in university libraries than is on the Internet on many topics, including the topic dealt with by this book, but there have yet to be great floods of knowledge-hungry students entering those libraries unless directed there by their teachers. Why would laptops change this for difficult, abstract, and/or arcane subjects? Indeed, it is with these types of subjects that teachers are particularly popular and useful.

28 Cf. Bauerlein, *The Dumbest Generation*. There is also an additional difficulty presented by the challenge of specifying learning as a means to an end versus learning as an end in itself. Broadly paralleling the distinction we have made between 'training' and 'educating,' there are some types of information that are useful for solving practical, hands-on dilemmas, and others that are more geared to the larger philosophical questions of life. Tapscott's approach cannot begin to address the latter.

29 Wikipedia, a free, collaborative encyclopedia, is useful for certain things, especially mundane matters and topics associated with popular culture and current events, but should not be taken as a sole source. A casual browse through it shows that many entries are marked by its overseers as suspect, incomplete, biased, and/or without sufficient references to constitute reliable sources of evidence.

30 Tapscott, *Grown Up Digital*, 134.

31 It is ironic for Tapscott's argument that many people blame the progressive movement for the widespread disengagement and sense of entitlement found among recent cohorts of university students. They argue that the pandering to students for the sake of bolstering their self-esteem has created these 'new learning styles,' which are not really learning styles at all, but rather self-indulgent excuses for laziness and the avoidance of the rigours of learning. In our view, as good as the progressive principles sound in theory, their wholesale implementation is not unproblematic, especially in mass education systems without unlimited budgets. Tapscott naïvely writes that the 'mass education idea … is being challenged' (p. 139) and provides two pages of advocacy for individualized learning. If it were only that easy to wish the old system away, it would have been done long ago. Certain aspects, such as interactive and collaborative learning, are clearly effective when they can be implemented, but this implementation is context-dependent, especially at higher levels of education, and is limited by the resources that societies make available to educators.

32 Winnie Hu, 'Seeing No Progress, Some Schools Drop Laptops,' *New York Times*, 4 May 2007, http://www.nytimes.com/2007/05/04/education/04laptop.html?_r=2 (accessed 25 April 2009).

33 Janice Tibbetts, 'Professors Declaring Classrooms Laptop-Free Zones,' *National Post*, 18 Nov. 2007, http://www.nationalpost.com/news/story.html?id=18a506fe-13c1-40dd-87c9-49d46100bdcb&k=21800 (accessed 25 April 2009).

34 Carrie Fried, 'In-Class Laptop Use and Its Effects on Student Learning,' *Computers & Education* 50 (2008): 906–14.

35 Christian Wurst, Claudia Smarkola, and Mary Anne Gaffney, 'Ubiquitous Laptop Usage in Higher Education: Effects on Student Achievement, Student Satisfaction, and Constructivist Measures in Honors and Traditional Classrooms,' *Computers & Education* 51 (2008): 1766–83.

36 Cf. Willingham, *Why Don't Students Like School?*

37 The New Media Consortium, *The Horizon Report: 2006 Edition* (Stanford, CA, 2006).

38 Eric Ribbens 'Why I Like Clicker Personal Response Systems,' *Journal of College Science Teaching* 37 (2007): 60–2; Doug Lederman, 'Proving the Benefits of Peer Instruction,' *Inside Higher Ed*, 5 Jan. 2009, http://www.insidehighered.com/news/2009/01/05/peer (accessed 25 April 2009).

39 Alan Groveman, 'Clickers, Pedagogy and Edtechtainment,' *Inside Higher Ed*, 20 June 2008, http://www.insidehighered.com/views/2008/06/20/groveman (accessed 25 April 2009).

40 Jay Hatch, Murray Jensen, and Randy Moore, 'Manna from Heaven or "Clickers" from Hell: Experiences with an Electronic Response System,' *Journal of College Student Teaching* 34.7 (2005): 36–9; Merrill S. Blackman, Patricia Dooley, Bill Kuchinski, and David Chapman, 'It Worked a Different Way,' *College Teaching* 50.1 (2002): 27–8.

41 Carla Carnaghan and Alan Webb, 'Investigating the Effects of Group Response Systems on Student Satisfaction, Learning, and Engagement in Accounting Education,' *Issues in Accounting Education* 22.3 (2007): 391–409.

42 Angel Hoekstra, 'Vibrant Student Voices: Exploring Effects of the Use of Clickers in Large College Courses,' *Learning, Media and Technology* 33.4 (2008): 329–41; Charles R. Graham, Tonya R. Tripp et al., 'Empowering or Compelling Reluctant Participators Using Audience Response Systems,' *Active Learning in Higher Education* 8.3 (2007): 233–58.

43 Graham et al., 'Empowering or Compelling Reluctant Participators Using Audience Response Systems.'

44 Jane Caldwell, 'Clickers in the Large Classroom: Current Research and Best-Practice Tips,' *CBE – Life Sciences Education* 6 (2007): 9–20.

45 Margie Martyn, 'Clickers in the Classroom: An Active Learning Approach,' *EDUCAUSE QUARTERLY* 2 (2007): 71–5.

46 Beth Morling, Meghan McAuliffe, Lawrence Cohen, and Thomas M. DiLorenzo, 'Efficacy of Personal Response Systems ("Clickers") in Large, Introductory Psychology Classes,' *Teaching of Psychology* 35 (2008): 45–50.

47 Carnaghan and Webb, 'Investigating the Effects of Group Response Systems.'

48 Caldwell, 'Clickers in the Large Classroom.'

49 See, for example, Blackman et al., 'It Worked a Different Way'; Caldwell, 'Clickers in the Large Classroom.'

50 April R. Trees and Michele H. Jackson, 'The Learning Environment in Clicker Classrooms: Student Processes of Learning and Involvement in Large University-Level Courses Using Student Response Systems,' *Learning, Media and Technology* 32.1 (2007): 21–40, 35.

51 Vicenc Fernandez, Pep Simo, and Jose M. Sallan, 'Podcasting: A New Technological Tool to Facilitate Good Practice In Higher Education,' *Computers & Education* 53.2 (2009): 385–92.

52 Ibid.

53 Ewen Callaway, '"iTunes University" Better than the Real Thing,' *New Scientist*, 18 Feb. 2009, http://www.newscientist.com/article/dn16624-itunes-university-better-than-the-real-thing.html?full=true&print=true (accessed 25 April 2009).

54 Jonathan Copley, 'Audio and Video Podcasts of Lectures for Campus-Based Students: Production and Evaluation of Student Use,' *Innovations in Education and Teaching International* 44.4 (2007): 387–99; Brian T. White, 'Analysis of Students' Downloading of Online Audio Lecture Recordings in a Large Biology Lecture Course,' *Journal of College Science Teaching* (January/February 2009): 23-7; Tomoko Traphagan, 'Class Lecture Webcasting, Fall 2004 and Spring 2005: A Case Study,' University of Texas at Austin, unpublished manuscript (accessed 29 April 2009).

55 See 'Rapid Development of Learning Objects,' http://meds.queensu.ca/medtech/assets/poster_rapid_mlo.pdf (accessed 25 April 2009).

56 David Harpp, 'Let's Enhance the Classroom Experience: We Should Provide Whatever Assistance We Can to Empower Students, Including Recorded Lectures,' *University Affairs* (March 2008): 40. Harpp teaches chemistry, and the video is needed 'to portray complex reactions, visualize chemical changes, examine modern inventions and show molecules in action.'

57 Suzanne Bowness, 'How Technology Is Transforming the Lecture,' *University Affairs* (December 2008): 14–7.

58　http://www.youtube.com/edu. Note, however, how few views the lectures have (at the time of writing, 22 Dec. 2009, the most popular one had only 95,926 views, while most had only a few thousand). There hardly seems to be a rush from the millions of university students around the world to view these. See, also, http://chronicle.com/wiredcampus/article/3684/youtube-creates-new-section-to-highlight-college-content?utm_source=at&utm_medium=en for a discussion of this development.

59　http://meds.queensu.ca/medtech/resources/info_podcasting (accessed 28 April 2009).

60　Larry Killen (Manager of Information Technology, School of Medicine, Faculty of Health Sciences, Queen's University), e-mail correspondence with James E. Côté, 21 March 2009.

61　http://meds.queensu.ca/medtech/assets/poster_rapid_mlo.pdf (accessed 26 April 2009).

62　Bowness, 'How Technology Is Transforming the Lecture.'

63　Harpp, 'Let's Enhance the Classroom Experience.'

64　Chris Evans, 'The Effectiveness of M-Learning in the Form of Podcast Revision Lectures in Higher Education,' *Computers & Education* 50 (2008): 491–8.

65　Mark J.W. Lee, Catherine McLoughlin, and Anthony Chan, 'Talk the Talk: Learner-Generated Podcasts as Catalysts for Knowledge Creation,' *British Journal of Educational Technology* 39 (2008): 501–21; Marco Lazzari, 'Creative Use of Podcasting in Higher Education and Its Effect on Competitive Agency,' *Computers & Education* 52 (2009): 27–34; Bowness, 'How Technology Is Transforming the Lecture.'

66　Aidín A. McKinney and Karen Page, 'Podcasts and Videostreaming: Useful Tools to Facilitate Learning of Pathophysiology in Undergraduate Nurse Education?' *Nurse Education in Practice* 9 (2009): 372-6.

67　Lee et al., 'Talk the Talk,' cite a 2005 study that reports that only '12% of U.S. Internet users ages 18 to 29 possess a working knowledge of what the term RSS means. Interestingly, the study found that a higher number of respondents overall (13%) understood the term "podcasting"'; see also Mark J.W. Lee, Charlynn Miller, and Leon Newnham, 'Podcasting Syndication Services and University Students: Why Don't They Subscribe?' *Internet and Higher Education* 12 (2009): 53–9.

68　Copley, 'Audio and Video Podcasts'; Traphagan, 'Class Lecture Webcasting.'

69　McKinney and Page 'Podcasts and Videostreaming'; Traphagan, 'Class Lecture Webcasting'; Adam C. Carle, David Jaffee, and Deborah Miller, 'Engaging College Science Students and Changing Academic Achievement with Technology: A Quasi-Experimental Preliminary Investigation,' *Computers & Education* 52 (2009): 376–80.

70 Dani McKinney, Jennifer L. Dyck, and Elise S. Luber, 'iTunes University and the Classroom: Can Podcasts Replace Professors?' *Computers & Education* 52 (2009): 617–23.

71 Carle et al., 'Engaging College Science Students.'

72 Harpp, 'Let's Enhance the Classroom Experience.'

73 Jane Secker, 'Lecture Capture Evaluation: Report of the Focus Group,' 5 June 2008, http://elearning.lse.ac.uk/blogs/clt/?p=292 (accessed 29 April 2009).

74 Òscar Celma and Yves Raimond, 'ZemPod: A Semantic Web Approach to Podcasting,' *Journal of Web Semantics* 6 (2008): 162–9.

75 An article on 'lecture capture' technology and faculty resistance, followed by numerous comments raising issues of intellectual property rights, along with other issues, is quite revealing of the obstacles facing the technological replacement of professors: Steve Kolowich, 'Fans and Fears of "Lecture Capture,"' *Inside Higher Ed*, 9 Nov. 2009, http://www.insidehighered.com/news/2009/11/09/capture (accessed 31 Dec. 2009).

76 http://www.blackboard.com/

77 But, see Brock Read, 'Have Wikis Run Out of Steam?' *Chronicle of Higher Education*, 30 April 2009, http://chronicle.com/wiredcampus/article/3744/have-wikis-run-out-of-steam (accessed 24 Dec. 2009).

78 For the sales pitch, see http://www.wimba.com/ (accessed 22 Dec. 2009).

79 Christal Gardiola, 'Studies in Second Life,' *University Affairs*, 1 Dec. 2008, http://www.universityaffairs.ca/studies-in-second-life.aspx (accessed 22 Dec. 2009).

80 http://en.wikipedia.org/wiki/WebCT

81 It is sometimes cited as a sign of things to come that MIT currently offers free access to 1,800 courses that reflect almost all the undergraduate and graduate subjects taught at MIT (http://ocw.mit.edu/OcwWeb/web/about/about/index.ht). While this is very generous on the part of MIT, according to the website, students cannot receive a free MIT credential because the on-line materials may not reflect the entire content of the courses, those using the on-line resources do not have access to MIT faculty, the 'courses' do not culminate into degrees or certificates, and thus studying the material on-line does not constitute an MIT education.

82 Elaine Allen and Jeff Seaman, *Staying the Course: Online Education in the United States, 2008* (Needham, MA: The Sloan Consortium, 2008).

83 David DeBolt, 'Universities See Double-Digit Increase in Online Enrollment, Study Finds,' *Chronicle of Higher Education*, 12 Nov. 2008, http://

chronicle.com/wiredcampus/article/3457/universities-see-double-digit-increase-in-online-enrollment-study-finds?utm_source=at&utm_medium=en (accessed 27 April 2009).

84 Ben Terris, 'Online University, Struggling to Attract Students, Loses Investors as Well,' *Chronicle of Higher Education: Wired Campus*, 9 Dec. 2009, http://chronicle.com/blogPost/Online-University-Struggling/9148/?utm_source=feedburner&utm_medium=feed&utm_campaign=Feed%3A+chronicle%2Fwiredcampus+%28The+Chronicle%3A+Wired+Campus%29&utm_content=Google+Reader (accessed 29 Dec. 2009).

85 John Crossley, 'Distance Learning Comes Closer to Home,' *Financial Post*, 6 Jan. 2009, http://www.nationalpost.com/related/topics/story.html?id=1146802 (accessed 27 April 2009).

The author of this article, John Crossley, is president of Meritus University, based in Fredericton, NB, which is owned by Apollo Group, Inc. Apollo Group has provided distance education for thirty years to a number of universities, including University of Phoenix, Institute for Professional Development, College for Financial Planning, Western International University, Insight Schools, Apollo Global, and Meritus University.

86 The University of Phoenix has some 115,000 students: http://www.carnegiefoundation.org/classifications/sub.asp?key=748&subkey=16977&start=783 (accessed 27 April 2009).

87 https://ecampus.phoenix.edu/ (accessed 27 April 2009).

88 http://www.open.ac.uk/ (accessed 27 April 2009).

89 Crossley, 'Distance Learning Comes Closer to Home.'

90 http://www.youtube.com/watch?v=e50YBu14j3U&feature=related (accessed 27 April 2009).

91 Another Kaplan ad, http://www.youtube.com/watch?v=F3nHvkJSNFg (accessed 27 April 2009), shows beaches, mountains, and streets with lines of chairs, and young people lounging at home using laptops. It begins with the question 'Where is it written that the old way is the right way? … Where is it written that classes only take place in a classroom?' The spot concludes with the question 'Where is it written that you can't change your life? That's the thing. It isn't written anywhere.'

92 'Washington Post Company,' http://topics.nytimes.com/top/news/business/companies/washington-post-company/index.html?inline=nyt-org (accessed 22 Dec. 2009).

93 Stuart Elliot, 'Do Online Universities Have Virtual Cheerleaders?' *New York Times* (12 Jan. 2009), http://www.nytimes.com/2009/01/12/business/media/12adnewsletter1.html?_r=3 (accessed 31 March 2009).

94 'Kaplan University,' http://www.ripoffreport.com/searchresults.asp?
   q1=ALL&q2=&q3=&q4=&q5=&q7=&q6=Kaplan%20University&
   searchtype=0
95 *Kaplan University Online Is a Ripoff,* http://www.youtube.com/watch?v=_
   I2Fgy23xYg&feature=related (accessed 27 April 2009).
96 'Accreditation,' http://online.kaplanuniversity.edu/Pages/KU_
   Accreditation.aspx (accessed 27 April 2009).
97 One study directly addressed the engagement issue by administering
   questions from the NSSE, adapted for the on-line medium (Chin Choo
   Robinson and Hallett Hullinger, 'New Benchmarks in Higher Education:
   Student Engagement in Online Learning,' *Journal of Education for Business*
   [November/December 2008]: 101–8). Based on data from three universities, this study found that on-line students reported more engagement
   when compared to NSSE norms for all institutions, but their engagement
   level was lower than institutions scoring among the top 10 per cent.
   However, it should be noted that some of the NSSE items bias the results
   in favour of the on-line medium and its requirements (e.g., the on-line
   courses require the use of technologies, which is an essential component
   of the NSSE benchmark for enriching educational experiences). In addition, the potential conflation between the medium of instruction and the
   size of classes was not addressed.
98 U.S. Department of Education, Office of Planning, Evaluation, and Policy
   Development, *Evaluation of Evidence-Based Practices in Online Learning:
   A Meta-Analysis and Review of Online Learning Studies* (Washington, DC,
   2009), xvii.
99 Pascarella and Terenzini, *How College Affects Students, Volume 2.*
100 Ibid., 101.
101 Ibid., 100.
102 Heather Kanuka and Jennifer Kelland, 'Has E-Learning Delivered on Its
   Promises? Expert Opinion in the Impact of E-Learning in Higher Education,' *Canadian Journal of Higher Education* 38.1 (2008): 45–65; Philip C.
   Abrami, Robert M. Bernard, Anne Wade, Richard F. Schmid, Eugene
   Borokhovski, Rana Tamim, Michael Surkes, Gretchen Lowerison, Dai
   Zhang, Iolie Nicolaidou, Sherry Newman, Lori Wozney, and Anna Pere-
   tiatkowicz, 'A Review of E-Learning in Canada: A Rough Sketch of the
   Evidence, Gaps and Promising Directions,' *Canadian Journal of Learning
   and Technology* 32.3 (2006): 1–70.
103 Kanuka and Kelland, 'Has E-Learning Delivered on Its Promises?'
104 Abrami et al., 'A Review of E-Learning in Canada.'
105 Jennifer C. Richardson and Tim Newby, 'The Role of Students' Cognitive

Engagement in Online Learning,' *American Journal of Distance Education* 20 (2006): 23–37.

106 Kanuka and Kelland, 'Has E-Learning Delivered on Its Promises?' 61.

107 C. Eugene Walker and Erika Kelly, 'Online Instruction: Student Satisfaction, Kudos, and Pet Peeves,' *Quarterly Review of Distance Education* 8.4 (2007): 309–19.

108 Doris U. Bolliger and Oksana Wasilik, 'Factors Influencing Faculty Satisfaction with Online Teaching and Learning in Higher Education,' *Distance Education* 30.1 (2009): 103–16.

109 Ibid.

110 Ibid.

111 Ibid.

112 Jack Stripling, 'So Many Students, So Little Time,' *Inside Higher Ed*, 24 March 2009, http://www.insidehighered.com/news/2009/03/24/heh (accessed 7 May 2009).

113 Michelle Rupe Eubanks, 'Online Study Ups Workload for Instructors,' *TimesDaily.com*, 18 Apr. 2009, http://www.timesdaily.com/article/20090418/ARTICLES/904185029/1011/NEWS?Title=Online-study-ups-workload-for-instructors (accessed 7 May 2009).

114 The Wired Campus, 'Tech Therapy: What's the Future of Online Learning?' 7 May 2009, http://chronicle.com/wiredcampus/article/3757/tech-therapy-whats-the-future-of-online-learning (accessed 20 May 2009).

115 Bennett et al., 'The "Digital Natives" Debate,' 783.

116 Tapscott, *Grown Up Digital*, 139.

117 Bauerlein, *The Dumbest Generation*.

7. Recommendations and Conclusions: Our Stewardship of the System

1 We do not mean aptitude tests like the American SAT. The admissions tests we have in mind would assess the ability to communicate in writing and speech at a level necessary for engagement in university courses requiring reading, writing, and discussion/debate.

2 We would add here that professional societies in each discipline should take the lead on this (e.g., the Canadian Sociological Association should set exit exams for the BA, MA, and PhD levels to ensure comparable learning outcomes among sociology programs across Canada).

3 Standardized exit exams will make professors and students behave more like partners in a cooperative process, rather than in conflict over, or complicit in, how little should be done for maximum rewards. Students should then respect professors' honest feedback on their performances,

so that they can improve sufficiently to pass the standardized exams, and professors will be motivated to challenge students to bring out their best performances.

4 Association of American Colleges and Universities, *Our Students' Best Work: A Framework for Accountability Worthy of Our Mission* (Washington, DC, 2004), 3.

5 Ibid.

6 Ibid., 3–4.

7 Ibid., 4.

8 Ibid., 5–6.

9 Quest University is a start-up university in Canada that is firmly based on liberal-education principles and an experiment that promises to provide a model for other Canadian universities that want to get on course, or back on course. Its approach is described as follows:

> Our name captures the essence of the academic journey our students will undertake when they join us. Quest speaks to a bold, personal mission – a journey of exploration and discovery, undertaken by those who are confident and pioneering, curious and passionate, and committed and resolute.
>
> A degree from Quest University Canada is not an end, but a beginning. Students will graduate with a heightened sense of preparedness for their entry into the global economy, post-graduate studies, or simply to be fully awake to all the possibilities of life. (http://www.questu.ca/ [accessed 31 Dec. 2009])

We visited Quest in April 2010, speaking with faculty members, sitting in on classes, and attending an awards ceremony. The engagement of the students is readily apparent in the classes, which are capped at twenty students, the dedication of the faculty is remarkable, and the school spirit is inspiring. A 'block course' system is used, whereby students take one course at a time per month, spend three hours per day in class (which incorporate Socratic dialogue and experiential, problem-based learning), and the remainder of the day/evening preparing for the next class and completing assignments. Quest participated in the 2010 NSSE, and many findings place it far beyond most higher education institutions in Canada and the United States in terms of fostering student engagement. Most notably, in terms of course engagement, 44 per cent of first-year students put in more than 25 hours per week in out-of-class study time (compared to only 10–20 per cent in other Canadian universities), and only 6 per cent put in 10 hours or less (compared to 42 per cent in other Canadian institutions) (David Helfand, President, Quest University, e-mail communication with J.E. Côté, 22 Aug. 2010). As noted in chapter 5, this is the level of effort most people would expect of a healthy institution of higher learning, but unfortunately it is not to be found in the vast majority of Canadian and American universities.

10 Association of American Colleges and Universities, *Our Students' Best Work*, 9.

11 Clive Keen and Ken Coates, 'Universities for the 21st Century: It's Time for Universities to Face the Challenges of Mass Education,' *University Affairs* (December 2006), http://www.universityaffairs.ca/article.aspx?id=1862 (accessed 22 Dec. 2009).

12 Andrew Park, 'Heck No, You Shouldn't Go,' *University Affairs* (March 2007), 43, http://www.universityaffairs.ca/heck-no-you-shouldnt-go.aspx (accessed 22 Dec. 2009).

13 'Rebuttal,' *University Affairs* (March 2007).

14 http://www.mphec.ca/en/Resources/AgendaEn.pdf (accessed 12 Jan. 2009).

15 Kuh, 'What Student Engagement Data Tell Us about College Readiness.'

16 Clive Keen, 'Universities for the 21st Century – *Nolens Volens*,' http://www.mphec.ca/en/presentationsandpublications/StrategicOptions.aspx. Double-click Keen's presentation to begin an automatic download of his PowerPoint presentation (accessed 12 Jan. 2009).

17 Clive Keen, 'Male University Transition Problems: A Guilt-free Explanation,' *Thymos* 1 (Summer 2007): 220–5.

18 See http://www.cegep.com/. CEGEP refers to Collège d'Enseignement Général et Professionnel or College of General and Vocational Education. The system website warns prospective students that they will need to put more effort into their courses than is the case in many high schools, including more reading, writing, and class participation. Here is how the website counsels students to prepare themselves for this increased workload:

> CEGEP is different than high school. It is a higher level of education designed to give you the 'smarts' and skills for university or the job market. By recognizing that it is different, you should be aware of some of the academic adjustments you will have to make next year.
> **Increased Workload.** If you're like the vast majority of new students, your CEGEP academic workload will increase significantly compared to high school. Instead of studying one or two hours per evening, you will have to prepare yourself for three or four hours of study. Since CEGEP students only have each course two or three times per week, expect that the interval between classes will be filled with assignments and required reading. Solution: Recognize that a fifteen-week semester is a seven-day

a week commitment and that weekends are not just 'party time.' Budget your workload so that it is spread out as evenly as possible throughout the semester. Make sure that you don't spend too much time on one course and neglect your other courses.

19 Keen ('Universities for the 21st Century – *Nolens Volens*') also calls for teaching loads that amount to 80 per cent of a professor's duties, with research allocated to 20 per cent. However, we believe that this would all but kill recruitment into an academic profession devoted to high-level knowledge generation. The PhD is a research degree, so where is the incentive for recruits to devote the time, effort, and money to earn a high-calibre PhD only to spend the vast majority of their professional careers teaching in an undergraduate classroom? Teachers' colleges could accomplish the goal of training teachers for an instruction-heavy system, but the entire research-intensive university system – which the rest of the world attempts to emulate – would collapse, and the economic benefits of such a system in knowledge-generation would be severely diminished.

20 Andy Furlong and Fred Cartmel, 'Mass Higher Education,' in *Handbook of Youth and Young Adulthood: New Perspectives and Agenda*, ed. Andy Furlong (London: Routledge, 2009).

21 Ibid., 123.

22 Ibid., 126.

23 Clark et al., *Academic Transformation*.

24 Richard J. Herrnstein and Charles Murray, *The Bell Curve: Intelligence and Class Structure in American Life* (New York: Free Press, 1994).

25 Murray, *Real Education*, 11.

26 Ibid., 16.

Index